Cuba Unspun

Cuba Unspun

by

Rosa Jordan

OOLICHAN BOOKS
FERNIE, BRITISH COLUMBIA, CANADA
2012

Library and Archives Canada Cataloguing in Publication

Jordan, Rosa

    Cuba unspun / Rosa Jordan.

ISBN 978-0-88982-289-4

    1. Jordan, Rosa--Travel--Cuba. 2. Cuba--Description and travel. I. Title.

F1765.3.J67 2012   917.29104'64   C2012-905362-7

We gratefully acknowledge the financial support of the Canada Council for the Arts, the British Columbia Arts Council through the BC Ministry of Tourism, Culture, and the Arts, and the Government of Canada through the Canada Book Fund, for our publishing activities.

Cover photo of children at Celia Sánchez Memorial in Manzanillo by Larry Doell.

Cover design by Greg Clover.

Author photo by Larry Doell

Map by Derek Choukalos.

Published by
Oolichan Books
P.O. Box 2278
Fernie, British Columbia
Canada V0B 1M0

www.oolichan.com

For Derek

Author's Note

One reason modern Cuba continues to be so mysterious and misunderstood is because virtually everything that purports to be information has been spun and re-spun. Cuban immigrants to the US have generated a phenomenal amount of negative press about the country they chose to abandon, while travel agencies describe it as an island paradise unparalleled in the Caribbean if not the world. The US government continues to spend millions of dollars annually spinning outright lies about Cuba, while the Cuban government would have us believe that every bad thing that ever happened on the island was the result of Yankee imperialism.

Some of the nonsense I believed prior to going to Cuba was that I would not be allowed to travel freely about the island or talk openly with people or them with me. I had also been told that Cuba was a socialist paradise where every second person was a college graduate and artists who showed any promise at all were state-supported. What I discovered was that almost nothing I thought I knew was completely true, and a lot of it wasn't true at all.

After fifteen years of traveling around Cuba by bicycle, bus, train, plane, truck, horse cart, and rental car; and spending time with Cubans in every walk of life from cops and cane cutters and black marketeers to students and doctors and government officials, I now have better idea of what is not true. But no certainty about what is. Even things that were verifiably true on my most recent visit a few months ago may not be true now. Cuba is very different from anyplace else. It has some aspirations and values that are the same as ours and some that are upside down to ours. The country is in a state of transition, and is constantly changing.

For these reasons I cannot say that what you read in this book is the absolute truth about modern Cuba. It is only what I have learned, in country and over time, and pass on to you, unspun.

Rosa Jordan

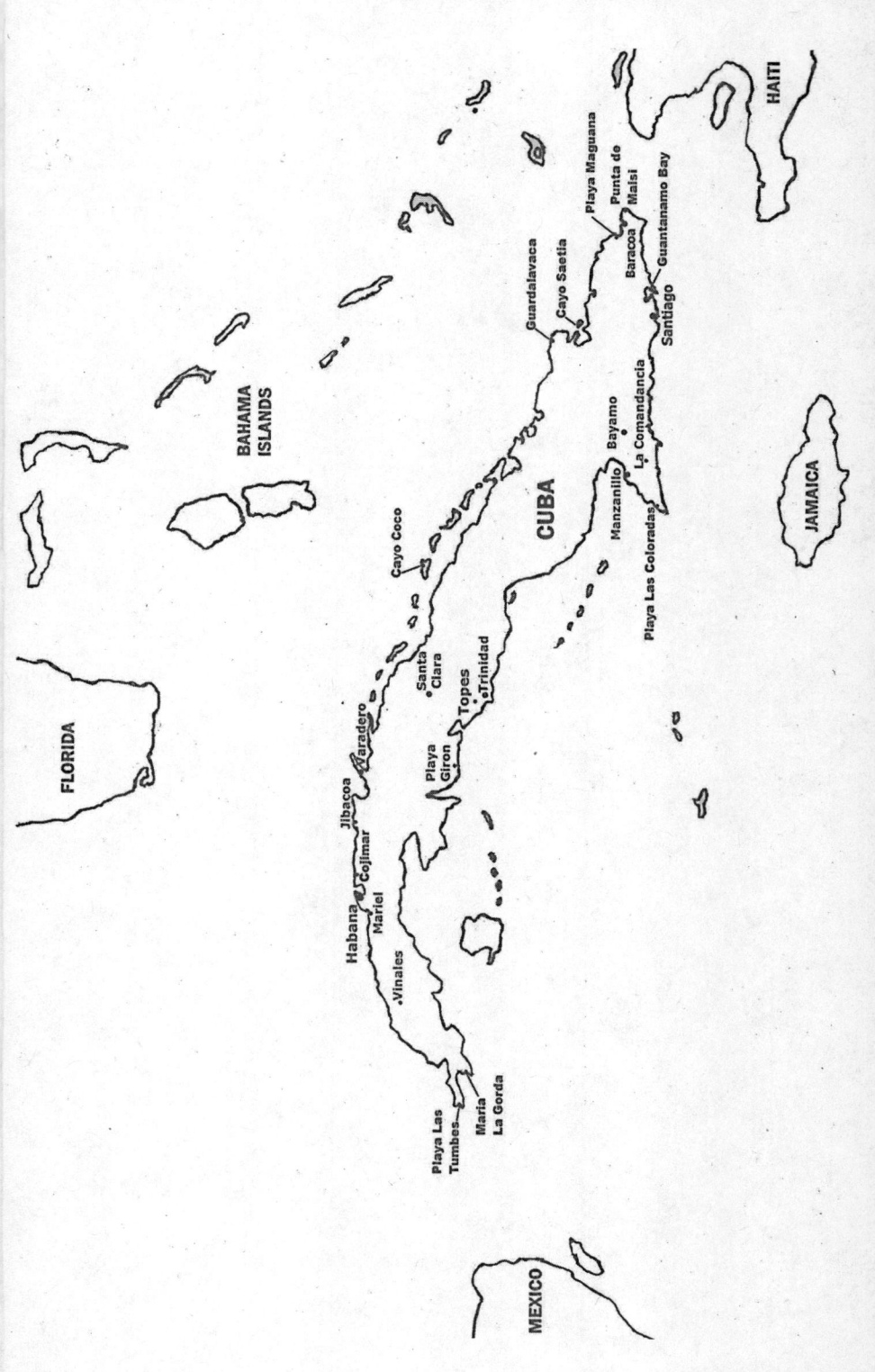

PART 1

CUBAN KISSES

My first Cuban kiss was only a fantasy, and it didn't happen in Cuba. It was in Florida. I was a pre-teen whose favourite pastime was watching a Cuban boy about ten years my senior paint signs. His name was José Martí but the sign shop owner thought he should have a more "American" name, so had dubbed him Marty Joe. Neither the shop owner nor I had a clue that José Martí was the most celebrated intellectual Cuba had ever produced, a name the Cuban youth must have carried with pride. We simply assumed that he would prefer one that sounded more Southern like Billy Joe, Bobby Joe, or Jimmy Joe, and never considered that what was familiar to our ears might have offended his.

Many hours that summer I stood at José's elbow. Scratching mosquito bites on one leg with the toenails of my other bare foot, I watched him letter signs and listened as his voice, a lilting mix of Cuban Spanish and southern drawl, painted vivid pictures of the island of his birth. The faster he talked the faster he painted, until at last he would drop the brush, leap to his feet, and dance hypnotically to some Afro-Cuban rhythm pounding inside his head.

In my mind's eye José merged into the scene his words created, dancing with black and brown friends on a white sand beach after swimming in warm blue waters and eating their fill of lobster boiled pink over driftwood fires that blazed all night. I could see their bodies swaying like palm trees, see waves rolling in behind them, and the yellow-orange of the imaginary fire. While José danced, his smile was the widest, his teeth the whitest, his laughter the most joyous I'd ever known. I longed to be there with him, and at times felt I could be if only he would hold his arms out to me and dance a little longer. And there would be kisses, ah yes, sweet, beach-salty Cuban kisses.

With jarring suddenness the dance would stop. José would sink back on the stool, fluid muscles bunched, and his face, still dripping sweat, would harden into the mask of a sullen twenty-year-old. Without a word he would pick up a brush and start painting again. The abrupt way it ended always put me off balance, left me feeling as if something precious had been snatched and smashed. It was no use trying to re-engage him. He painted in silent fury and wouldn't speak again except to tell me to leave him alone; couldn't I see he was busy?

I would go then, but kept coming back all that long hot summer, unable to resist those glimpses of a magical place called Cuba that he couldn't resist creating for me. It was my private fantasy that he would someday return and take me with him. One afternoon I asked him outright, "Marty Joe, you gonna go back to Cuba after a while?"

Without taking his eyes off the sign he was lettering he said, "Rosita, you dirt poor, but your family have chickens and a few head of cows. People in Cuba way more poor than that."

I was too stung by being called "dirt poor" to absorb the comparison. In a voice made small by hurt and disappointment, I said, "I thought you wanted to go back."

It seemed an eternity before the answer drifted over his shoulder. "Nobody want to go back to that kind of poor."

I stopped going to the sign shop after that, perhaps to avoid being confronted with the harsh economic realities of his past and my present. Also, I was entering junior high and other things occupied my time. I don't know what became of José. But a decade later the fantasy of going to Cuba resurfaced in a different form, sparked by circumstances that could hardly have been more different.

Head Trips

I was a waitress in a South Florida restaurant frequented by affluent cigar-smoking Cubans who had recently relocated to the States, lock, stock, and liquid assets, to escape the anticipated confiscation of their property. These were men who would become mover-shakers in Florida's construction, real estate, sugar, banking, and drug-trafficking industries, but even Floridians far more sophisticated than I couldn't know that in 1960.

As a 21-year-old, I was as politically unaware as one could be. I had dropped out of high school five years earlier. Juggling three low-paying jobs, there was no time to read books or even newspapers beyond a scan of headlines as I cleaned up those left behind in the restaurant. I had only seen pictures of Fidel Castro, and understood that he headed the government in Cuba. I had no idea why or how he had overthrown the previous government, but I learned why the restaurant's customers hated him from their daily conversations.

"You mark my words, the bastard's going to grab every moneymaking enterprise in Cuba and turn it over to his Commie pals."

"Kennedy won't let that happen, not with all the Americans have invested there."

"It's the Cuban people who have to stand up to him. If they're too stupid—"

"Haven't you heard? He's going to teach all the monkeys

to read." (Laughter.) "Every cane cutter's kid will go to college at government expense."

Being myself the daughter of farm workers and having dropped out of school for lack of money, someone who promised a college education to the kids of seasonal farm workers didn't sound bad to me. But what did I know? I stood by their table, as invisible as the pot from which I refilled their coffee cups, and listened in silence as their voices rose in conversations that ran along these lines:

"As if a *campesino* would know what to do with an education if he had it! My son's at the University of Havana right now, and having a hell of a time."

"It's all this revolutionary ballyhoo. It's got them confused. Mine's there, too, and if I don't bring him over soon, he could get mixed up with them. He's already talking about dropping out and joining some so-called literacy brigade."

"My daughter's got the bug, too, but I blame her mother for that. Says she can't leave because of her parents, but it's more than that. I think she's in love with the bearded sonofabitch."

I wasn't in love with the "bearded sonofabitch" the way wannabe revolutionaries all over the world were, but I was intrigued. I began reading beyond newspaper headlines, trying to learn more about this Fidel Castro person. South Florida papers were hardly a reliable source of information, but from them I did get a sense that he might be something along the lines of a Spanish-speaking Robin Hood. There was widespread speculation that he intended to strip the rich of their wealth and use the money to make health care, educational opportunities, and better housing more available for the island's poor. From where I stood, at the bottom of Florida's economic ladder, that sounded pretty good.

I looked at a map and saw that Cuba was barely 300 miles from where I lived. One day I counted the few dollars

I had managed to save from my three jobs, and sidled into a travel agency. I looked over the rack of brochures, and not seeing one for Cuba, asked the agent if she had any.

"No, honey," she answered in the voice one uses with a child who ought to know better. "And I'll bet *you* don't have a passport."

When I admitted that I did not (I had not even known a passport was required to travel abroad), she informed me that Cuba was dangerous and I did not want to go there. But I *did* want to go there. Humiliated by the way the agent had talked down to me, and not knowing where to turn for information about Cuba, I sat down and wrote a letter that I addressed, simply: "Fidel Castro, Havana, Cuba." I asked if it was really dangerous there right now, and if it would be okay for me to visit.

What did I expect? That he would issue a personal invitation, as José had not those many years ago? Tell me how to get there and greet me with a kiss? Or maybe just answer my letter with words that would let me decide for myself whether he was some bearded devil or a romantic figure I might love from afar?

In fact, I did get a reply to that letter. Not from Castro, of course, but from someone who politely refrained from ridiculing my abysmal ignorance. The letter assured me that Cuba was quite safe. They would welcome my visit, and here was a number I should call when I arrived for any assistance I might need.

I did not go. It wasn't just that I lacked a passport and the money for a trip to an island just a few hours away. It was because I had a much further distance to travel before I would have anything approaching an education that would give me a context in which to understand the insane politics that governed US-Cuban relationships.

In the decades to follow, I passed through marriage, divorce, child-rearing, university, and a fire that destroyed my home. I became a freelance journalist, a social justice activist, and a citizen of Canada. Only after all that did I find myself again planning a trip to Cuba. Although "planning" would hardly be the operative word.

I was in the San José, Costa Rica airport with ten days to kill between visits to environmental projects I was facilitating in Guatemala and Ecuador. What to do? Rent a car and explore Costa Rica? Relax on the beach? Bus north to Nicaragua and visit friends there? As I stood at the airline counter considering my options, I noticed that a flight was departing to Havana in just two hours.

Spontaneously, I asked the ticket agent, "Are their any seats left on that flight?" When she said there were, I asked, "Do you think I'd have time to get to the embassy to get a visa?"

"That's not necessary." She smiled. "I can issue you a tourist card right here."

Within moments I held a tourist card and ticket to Havana.

I was aware as I waited for the flight that the sudden decision had been prompted not only by a desire to fulfill a dream I'd had years earlier, but also by anger. Although I had lived many years in Canada and no longer traveled on a US passport, it rankled me that the US government made it difficult if not impossible for its citizens to visit Cuba. Just a few months earlier an article had appeared in the *Washington Post* about two kids, classmates of then-President Bill Clinton's daughter, who had scheduled a beach-and-biking vacation to Cuba. Shortly before the intended trip the children had received letters from the US Treasury Department informing them that if they went to Cuba they could face ten years in jail and a fine of up to $100,000.

How many millions of Americans had been dissuaded from travelling to Cuba by government regulations, travel agents, and media that kept them in the dark about that country? How many, like me, had allowed their own ignorance to prevent them from feeling the kiss of Cuban sunshine?

Havana~Anna's Place

I exited Havana's José Martí airport with a Swiss man named Paul who had been my seatmate from Costa Rica. He offered me a ride into the city with him and his Cuban fiancée, Fresa, who he expected would be there to meet him. She was there, a vivacious black girl who leapt into his arms and smothered him with kisses before he reached the curb. But the rattletrap '59 Chevy she and her friend Luna had arrived in was not licensed to transport foreigners. A polite but firm policeman instructed Paul and me to take one of the waiting taxis. The women screamed in his face but he simply ignored them as he removed our bags from the trunk of their car and placed them in a taxi.

Earlier I had asked Paul if he knew a good guest house in Havana. He had thrown his arms wide and said, "All Havana is a guest house." He explained that Cubans had recently been given permission to rent rooms in their homes, and hundreds of families were doing that to earn foreign currency. Later such family-run businesses would have to purchase a permit, pay taxes on the income, and meet various criteria. Only two rooms in a home could be rented and those had to meet certain standards—a lockable door, access to a functioning bathroom, etc. And the owner must live on the premises—this to prevent the re-emergence of an absentee landlord class. But as of then, 1996, the bed-and-breakfast business in Cuba was not that regulated.

I went to the guest house where Paul was staying with Fresa. It was in Vedado, one of Havana's nicer suburbs, a large house that could have served as a B&B anywhere in North America. The casa owner, Anna, was a retired school teacher. She knew Paul and Fresa from previous stays, and Luna was a neighbour who had (for a fee) offered to collect Paul at the airport in her old car—the one we had not been allowed to ride in because taxis were already being regulated. Anna greeted each of us with what I would soon learn was the standard grownup greeting kiss, a smack in the air alongside each cheek. However, not yet having got the hang of it, I planted a peck flat on Anna's cheek.

We were still standing in the living room when a public service announcement came on television, cartoon characters doing a little song and dance routine announcing that it was time (nine o'clock) for small children to go to bed. A man introduced as Anna's son entered with his five-year-old daughter. The child ran to Anna, Luna, and Fresa to kiss them—a childish smack on the check like the one I had given Anna. Then, hesitantly but not unwillingly, the little girl kissed me as well. Having become accustomed to the fear North American children show toward strangers, I was touched almost to tears by the gesture. I hadn't realized how much I had been missing the spontaneous hugs and kisses that used to be part of the interaction with almost any small child. Later I would notice that young girls in or nearing adolescence did not kiss friends and relatives, but demurely turned a smooth-skinned cheek to receive a kiss.

As soon as Anna's granddaughter was put to bed, the volume on the television was turned up and everyone in the room sat down as if in a trance. Paul whispered in Fresa's ear, but she shook her head and focused on the screen. I wondered what had drawn their attention so raptly. A speech by Castro perhaps? But no. It was a Brazilian *novella*, which I soon discovered was as much an institution in Cuba as Monday night football in the States or Hockey Night in Canada.

When the soap opera ended, Anna shuffled off to the kitchen to make coffee. Again Paul tried to coax Fresa to their bedroom and again was rebuffed with the Spanish equivalent of "later, darling." She wanted him to take her and Luna out to dinner and dancing. She squirmed in his lap and gave him kisses that in no way resembled the *pro forma* ones with which Anna had greeted us or the chaste ones bestowed by the child. It was clear that if Paul was to get what he wanted it would only be after Fresa had got what she wanted.

Luna, I learned, was a dancer in a salsa troupe soon to tour Europe. She and Fresa were *jineteras,* although I did not yet know that word. The direct translation for *jinetera,* or in its masculine form, *jinetero,* is "jockey." In the Cuban context, it means someone who is hustling to get ahead. That is considered admirable in North America, but in Cuba, admirable is being a team player and working for the good of community and nation. Hustling for the personal benefit of yourself or your family is tolerated, but is not considered particularly noble.

But this was 1996 and these were difficult times. Six years earlier the Soviet Union had collapsed and aid to Cuba had been terminated. The nation's over-dependence on that aid and failure to achieve food and energy self-sufficiency during three decades of Soviet largess made the sudden withdrawal of foreign aid an economic disaster. In any other poor country it probably would have been a humanitarian disaster as well, but in Cuba it only created a decade of hard times. Very hard times.

Everything—food, soap, shoes, gasoline—was rationed, and rations were cut to the bare minimum. Suddenly everyone from fishers in seaside villages to high-level government decision-makers looked for ways to stave off hunger. The steps taken by the government were rapid and varied, putting a lie to the notion that a centrally-planned economy can't respond speedily to crisis. In a huge nation like the USSR, maybe not. But in a small one like Cuba it not only can be done but was done during the "Special Period" of the 1990s.

Debates raged in the National Assembly and policies were reversed. Previously, in an attempt to maintain some degree of economic equality (one of the main values of the Revolutionary government), ordinary Cubans were not allowed to have foreign currency. They were supposed to get by on what they could purchase with *moneda nacional*— that is, Cuban pesos. The government tried to lay hands on whatever dollars came into the country, as foreign currency was required to purchase what the nation needed from abroad, primarily food and petroleum.

After the loss of Soviet assistance the Cuban government needed hard currency more than ever, but it approached the problem in a more effective and less restrictive way. Laws were changed to allow Cubans to have and use dollars. At the same time, the government opened "dollar stores" all over the island. These sold both the consumer goods Cubans desired and some items previously supplied by the state at near zero cost—things people can live without but don't want to, like soap, shampoo, and feminine hygiene products.

Once island Cubans were allowed to have and use dollars, friends and family members living abroad could send "remittances" to help those back home who were in need. Island Cubans could take that foreign currency to a government-operated dollar store to purchase what they needed, and the government, with the dollars it raked in, could buy petroleum from Venezuela to generate electricity, or rice from China to be distributed to Cuban families at prices that even the poorest could afford.

Meanwhile, faced with insufficient funds to purchase fertilizers, a US embargo, and farm equipment sitting idle for lack of fuel and spare parts, many government officials advocated breaking up the big state-owned farms. They argued that small plots should be distributed to families and cooperatives that were willing to till the land in the old pre-industrial way. To facilitate this change, thousands of water buffalos were imported to provide animal traction and manure. Horse-drawn carts became commonplace even in cities, and cart horses were fitted with manure-catchers to collect organic fertilizer.

But all that was taking time, and folks like Anna, Luna, and Fresa were not farmers. If they wanted more than what was available with their ration card, well, pesos didn't go far. Dollars did. The easiest way to acquire dollars was intimately linked to a far greater change that had come about in the five years prior to my arrival. That was the government's decision to pursue recreational tourism.

Recreational tourism had always been an anathema to Fidel Castro, and more so Celia Sánchez, the most influential person in his life during the war and for two decades afterwards. They were sickened by the moral degradation that characterized Cuba's Mafia-controlled gambling-and-prostitution tourism of the 1940s and 1950s, and were determined to replace that "dirty tourism" with "clean tourism." During the 1960s, this took the form of tours to schools, factories and hospitals to show off the Revolution's efforts to improve the lot of the masses. In the 1970s, "clean tourism" was expanded to include medical services, whereby people from all over the world could come to Cuba to receive quality medical care at the hands of good, German-trained Cuban doctors.

But "clean tourism" did not generate enough hard currency to save an economy that in 1990 was knocked to the ground by the sudden withdrawal of $30 billion per year in Soviet aid. To make matters worse, sugar prices were down on the international market, hurricanes were doing massive amounts of damage nearly every year, and the US embargo was still in place. Something about the Cuban economy had to change. What changed most radically was the government's attitude toward recreational tourism. By the time I arrived in 1996, the Cuban government had signed joint venture agreements with many international companies, and resorts were beginning to line its finest beaches. Resorts brought foreign visitors and they brought dollars.

At that point, many Cubans began to do what they could to ensure that some of those dollars were spent outside the resorts. All over Havana I would meet women like Anna who had turned the family home into a guest house, and younger ones, male and female, who reverted to a still older method of separating foreigners from their money.

What made this unusual in Cuba was the way that what we would call prostitution (and in Cuba is called "transactional sex") was accepted by young people's parents and integrated into family life. To some degree this was a matter of necessity. UN statistics indicated that the average Cuban's daily caloric intake during the first half of the 1990s fell from 3000 to 1900. No doubt about it, many families were truly hard up. If a girl went dancing and came home with a foreign *novio* (fiancé or serious boyfriend), her welcoming family frequently benefited as much from the man's generosity as their daughter. Natural Cuban hospitality caused families to spontaneously share what little they had, and that in turn was repaid with gifts ranging from aspirin and groceries to bicycles and refrigerators.

Another thing that kept families from freaking out when their daughters turned to something that greatly resembled the world's oldest profession was that Cuba has a good family planning program, plus support, via the *libreta* (ration card) for any children that might be born from such partnerships.

Then there was the influence of recent history. During the Revolution's heady early days, many young women participated in literacy campaigns and work brigades far from parents' watchful eyes. More than a few of those mothers and grandmothers of today's generation had become pregnant and given birth to children out of wedlock. In Cuba there is no stigma attached to having a child, in or out of marriage.

Havana ~ Deisy's Place

This I learned later when I rented a room in Deisy's home in Havana's western-most suburb, Santa Fe. Once a beach community for Habaneros who chose to live near the city rather than in it, Santa Fe had, in recent years, become less appealing. Formerly well-maintained yards had been in-filled with small houses serviced by amateur plumbing and wiring that met few if any building codes.

Building on the property of a friend or family member resulted largely from the island's land tenure system. There *is* private ownership of homes—over 80% of Cubans own mortgage-free houses or apartments. However, for the fifty years between 1961 and 2011, ownership lasted only as long as some family member lived there. If no family member remained in the home, the owner could trade it for another place to live in Cuba but could not sell it outright. If no trade was made and every family member left, the house reverted to the government to be passed on to some other family (or in the case of mansions, converted into schools, clinics, or museums). This was the situation when I first visited Cuba, and would remain so until 2011, when laws changed to allow home sales.

As the population in Cuba increased from seven million in 1960 to eleven million by 2000, the difficulty of acquiring land for home construction was partially overcome by building on the lot of an existing home. This was so prevalent in Deisy's neighbourhood that she had been unable to find even a few metres of someone's back yard upon which to build a place. What she had done instead was buy the flat *roof* of an existing house. There, over a period of three years, she had constructed a small apartment. What she paid for the roof was a large television acquired from a foreign boyfriend. What she paid for materials and labour, well…

Deisy was a shapely 29-year-old with tawny blonde hair. She had a lifestyle that combined, in a discreet way, what Anna, Fresa, and Luna were doing: namely, renting out a bedroom when she could, bartering things she had for things she needed, and looking for a foreign boyfriend.

For a while Deisy considered herself engaged to a Danish ship's captain. She may have been in love with him, and certainly had been in love with the dream that he would marry her and take her to live abroad. But his shipping line had ceased to make runs to Cuba, and when he stopped writing she resigned herself to never seeing him again. By the time I was a guest in her house, she had a new boyfriend. He was a Cuban expatriate living in Canada, uninterested in marriage as he was already married. Deisy was quite satisfied with the arrangement. She seemed not to mind seeing him only when he came to Cuba on business. And she definitely did not mind that she was pregnant by him.

She told me about her pregnancy by way of explaining why she would be out all day, and which flower pot the key would be hidden in if I got back before she did. A neighbourhood health team had come by, as it did every month, to ask if anybody at this address was pregnant. Pregnant women were required by law to go for testing as soon as they became aware of their condition. It was the health team's job to identify pregnant women and make appointments for checkups and ensure follow-up.

"I'll get a pelvic and a blood test and psychiatric exam," Deisy explained.

"That's good. What's the psychiatric exam for?"

She looked surprised. "Why, to find out if I'm okay about having a baby. Don't they do that in your country?"

"I don't think so. What if a woman isn't okay with it?"

Deisy shrugged. "She could have an abortion. Or if she doesn't want either a baby or an abortion, the state will put it up for an adoption. Although I can't think why a woman would go through all that if she didn't want a kid in the first place."

Deisy did want a baby, much more, she said, than she wanted a husband. "Why not? Babies are nice, no?"

I watched her dress for the doctor's appointment, brushing honey-blonde hair and rubbing lotion on strong bare arms and legs, and thought, "Why not?"

Her Cuban-Canadian boyfriend, who happened to be in Havana just then, came by to drive her to the doctor. Off they went, cheerful at the prospect of having a child who would not be a big financial burden on either of them. There would be no hospital or medical bills, and the baby would get a ration of food just as Deisy did, plus the litre of milk per day doled out to all Cuban children under the age of seven. Mommy would not work, but very likely would continue the kinds of barter she and her neighbours were all doing during this Special Period, as a means of acquiring things that the government did not provide. Plus, there would be periodic gifts from Papí when he came to Havana on business, and dropped by to receive a sloppy baby kiss from his and Deisy's child.

Women on the Make

I soon tired of staying at Deisy's place with its blaring TV and constant flow of visitors. I needed a bit of quiet, and asked if she knew of a beach place where I might hole up for a while and do some writing. She suggested Villa El Salado (later Villa Cocomar), about fifteen kilometres west of the city.

I had not known what "villa" signified in Cuba, but when I got to Villa El Salado I saw that it consisted of individual cottages scattered over well-maintained grounds. Some were by the pool, others faced the ocean. I asked for one of the latter, which offered the tranquility I desired. The place gave me yet another glimpse into the world of Cuban kisses, and who was exchanging what for what with whom.

While having lunch by the pool I observed that the clientele consisted almost entirely of men middle-aged and older, their sizeable pot bellies overhanging small swim trunks, each accompanied by a much younger woman. At first I thought they were all Cubans and I had stumbled into the kind of place where, in other Latin American countries, men bring women they prefer not to be seen with by someone who might tell their wife. However, poolside chatter soon informed me that only the girls (and many of them *were* girls, not women) were Cuban. The men, as far as my ear could discern, were Italian, Spanish, and Mexican.

Later I learned that travel agencies in those three countries had begun to run charter flights to Cuba specifically for sex tourists. It was possible to find ads on the internet that offered Cuban sex partners, black or white, male or female, hetero or gay. The ugliest side of that was not even what I was seeing there at Villa Salado. It was to be found in fenced-and-guarded, all-inclusive resorts developed by Spanish and Italian companies. Sex tourists would be flown in from a particular country and provided with services that included (for an additional fee, of course) a sex partner.

I stumbled onto only one such place these during my rambles around Cuba but it is likely that there were others during the early years of Cuba's move into recreational tourism. This would seem to have been confirmed in 1997, when several high Cuban officials were brought down over the scandal. Minister of Tourism Osmany Cienfuegos was removed from office, not charged but in disgrace nonetheless. The consensus was that if he hadn't known that sex tourism was going on in some all-inclusive resorts jointly owned by the state and foreign companies, he certainly should have.

Several laws were subsequently enacted, aimed at preventing Cuba from developing the kind of sex tourism that disgraces countries like Thailand. One law prohibited Cubans from entering a foreigner's hotel room. That was followed by laws prohibiting homeowners from renting rooms to Cuban-foreign couples unless they could prove they were married.

If the government was slow to react (it did not implement these laws until around 1997), it might have been because Castro recalled that one of his few political defeats had been dealt by prostitutes. In 1959, just after the victory of the Revolution, prostitution and gambling were declared illegal. Havana's prostitutes, supported by croupiers from the casinos, took to the street in protest. How could the new government throw thousands out of work without offering alternatives? Upon reconsideration, the young rebel leaders (who were not as puritanical as all that) agreed that prostitution and gambling would not be made illegal until training programs for other professions could take effect.

Once basic necessities were provided to the entire population, and education and jobs were readily available, there were few reasons for a person to go into prostitution. Cuba had never been as sexually repressed as other Latin countries, so Cuban men rarely relied on prostitutes for sexual gratification. Once recreational tourism was replaced with the "clean tourism" of health care and government-sponsored political tours, there were not many opportunities to earn money by prostituting oneself to foreigners anyway.

At least that was the way it *had* been. But on my first visit to Cuba in 1996, recreational tourism was on the rise. So was prostitution, and the new laws aimed at curbing it had not yet been enacted. Faced with hard economic times, many young Cubans were selling their kisses—and more.

I wanted to talk to the women at Villa Salado but it was not easy, as their male escorts were usually close by. The girls would stroke them with pretty lacquered fingertips and hold out palms to be filled with money with which to buy something from the bar or boutique. The money would be handed over, the man rewarded with a light kiss that promised more, and off she would go to make her purchase. Whatever amount she had been given, I never saw any change being returned.

One day, chatting with two girls in the restroom, I asked how they had met the men they were with. They said they had met them at the Copacabana, a hotel with a disco open to the public. However, they were more guarded than Deisy had been, and our conversation went no further.

Another day I met three teenagers on the beach who said they had come out for a walk because they were bored with the "old men" who had brought them there. I shared my sunscreen and they became conversational, asking questions about my life and answering mine about theirs. They too had met their men (picked them up would be more accurate) in discos or outside hotels. They said no pimps were involved. As they revealed more of the relationships (if such short-term liaisons could be called that), it seemed to me that they were not getting as much as Deisy was from hers, or even as much as Fresa, who seemed genuinely fond of Paul. All these girls were getting was money and a chance to spend a day or two at a pleasant beach resort.

When I asked if they were practicing safe sex, they answered almost in unison, "Of course. We're not stupid." Another piped up, "Cuba is not like Miami, where *everybody* has AIDS."

"Not everybody," I countered. "But the rate of HIV-AIDS infection is high there. It is also very high in countries like Mexico, Spain, and Italy."

They exchanged glances that suggested that they had taken my point about their sexual partners not necessarily being disease-free, but the next remark from a bubbly brunette seemed to reassure them. "There aren't many cases in Cuba," she bragged. "And anyway, Cuba's going to find a cure."

Cuba did have the lowest rate of infection in the Caribbean, and it was dropping at a time when the US rate was climbing. Still, their behaviour struck me as risky and their confidence in Cuban scientific prowess more than a little naive.

I hope I have not left the impression that a majority of Cuban women, and only women, were involved in prostitution in 1996, because that would be totally incorrect. However, the Special Period of the 1990s was a time when there was more of that than there had been a decade earlier. And more than there would be a decade later, after laws had been put in place to curb such activity, and the economy was again on the upswing.

A Cuban Man

I had been warned by some who had visited Cuba before me that Cuban men were rather wonderful and I should not be surprised if I found myself involved with one. But perhaps because of my age, or because my personal life was well-grounded in a satisfying long-term relationship, that didn't happen.

In fact, the only Cuban man to hit directly on me was gay; this on a later trip to Cuba when he sat next to me on the plane. A chatty 22-year-old, Carlito had been on an eleven-month work visa to Guatemala but was returning early, he said, because the treatment of gays was horrible there. Although there were tons of consumer goods on offer, he had had to work unbelievably long hours to afford the things he wanted, and going out at night was terribly dangerous. Several of his friends had been attacked by gay-bashers. One, badly beaten, had been unable to gain admittance to hospital or find a doctor in Guatemala City willing to care for him.

"They hate gays there. *Hate* them," he repeated. "They say it used to be bad in Cuba, but I don't think it was ever that bad!"

With no prompting from me, he regaled me with stories meant to show how accepted gays were in Cuba now. No Cuban doctor had ever discriminated against him, he said. In fact, many doctors were gay. He and his openly gay friends hung out unmolested on the Malecón, La Rampa, and at favourite beach cafes in Playas del Este.

This led to a conversation about dance and music, but when I asked which Cuban bands playing *la trova* (folk music) he liked best, he dismissed them with a wave of the hand. He loved American disco and had bought as many CDs as he could afford in Guatemala, some because they were personal favourites and some for resale.

He said that when he got home to Havana he planned to re-register for university, which he had dropped out of the year before in order to "have fun." Only when I asked about his parents did a cloud pass over his face. "They don't want to have anything to do with me," he said. "Not since I told them I was gay. That's why I will live with my grandmother. She accepts me as I am."

Carlito went through Immigration just ahead of me, and asked, when I had come through as well, "Did you hear what she said to me? She said, 'You know there's a lot of AIDS in Guatemala. Be sure to get yourself tested right away.' You see," he added with a proud smile, "Cuba looks after us. The test will cost me *nada*."

He hung around a bit longer as we collected our luggage. I could tell that he was hoping that I might be a "fag hag"—one of those women of a certain age who enjoy or even prefer the company an agreeable young man whom they know won't be hitting on them for sex. I did take the phone number he gave me, and said, when he repeated his offer to show me around Havana, that I'd think about it.

But as Carlito bade me goodbye with a warm kiss such as a boy might plant on the cheek of his mum, I doubted I'd call. Given the age difference, our different sexual orientation, and his enthusiasm for American disco and mine for Cuban folk music, what were the chances of a mutually satisfying night on the town?

Interestingly, I did see Carlito again, perhaps twice, but I am not sure about the first time. It was several years later in Playas del Este, a popular beach area close to Havana. I was driving past Mi Cayito, an outdoor café on a tiny island in the middle of a small lagoon, connected to the mainland by a footbridge. Normally the place is quiet in mid-afternoon, but this particular day it swarmed with young men. I knew that Mi Cayito was a gay hangout, but I had never before seen any gay crowd in Cuba like the one now spilling off the little island and filling the street. As I stopped to let a group cross to the road to the beach, I thought I saw Carlito. But it was a long time since we had been seatmates on that flight from Guatemala and I wasn't sure it was him.

I asked a man on the side of the road what was going on. He said it was an event called *Junto a Tí* (Together with You), which I knew only as an album by the Havana musician Joel Gulian. Later I learned that "Junto a Tí" was also a grassroots movement working to prevent the spread of HIV among men who had sex with men.

The next time I saw Carlito—and this time it was definitely him—was in 2009, in a conga line near Havana's Parque Don Quixote. I was amazed that he had changed so little in ten years, and even more amazed when I called out and he recognized *me.* He left the conga line and greeted me as if it was only last week that we had parted at the airport.

"What's this?" I asked when we had exchanged air kisses. "A gay pride parade?"

"Gay *pride?*" He gave a scornful laugh. "We don't celebrate our gayness in such a trivial way. This is to publicize IDAHO." At my blank look he spelled out the acronym. "International Day Against Homophobia and Transphobia."

"Oh!" I said, still stuck on the word "trivial." The conga

line included both men and women, many in fairly bizarre costumes, clowns on enormously long stilts, kissing same-sex couples, drummers, and somebody carrying a giant, rainbow-coloured flag.

I knew Raúl Castro's wife Vilma Espin had got through a law decriminalizing homosexuality way back in 1979, and on that plane ride with Carlito in 1999 he had said that he didn't feel discriminated against in Cuba. Still, Havana wasn't San Francisco, and this event looked like something I would expect to see in San Francisco. Or no, not quite. In San Francisco there would have been more nudity and leather, and would have numbered in the thousands, while here there were two hundred at most. True, metro San Francisco has a population of 7.5 million, while Havana's is less than 2.5 million. Still…

"Whatever it is, it looks like fun," I observed.

"*Claro,*" Carlito said airily. "Cubans know how to have fun. But it ought to be more than that, don't you think? Like last year, there was the Junto a Tí event to raise awareness about AIDS."

"That's great!" I said, with sincere approval.

Carlito beamed, and indicated an attractive woman at the head of the conga line who looked to be in her late forties. "Do you know who that is?"

"No," I said. "Should I?"

He leaned close and whispered, "She is Mariela Castro. Raúl's daughter."

The *president's* daughter? I tried to imagine Chelsea Clinton or audacious little activist Amy Carter or even Reagan's rebel daughter leading a gay-lesbian-trannie event while their respective fathers were in office. Unimaginable. Safety issue alone would have made such exposure impossible for the daughter of a US president, even if the whole block-long conga line was made up of cross-dressing security people.

"We are having panel discussions about gender issues later on," Carlito informed me. "There will be a screening of *Fresas y Chocolate*."

I had seen the award-winning film, written in 1990 about life as a gay in Cuba of the 1970s, and remembered that Carlito had said on the plane that he did not think things were ever "that bad" in Cuba. But then, he had barely been born in 1970. Apart from stories like the one in the movie, what would he know of the bad old days? His personal basis of comparison was between the violent homophobia he experienced in Guatemala and a relatively accepting society (excluding his own parents) in Cuba.

"It's amazing to run into you after so long. How have things worked out for you?" I asked. "Did you go back to school?"

"Oh yes. I am a doctor now. Actually, a dentist." He flashed a tooth-perfect smile.

Someone in the conga line called to him. He turned to go. Blowing me a farewell kiss, he added, "And I'm getting married!"

Married? Had he gone straight, or—

"Wait!" I shouted after him. "You mean gay marriages are *legal* in Cuba now?"

"Not yet," he called back cheerfully, as the conga line opened to let him back in. "But when they are, Tomás and I will be ready."

PART 2

REALITY CHECKS

When I first traveled abroad some long time ago, my main purpose was to feed an irrepressible restlessness. It did not occur to me that I would receive an education—or needed one. I had recently graduated from UCLA with a degree in political science, and from living in Southern California I imagined I knew more about Latino culture than I actually did. A year after graduation I had headed south, oblivious to my own ignorance. It took a year in Mexico to open my eyes to how much I didn't know. There was still a vast amount I didn't know, but at least I was no longer viewing Mexico through the lens of my imagination. By the time I left, I was seeing, and sometimes understanding, bits and pieces of its reality.

Later, with improved Spanish and a little more awareness, I struck out for South America. Again there was the painful discovery of how much I did not know about each country, and how much of what I thought I knew was inaccurate. At times I felt as ashamed as the teenaged waitress I had once been, who had not even known that a passport was required to travel abroad. My desire for adventure gradually gave way to the need to understand why things in other places were the way they were.

In those days most of my Western Hemisphere travels were in Central America. Few places could have been more dangerous during the 1980s and 1990s than the war zones of Central America, where priests were beaten to death on university campuses or while saying Mass, where women were routinely tortured, raped, and murdered, where whole villages were driven into exile or massacred. I was but one of many journalists, missionaries, students, and backpacking adventurers who became so politicized by what we saw that we left off what we were doing to try to help victims of the violence. In the eyes of some North Americans this made me as good as a Communist. But I had no ideology. What I had was a visceral reaction against men with guns. When they turned guns on unarmed civilians, I had no trouble deciding whose side I was on.

Little by little North Americans became aware of the horrors Central American governments were inflicting on their own people. Canada, I believe, protested sooner than the US because it was not in the business of propping up the region's most vicious regimes. But eventually articles about atrocities in Central America went mainstream. Awareness of what was going on south of the border came slowly but it did come. Except where Cuba was concerned.

What *was* going on in Cuba? The US media routinely portrayed Cuba as the most repressive nation in the Western Hemisphere. Cubans who wanted to leave their homeland were said to be proof of this. Reports on Cuban emigration never bothered to put the numbers into context. To have done so would have revealed that the percentage of Cubans leaving the island were about the same as those leaving capitalist Puerto Rico—and far fewer than those fleeing war-ravaged countries like El Salvador and Haiti.

I never believed that things were as bad in Cuba as the media made them out to be, yet I delayed going there until 1996 because I had allowed myself to be deceived on one account. Many times I heard that there was no freedom in Cuba and if one went there one would not be allowed to travel freely. I travel for many reasons but above all to see and understand. I wasn't keen on going anyplace where I wouldn't be allowed to do that. Thus my long delay in getting to Cuba to see whatever could be seen in a country where, by all accounts, I would be prevented from moving about freely.

I have already described my first trip there. I was not shadowed by government spies or prevented from staying in the homes of ordinary Cubans, where we discussed anything and everything. However, when I tried to tell North Americans about how freely I had wandered during that ten-day visit, most simply did not believe me.

Canadian friends, many of whom had vacationed at Cuba's new all-inclusive resorts, suggested that maybe I was allowed to move around easily because I was a foreigner. Wasn't it common knowledge that Cubans were watched all the time and had very little freedom? Some Cuban staff at their hotels seemed reluctant to socialize with them after hours, and, well, you just couldn't tell, could you?

My US friends were even more convinced of the lack of freedom in Cuba. Many said that what I told them about being able to mix and talk with ordinary Cubans could not be true. Either I had slipped under the radar or else my Cuban friends and I were being watched without my realizing it. I just hadn't been there long enough, they insisted, or been in the right places, to see what a repressive society it was.

I believed they were wrong about that, but they were right about one thing: ten days in the country had not made me any kind of authority. It had, in fact, left me with exactly the same frustration I had had so many times before in other places: a sense of my own abysmal ignorance about what was really going on. Either I had to shut my mouth about how things were in Cuba or else go back, travel further afield, and learn more than I had on that first trip.

Having become a Canadian citizen I could now go to Cuba whenever I liked. However, getting *to* Cuba was a lot easier than getting around there. The US embargo and no more Soviet subsidies meant that gasoline was scarce. Transportation options outside Havana and resort enclaves were limited. On my first visit, in 1996, every street corner and highway intersection swarmed with crowds of Cubans looking for motorized transport.

This situation would gradually become less acute, but fifteen years later, hours-long waits for any kind of transport vehicle was still a noticeable characteristic of Cuba. At any time during the first decade of the 21st century, ask any Cuban what their major problem was and the reply would likely be *"Transportación."*

Automobile-owning Cubans could get gasoline at very low, subsidized prices but were rationed to as little as one litre per month; thus most saved their allowance for emergencies. More gasoline could be purchased for dollars, and there were rental cars, so that was an option for foreign visitors. Travelling by bicycle was also an option. I liked the thought of cycling but was a little short on confidence. I had not even owned a bike since college. Besides, there were no cycling guides for the island. So for my second trip to Cuba I opted for the rental car.

A Canadian friend, Dianne Dennis, offered to go with me and share expenses providing we spent a fair bit of time at the beach. This seemed a good plan. I had not seen many Cuban beaches on my previous trip and there was one thing about those I had seen that intrigued me. It was that so many ordinary working-class Cubans lived on or within easy walking distance of the ocean. In Habana del Este (East Havana), about 200,000 people lived in public housing built on what in Vancouver, Miami, or Los Angeles would have been considered prime waterfront real estate. Many beachside communities east and west of Havana consisted of modest privately-owned homes. This convinced me that a beach-to-beach itinerary didn't have to mean resort-to-resort. There were probably Cuban communities on the coast as untouristed as towns in the interior.

I did know that the government, having taken the decision to rebuild the economy with recreational tourism, had designated many of the island's most beautiful beaches for resort development. In fact, one government planner told me that every fine beach in Cuba was slated for development, not immediately of course, but in five, ten, or twenty years. He said that plans had already been drawn up and locations prioritized. Hearing this gave me an extra incentive to get to beaches that within a few years were likely to go from wild to resortified.

Varadero

Dianne and I arrived in Cuba, rented a car at the Varadero airport, and drove to Peninsula Hicaco, where Varadero, the Cuban equivalent of resort-saturated Cancun, is located. Holiday seekers had begun spending beach vacations here as long ago as 1887. In the old days they traveled the one hundred kilometres from Havana to Matanzas by train and covered the remaining forty kilometres in a horse-drawn carriage.

Over the next half century Varadero evolved into an exclusive beach enclave for the very wealthy. In the 1920s, Irénée DuPont, having made millions from the manufacture of munitions during World War I, built a mansion called Xanadu out on the peninsula a kilometre or two northeast of town. The notorious Chicago gangster Al Capone built a beach house a few kilometres to the southwest.

Between La Casa de Al and Xanadu was the little town of Varadero. It had an atmosphere and architecture similar to Key West, Florida—hardly surprising since Key West, less than 150 kilometres across the Strait of Florida, started growing at about the same time. Dictator Fulgencio Batista, who controlled Cuba from 1934 until 1959, had a beach house in Varadero, too—a Spanish-style compound called Cuatro Palmas (Four Palms).

Following the victory of the Revolution, those properties were confiscated. Xanadu and La Casa de Al were opened to the public as upscale restaurants. Cuatro Palmas was used first to lodge and train high school and college students as teachers for the Revolution's anti-illiteracy campaign. Later it was turned into a hotel and remains that today.

Given Varadero's history as a vacation spot and the fact that the infrastructure was already there, it was logical that Cuba's first and most extensive resort development would be on Peninsula Hicacos. The peninsula angles out from the mainland like a thin thumb, fringed by twenty-two kilometres of white sand beach on the open ocean side. On the opposite side of this slim finger of land, the Bay of Cárdenas offers sheltered harbour for all manner of pleasure craft. Varadero's proximity to Havana, only two hours away, adds to its appeal.

Dianne and I were not planning to overnight in Varadero or at any of the nearby resorts. Instead, we drove fifteen kilometres beyond the town, almost to the end of the peninsula. The area was still in native vegetation. It featured such interesting things as small caves with pre-Columbian drawings, a giant cactus said to have been growing there when Columbus landed, and Laguna Magón, where generations of slaves worked and died extracting salt for curing meat supplied to Spanish ships. Havana friends had told me that this last hotel-free bit of the peninsula had a *campismo*—the

Cuban version of a campground. That was our destination.

We pulled into the campismo around dusk. After inspecting an A-frame hut and seeing that it was not mosquito-proof, we opted to pitch our own tent on the sand. The temperature was as perfect as we Canadians could imagine, but to Cubans the 22° Celsius was cold. No one was around except two young men there to look after the place. They did say that the next day, a Saturday, the campismo would be full.

Thus Dianne and I spent the night on one of the most beautiful beaches in the Caribbean, known internationally for its all-inclusive resorts but which we had entirely to ourselves with nary a hotel or tour bus in sight. We woke to a blue sky decorated with small puffs of cloud turned pink by the rising sun. Moments later we crawled out of our tent and crossed the beach. Dianne, a tall athletic woman with a mass of dark hair, splashed into the turquoise sea like a dolphin, I right behind her.

The fragility of paradise was brought home to us an hour later when we paddled in from a perfect swim in the crystal clear water. Although there was still not a soul in sight, the morning calm was being shattered by disco music over-amplified to the point of distortion. It came from an outdoor speaker almost as large as the economy car we had rented.

I found the two young men who had checked us in and asked how long the noise was likely to last. As it was only eight a.m., I supposed they were testing the speakers for some event later in the day. One of the boys cheerfully explained that the music had been turned on because bus-loads of Cuban high school kids would be arriving shortly to spend the weekend. There would be continuous music until they left on Sunday afternoon. He danced a few steps across the hard-packed sand and turned to me with an inviting smile. "You and your friend like to dance, yes?"

I had not been in Cuba long enough to perceive how foreign women of every age are seen there, and was charmed by the young man's desire to dance with a woman old enough to be his mother. Had I stumbled onto the one culture in the world with so much gender equality that it was as acceptable for a young man to be attracted to an older woman as it is for a young woman to be attracted to an older man?

I had, but not for reasons I yet understood. I would figure them out eventually, but only by referencing my own culture as well as Cuba's.

Who will forget the gorgeous young women who surrounded pudgy, over-the-hill Henry Kissinger when he was at the height of his power, or his reply when asked what it was about him they found so attractive: "Power is the ultimate aphrodisiac."

So it is in Cuba today. The comparative wealth of a foreign woman identifies her at once as a powerful person. It would have been pointless to explain that Dianne and I were not wealthy. How could we *not* be when it took a Cuban two months to earn what we spent daily on our rental car alone?

Even greater proof of our power was that we were free to travel as we pleased, in Cuba and out. I have often spent long periods in Cuba without meeting any Cuban who wants to leave for good, but never a day that I didn't meet some who longed to travel. Many do travel, of course; it's one of the most coveted perks offered by the government because travelling on the government dime is the only way most Cubans can afford it. But many more, lacking the personal resources or any reason for the government to sponsor them, will never have the resources to travel abroad.

Never mind my blue-green eyes, always perceived as pretty in cultures of darker complexions, or the fact that I'm small, also a plus in countries where the average man is not particularly tall. What makes me and all other foreign women attractive in Cuba is that combination of wealth and freedom to travel; in a word, power. It is not, of course, the kind of power Kissinger meant. But it is the kind of power most Cubans crave.

It would be easy to denigrate young men who fall for older foreign women as gold diggers, and the women who seduce them as cradle-robbers. I wouldn't deny that there are sexual predators in Cuba as much as anywhere else, but there are also attractions at work which are powerful and genuine. At least in the beginning.

It was a Londoner, herself happily married to a Cuban, who described to me what she saw at a Cuban festival in London, which is probably not uncommon in the evolution of such relationships.

"The place was swarming with older women with young Cuban partners. It wasn't the age difference that struck me; it was the power difference and how the women used it. They paraded around with their Cuban lovers on the emotional equivalent of diamond-studded leashes."

Whatever those young Cuban men thought they were getting into by way of a relationship with a foreign woman, it probably wasn't that.

Of all this I was innocent that morning on Varadero beach, and I expect the young man gyrating across the sand in front of me was, too. Given the tropical beauty of the beach, the intense blue of sky and sea, and the blood-churning disco rhythm, I might have taken his hand and, at least for the duration of a dance, played at being younger than I was. But a bus rolled in just at that moment and spilled out scores of lively teenagers.

He went off to do his job of checking them in while the kids surrounded me, an unexpected exotic on their beach.

They wanted to practice their English, asking questions about my country and how I liked theirs; wanted to see inside our tent and marvelled at how easy it was to take down. And when it was clear that we were leaving, wanted to exchange addresses in hopes of turning a casual meeting into a long-term friendship with these two unimaginably powerful women.

Driving East

Dianne and I paused in Varadero only long enough to grab a cup of coffee. Then we headed east on the Circuito Norte, a poorly-paved highway that runs more or less parallel to Cuba's north coast. Along the way we planned to take side roads leading to various offshore islands, each connected to the mainland by a recently built causeway.

Each island, on its open ocean side, has a long beautiful beach. Where there are reefs, snorkelling and scuba diving is outstanding. Foreign investors were already competing for sites on the nicest beaches. The Cuban government found it helpful that there were no communities or permanent residents on the islands to be disturbed by development; thus large resort complexes could be built without depriving Cubans of mainland beaches that they had traditionally enjoyed.

One more advantage of the offshore islands, rarely mentioned but important to the government, was that locating tourist facilities on offshore keys far from major population centers would reduce opportunities for foreign visitors to seek out Cubans for sex—or for Cubans to offer that service.

As we headed east from Varadero, the first island on our itinerary was Cayo Santa María. We were planning to camp there but that was not to be. The forty-eight-kilometre causeway was so new that, unbeknownst to us, it wasn't even open yet. About twenty kilometres along, driving a bit too fast on the brand new totally empty highway, I hit a rock that had rolled into the road. Blam! There went a tire! We inspected the damage and saw that the rim had been damaged as well. So—change of tire and change of plans. We headed back to the nearest town, Caibarién, to find someone to make repairs.

Entering Caibarién, we asked a teenaged boy if he knew where we might find a mechanic. He said there were lots of people in town who could fix a flat, but he had to think a minute before he recalled someone who had the tools to fix the rim. When the name came to him, he hopped into the back seat and directed us to the house.

The mechanic looked at the damage and listened sympathetically as I described how it had happened. He explained that the causeway leading to Santa María was open only for buses carrying labourers out to hotels still under construction. Even if we had reached the end of the causeway, security people there would not have allowed us to come onto the island.

The mechanic quickly separated tire from rim and went to work on the repairs. His wife came out of the house and invited us to wait inside. We gratefully accepted her invitation because by then it was blazing hot.

In the small living room I noticed a dark-haired doll in a yellow dress, prettily seated on a shelf. I asked if the doll was special.

The woman gave me a sly, sideways smile, and said, "When Catholics visit, she is Santa Barbara. When Santerians visit, she is the goddess Ochún. When the Baptists come, she is just a doll."

It took the man about an hour to fix the tire and rim. When we returned to our car, we were amazed to see that he had not only straightened the rim but had even got hold of some silver paint and dabbed it onto the hammer marks so it was nearly impossible to see where the dent had been. We paid him for his work, thanked his wife for her hospitality, and asked her to express our appreciation to whichever god she figured was responsible for guiding us to their house. Then we went on our way.

Along Cuba's North Coast

Having learned that we could not get to Cayo Santa María, we continued east to the next causeway and drove out to Cayo Coco. There were already several big resorts on Cayo Coco as well as one on an adjacent key called Cayo Guillermo. We figured that we would have no trouble finding somewhere on Cayo Coco's twenty kilometres of white beach to pitch our tent. We found a suitable beach away from the resorts and had just jumped in for a swim when I noticed a small building surrounded by native vegetation. It was on a bluff with a view of the beach for a long way in either direction. If someone there had not spotted us already, they would soon. Thus it seemed unwise to behave as if the beach belonged to us—which it did not. Better to ask if it was okay to camp there.

A kindly man in charge of what he explained was a weather research station said, with some hesitation, that he thought it would be okay to camp there for the one night. His two female co-workers objected. They pointed out that camping wasn't allowed outside campismos and there was no campismo on Cayo Coco. But their greater concern seemed to be for our comfort. I insisted that our tent *was* comfortable, but they remained unconvinced. "It is better you don't sleep on the beach. There are no facilities for camping, no bathroom or anything."

"The sun is setting already," I pointed out. "The causeway

is almost thirty kilometres long and then there is the drive on to Morón. For sure it will be dark before we get there. And it has only one hotel. We don't even know if we can find a room."

"*Sí, sí.*" The women acted as if this was so obvious as to not even require discussion. "Don't worry, you just come with us."

They led us to a small bedroom with two bunks. "We have students who come during the week," one explained. "But this is the weekend so they've gone back to town. You can sleep here tonight."

And so we did. Dianne and I told each other that we would have preferred our own tent down on the beach, but there was no denying that it was nice to have a flush toilet and a shower to wash away sand and sea salt before tucking in.

The next day we continued east, having slept well but having eaten only a few crackers we had stashed in the car. The Circuito Norte was mostly flat and somewhat boring. The small towns we passed through had nothing resembling a restaurant. By noon I was getting grumpy from low blood sugar. Suddenly a red hen dashed in front of the car. I slammed on the brakes, missing the chicken but stalling the engine.

"Dumb thing must be trying to commit suicide," I grumbled. "Why else would she run out in front of what was probably the only car to come by all day?" I sat there for a minute, then pulled off onto the shoulder and got out.

"Where are you going?" Dianne asked.

I grinned. "Where there are chickens there are eggs, Dianne. I'm going to find us some breakfast."

By then the chicken was nowhere in sight, but there were three small cinderblock houses in the direction it had run. I knocked on the first door and asked the little girl who opened it, "Do you have any chickens?"

She shook her head and pointed to the house next door. "They do," she said. In the charming way of small children in Cuba, she then took me by the hand and led me to the neighbour's house.

The front door was open. Just inside, sitting in a spot of sun, was a man in a rocking chair. He was wearing only swim trunks. Across his abdomen was a long, recent scar. He did not rise when I appeared in the doorway. Before either of us could speak, the child said importantly, "She wants to see the owner of the chickens."

He called into the kitchen. "Yudy!" Then turned back to me and asked, "Did you run over one?"

"Almost," I admitted. "But no. It's just, my friend and I, we haven't had breakfast and—" Yudy appeared in the doorway and I finished hopefully, "We were wondering if we might buy a couple of boiled eggs from you."

It seemed to take them a second or two to absorb this unusual request. Then Yudy said, "But you said you haven't had breakfast. Would you like me to fix you something?"

"Well, uh, sure. But just a couple of eggs would be fine."

"I'll fix you something," she insisted. "Sit—or no, go get your friend. You can talk to my husband while I make the eggs. You like them scrambled? Or in a *tortilla?*"

"Scrambled would be great," I said, not knowing what she might put in a tortilla, which in Cuba is an omelette, not the kind of flatbread called tortillas in North America.

When I returned with Dianne the man was still sitting in the living room, having only turned the rocking chair slightly so as to remain in the spot of sun coming through the open front door. He motioned us to a seat on the sofa.

"Excuse me for not getting up," he said. "But I am just home from hospital." He glanced down at the scar. "It was a serious operation, with some complications. I was there for a month. I was told to sit with the sun shining on my skin for an hour every day. That, and some cream they gave me, is supposed to help. They say the healing, inside and out, will take another month."

"Then you will be well enough to go back to work?" I asked.

He shrugged. "Maybe, maybe not. I get the same salary during convalescence as I got while I was in hospital. The same as my normal salary."

I translated all this for Dianne. She said, "Wow!"

He looked from one of us to the other. "You are Canadian? Or English?"

"Canadian," Dianne replied.

"Then your government provides you with the same health benefits as here in Cuba, right?"

"Not full salary," she said. "And a lot of drugs aren't covered either."

He looked disappointed. "I thought Canada had a better health care system."

I grinned ruefully. "No—just better than what the US has."

"Of course," he said complacently. "In the US hospitals are only for the rich."

"Well, not only. There are hospitals where people without money can go," I explained. "But they are not as good."

Again he shrugged. "In a way it's like that in Cuba. We have our medical tourism, with special facilities for foreigners who can pay in dollars. I have never been inside one but they are probably nicer than hospitals for ordinary Cubans. I don't think the doctors there would be any better, though. I got the best care, really, the very best. When they couldn't do the procedure locally, I was taken by ambulance to Havana. It didn't cost me a centavo."

We were still talking about the Cuban medical system

and details of the gastrointestinal operation he had had when Yudy reappeared in the doorway and motioned to us. "Come. Breakfast is ready."

Dianne and I traipsed into the kitchen. On a small table sat two plates, each with a heap of scrambled yellow eggs, bright red sliced tomatoes, and a piece of bacon, thick-sliced, country style. I think our appetites told Yudy more than our enthusiastic words just how much we appreciated the food. But even as we ate I worried that we might be taking food out of the family's mouth. Of course we'd pay for the food but given Cuba's shortages, where, for example, would they find more bacon?

When I tactfully put this question to Yudy she explained that was no problem in her community because, "We don't depend on the libreta. I have chickens and they produce more than what my husband and I need for ourselves." She pointed to the house where the child lived. "That family has plantains and a huge avocado tree—enough for all the neigh-bours. And there," she pointed across the highway, "that man raises pigs. We trade back and forth. You understand?"

This explanation and others allowed me to grasp that while the food rations all Cubans received from the govern-ment ensured that nobody starved, those living in rural areas typically ate better than many in the city who were not able to produce their own food—or chose not to. That last of course would change, and in fact was changing even then. A year earlier, while staying with Deisy in Santa Fe, I had met a young woman working with an Australian NGO called "The Green Team," which had as its mission urban food production.

"The first five years were unbelievably hard," the Aussie woman had told me. "A lot of city folks think they are too good to garden. It's like, 'this is what we fought the Revolution for—to get away from hard labour on the farm.' Government officials were very suspicious of us, too. But then came the withdrawal of Soviet aid and suddenly they were like, 'You want to start gardens in schools? Seniors centers? On hospital grounds? No problem! What can we do to help?' We were encouraged to start gardens all over the place. I'd say there are at least 20,000 urban gardens in Havana now."

When I remarked that I hadn't seen very many gardens on my strolls around the city, the Green Team girl pinned me with a single question: "And how many balconies, roof-tops, and backyard patios have you seen?"

Point taken. I would later learn more about how food production in Cuba was changing. However, as we all but licked our plates clean there in Yudy's kitchen, what I was learning was how, even in these hard times, rural Cubans managed to eat pretty well.

In other Latin American countries I had often scolded backpackers for accepting hospitality without repaying it in some way. The last thing I wanted was to be one of those travellers who take such delight in vacationing on the cheap that they cheerfully take advantage of the generosity offered by people infinitely less well off than they are. But in Cuba the issue of what to give local people in exchange for what they gave us was a tricky one. It wasn't made easier when we asked, "How much do we owe you?" and rural people like Yudy often said *"Nada."*

If we pressed the point, they would throw up their hands and say, "It doesn't matter. Whatever you feel like."

The issue was further compounded by the fact that Cubans had not engaged in modern commerce for nearly half a century. They had been taught that one should share whatever one had to share, and that charging for goods and services was not a particularly nice thing to do. However, that did *not* mean that those who shared expected nothing in return. While it was not polite for them to ask for anything, neither was it polite for the receiver to fail to reciprocate in some way. With neighbours that was easy, but what about transients like us?

What Dianne and I decided at the outset of our trip was that if we asked for something we would not fail to pay, even if the person said payment wasn't necessary. Nor would we pay a ridiculously small amount simply because the people in question were so unaccustomed to commerce that they had no idea what their service was worth—like the mechanic in Caibarién who had asked only US$1 for the hour he spent repairing our tire and rim. Insofar as I knew or could guess what the same thing would cost in Havana, that was what we paid.

Now, knowing that in Havana we would have paid about US$2.50 each for a breakfast like the one Yudy served us, that was what we paid. It didn't matter that her husband's salary might be only $15 a month. We would not have hesitated to pay $5 for those two breakfasts in the city, so why should Yudy not get the same? Poverty, I reasoned, was not a good excuse for paying poorly.

However, this solved only part of the problem. On my first visit the year before, I had learned that Cubans would incessantly be doing favours for which they simply *would not* accept money. In many cases the very offer of payment seemed inappropriate, as it would have turned a simple act of kindness into a commercial transaction. So we had looked for a way to handle that, too. Our solution was to bring for our own use only what we could stuff into our carry-ons, and to max out our checked luggage allowance (which in 1997 was twice what it is now) with items that were hard to get in Cuba. As a result, the trunk of our car was stuffed with things to share with Cubans struggling with shortages caused by the embargo and Special Period restructuring of the economy.

We did not give away things willy-nilly, but were always looking for situations where a gift might be appropriate; for example, a baseball for the boy who had helped us find the mechanic, blouses left behind in Cayo Coco for the two women who had insisted we use their spare room, a box of crayons for the little girl who guided me to Yudy's house. On this trip, and every other I made to Cuba, there were five or ten such situations each day. Many occurred as a result of a phenomenon I haven't yet mentioned—hitchhikers.

We had barely pulled out of the rental car lot at the airport when we picked up our first hitchhikers, two girls who had just got off work and were on their way home in a town about ten kilometres away. When we stopped to let them out two more young women, heading to work in Varadero, asked for a ride. The directions they gave us for getting to the campismo at the end of the peninsula was our first lesson in how valuable it was to have someone local in the car to help us get where we wanted to go. We started by picking up only women and children. Then began stopping for whole families, who would squeeze gratefully into the back seat.

We had brought many pairs of children's shoes, and as a small child sat with his or her feet dangling off their parents' lap, it was easy to compare the size of those feet with shoes we knew we had in the trunk of the car. While the adults were reluctant to accept anything for themselves, they never refused a gift for their children. After all, seeing that children had the best available—that *was* the Cuban way.

Even with hitchhikers the gift-giving was not a one-way deal. Adults who caught rides with us often insisted that we take some of the fruit most carried with them for travel food and for sharing with whoever they were going to visit.

When we stopped for the night, either Dianne or I always had to check around and under the car seats to collect mangos, avocados, bananas, pineapples, and other fruit gifts that had ended up there. More than one night, when we camped in an area where no food was available, that was what we had for dinner.

I had been told by a Cuban official that when it came to selecting beaches for development, top priority went to Varadero where infrastructure already existed. Second priority, he said, was being given to islands like Santa María, connected to the mainland by recently-built causeways. But as we continued east along Circuito Norte, we noticed that the government's plan to put resorts on several keys along its north coast had been put on hold. Whatever Cuba's contribution was to have been toward the joint ventures—presumably roads and other infrastructure—the Special Period had made it difficult to follow through. Our map showed a road leading to a causeway that connected Cayo Romano to the mainland. However, the road was impassable due to heavy rains. We ran into the same problem when we tried to get to the causeway leading to Cayo Sabinal. Only a horse, bicycle, or sturdy trekker could have been certain to make it all the way to the causeway and across the island to what was reputed to be an extraordinarily beautiful beach. "Come back during the dry season," the locals advised.

I determined to do that, and did, but it took three trips at different times of the year to finally get to those islands. In 2012, Cayo Romano and Cayo Sabinal were still uninhabited and showed no signs of development beyond causeways to the mainland.

Further along, in the province of Las Tunas, we were told by residents in two tiny communities—Las Bocas (The

Mouths) and La Herradura (The Horseshoe)—that one day the government would build hotels there, tourists would come, and there would be something other than fishing to sustain them. It was easy to believe this, for each of these communities had *two* beautiful beaches—one on the bay and one on the open ocean. But the apparent abandonment of far more ambitious projects on Cayo Romano and Cayo Sabinal made me wonder. Of course tourism infrastructure would line these beaches "someday," and the locals would probably be glad of it. But in the meantime, I was glad to have reached Las Bocas and La Herradura in time to experience the easy camaraderie of local folks who had not yet hosted so many foreigners that their own culture had begun to change.

I need not have hurried to get there. When I visited Las Bocas and La Herradura again in 2012, they had barely changed. There were a few private homes licensed to rent rooms, and a few tourists, enough, I suppose, to sustain those little B&Bs. Several women served home-cooked meals of fresh seafood, both contraband and legally caught, but neither village as yet had a hotel or regular bus service. The streets were still sand and it was still easy to walk for kilometres along the beach without seeing anyone other than local residents.

The main change I saw when I returned in 2012 was that most of the sand on the long oceanfront beach had been washed away by a recent hurricane, leaving a rock-and-rubble-strewn coastline. It occurred to me that the disappearance of its once gorgeous beach might be the very thing that precluded resort development in this location.

From La Herradura we swung inland to Holguín, then back to the beach at Guardalavaca—an amusing name that translates as "guard the cow." Apparently there had once been pens there that held cattle, bought by Spanish ships to feed their crews on the voyage across the Atlantic.

However, the town, if it could be called a town, was not as pleasing as its name. The beach, yes, was beautiful. Snorkelling and scuba diving was good and easily accessible at a long reef 100 metres from shore. Two resort complexes contained all the usual facilities sought by those who opt for that kind of vacation. What Guardalavaca lacked, with its poorly planned development, was any sense of community. Most resort employees did not live in town near the beach. They lived about five kilometres away in a large housing development. Often such residential complexes are situated on the waterfront, thereby offering those who live in the apartments beautiful views and easy access to the beach. However, the planners had not done that in Guardalavaca.

I considered this a real planning deficit until, a decade later, in Baracoa, I saw the destruction of ocean-front public housing units wrought by a recent hurricane. That may have left those living a few kilometres back from the sea feeling that the planners hadn't made a mistake after all.

Dianne and I tramped about Guardalavaca looking for an isolated section of beach to camp. Not finding anything suitable, a little after dark we decided to pitch our tent at a spot on the beach midway between a hotel and some vacation apartments. We had trouble falling asleep, as voices sometimes carried to us from a nearby path. I had just drifted off when I heard a soft feminine voice calling, *"Compañeras?"*

I unzipped the tent and looked out. A stout woman in a bathrobe stood there looking worried.

"I am sorry to disturb you," she apologized. "But this is not a good place to put your tent. It is against the rules to camp on this beach. The police will be by soon." She pointed to the path. "They make rounds every two hours."

"Oh crap," Dianne muttered sleepily. "Did I hear her say something about *policia*?"

"Unfortunately, yes," I told Dianne. To the woman, I said, "Thank you for telling us. We don't know the area. We tried to find a place farther out of town, but the road in both directions leads away from the beach."

"You *want* to sleep on the beach?" she queried.

"Well, yes," I told her, wondering why else she might suppose we were here.

"Then move your tent over under the deck of my apartment." She pointed to the nearby beachfront apartments, each with a deck that extended over the sand, to within a few yards of the surf. "The police will not be able to see it there."

We didn't really want to put our tent under her deck, even though she said her family, who had rented the place for the week, was already in bed and we wouldn't hear a thing. But neither did we want to be awakened again in an hour by a police patrol telling us that camping on this beach was not allowed. Above all, we did not want to seem ungrateful to a Cuban woman who, in the middle of the night and already dressed for bed, had put on her robe and come trudging down the beach to explain the rules to two *nortamericanas* and offer them a safe alternative.

It was a characteristic I would come to cherish about Cubans; their way of not interfering with whatever inexplicable thing the foreigner is doing unless they see that they are headed for trouble. Only then will they insist, really insist, that you do their version of the appropriate thing.

Women's Day at Playa Maguana

From Guardalavaca we continued east along the coast. I was curious about Cayo Saetía, another island connected to the mainland by bridge, but I had heard that it was a hunting preserve for Cuba's military brass so decided to give it a miss. When I did get around to visiting Cayo Saetía in 2005, and again in 2008, I would discover that the hunting had been more or less phased out, leaving behind only a small comfortable hotel and yet another island jewel bypassed by heavy tourism.

Dianne and I were within eighty kilometres of the eastern tip of Cuba when we came to Playa Maguana. We were ready for a beachcombers' paradise and miraculously, this was where we found it. Maguana's pale gold, gently curving beach was caressed by translucent water and backed by palms and sea grape trees. The only lodgings for visitors was a small "villa"—basically somebody's former beach house— with four rooms for rent and a front porch so close to the water that waves practically lapped up under it during high tide. We did not need a room as we had our tent, but we thought we might need the villa's restaurant because we did not see anything that resembled a community.

However, there was a community. We had not seen it when we drove in because the huts were concealed by the lush tropical vegetation that characterized this part of the island. After pitching our tent and toasting awhile on the beach, I went exploring. What we had taken for thick forest covering the half-mile between highway and beach was in fact a populated area. Along meandering sandy footpaths lay at least two dozen wood frame huts with palm-thatched roofs. Most had rough-hewn wooden floors, but some floors were of hard-packed earth, especially in the open-air sheds at the back of each house where the cooking was done.

The houses did not appear to have been there very long so I asked how they came to be. A local resident named Pedro explained, "The government is responsible for providing housing. Until the Special Period it did pretty well, although it never quite keep up with the demand. You can see, in Baracoa, a lot of apartment blocks right on the Malecón, with balconies facing the bay. There is a waiting list for those apartments, though. Here at Maguana the government built a clinic and an elementary school but no houses. We got tired of waiting so we built our own."

"Everybody built their own house?" I asked, looking down the long sandy track that disappeared into the forest.

"Everybody around here," he said. "But some prefer living in town in whatever they can find. The ones like me who have stayed, we like living by the sea, like catching our own fish. And here," he motioned toward the villa, "the tourists come."

Before I could ask what benefit a four-room lodge could provide by way of tourism income, he asked a question that provided something of an explanation. "You and your friend, would you like my wife to fix dinner for you? It is better than the villa restaurant. Cheaper, too."

Well, yes, I thought. We'd have a fresh seafood dinner, a bargain at US$5 each, and the family would earn $10, almost equal to the monthly wage of a cane cutter. I did not see how *all* the families living there could earn a living from tourism, but at least some of them would benefit from the trickle of foreigners who fetched up on their beach. Their health care was free, their kids' schooling was free, their housing was free, and most of their food was free, acquired through government distribution or else taken from the sea and surrounding fruit trees. It was a simple life, could call it a life of poverty. But given that subsistence safety net and the possibilities offered by education for at least some of their children, it was nowhere near as harsh as the poverty I had seen on other Caribbean islands and throughout Latin America.

My visits to little hand-built cottages up and down the

sandy lanes of Maguana resulted in an invitation for Dianne and me to join the community next day for a fiesta celebrating International Women's Day. We didn't have to worry about the time because when the time came—that is, when music being blasted from outdoor amplifiers set up on the school soccer field reached us—a number of locals came to escort us to the dance. The loud music made it seem like a high school dance and many teens were in evidence. But there were also elders, middle-aged people, young parents, and little children. A few speeches were tossed off about the contributions of women to home and country, then everybody got down to the real reason for the fiesta: dancing. This was literally a "dance till you drop" experience, and I admit that Dianne, younger and much in demand, lasted a lot longer than I did.

Between the friendliness of the people and the beauty of the beach we had some difficulty leaving Playa Maguana, and so dawdled there too long for what was meant to be a reconnaissance trip around the entire island. Eventually though, we brushed the sand off our feet, climbed into the car, and drove the remaining twenty-one kilometres to Baracoa.

Columbus reached the Baracoa area in 1492. He sailed a short distance inland on a deep clear river. The flowering and fruit-laden trees to water's edge, filled with singing birds, induced him to write in his journal that this island was "the most beautiful land that human eyes have seen."

Baracoa was a Taíno village then. Now it is a quaint town with three pocket-sized parks well-used by local folks and tourists alike. One park has a bust of the Taíno chief Hatuey who led a fierce guerrilla war against Spanish invaders, thus going down in history as Cuba's first revolutionary. When Hatuey was finally captured, a Dominican priest, Bartolomé de Las Casas, tried to save him but failed. Las Casas wrote of

Hatuey's execution: "A Franciscan monk, a holy man, spoke as much as he could to him in the little time that the executioner granted them, about God and some of the teachings of our faith, of which he had never before heard. He told him that if he would believe what was told him, he would go to heaven where there was glory and eternal rest; and if not, that he would go to hell, to suffer perpetual torments and punishment. After thinking a little, Hatuey asked the monk whether the Christians went to heaven. The monk answered that those who were good went there. The chief at once said, without any more thought, that he did not wish to go there, but rather to hell so as not to be where Spaniards were." And so the pyre was set alight.

Apparently the Spaniards had God on their side because in addition to steel, gunpowder, and an astonishing capacity for cruelty, they brought germs that felled the indigenous population like nerve gas. Within fifty years, few if any were left.

I loved Baracoa but hanging about to soak up its history and charm would have to wait for another trip. Like many first-time visitors who set out to see "all of Cuba" in two weeks, Dianne and I had not grasped the reality of how big the island is. It had seemed small on the map, but after days of driving, we realized that Cuba is small only in comparison to continent-sized countries like the US and Canada.

Now, having visited only a few of the prettiest beaches along the north coast, already it was time to head back to the Varadero airport, 900 kilometres away. We checked the map and figured that if we put in one long day of driving up the centre of the island we would just have time to hit two interesting beaches on the south coast: Playa Ancón near the town of Trinidad, and Playa Girón at the mouth of the Bay of Pigs.

There were fewer buses running on Sunday and many people hitchhiking, a lot of them well-dressed and on their way to church. Most were going only a few kilometres, which meant continuous pickups, drop-offs, and more pickups and drop-offs. A whole family would sometimes squeeze into the back seat of our compact car, children layered in their parents' laps. Frequently one of the adults would lean forward to give us a religious tract promoting one evangelical denomination or another: Baptist, Methodist, Pentecostal, Seventh Day Adventist, Latter Day Saints, and others. Sometimes this "gift" was accompanied by an invitation to join them at church services, or even a proselytizing spiel.

I, who understood Spanish and therefore could not tune out the sermon as easily as Dianne, soon grew distinctly cranky.

As Dianne, who was driving, stopped to drop off one persistent Jehovah Witness, I snapped, "That's it. One more person hands me a religious tract and we don't pick up any more Sunday hitchhikers!"

Just then a family with babies in arms waved and Dianne stopped. It was, after all, late morning and dreadfully hot. They were barely settled in the back seat when the woman leaned forward and asked, "Have you been born again?"

"I hope not," I said shortly, and turned on the radio to preclude further conversation. Immediately an evangelical sermon came on. I switched off the radio and grumbled to Dianne, "Proselytizing used to be illegal in Cuba. Five years ago they changed the law, and now, in the name of religious freedom, this is what we get."

"I thought Cuba was a Catholic country," she remarked.

I had thought so, too, but later, looking up the statistics, I learned that even before the Revolution, when 80% of the Cuban population claimed to be Catholic, the Church itself had judged that only 10% were active. Despite the Revolutionary government's coolness to all religions, there had been only a slight drop in the number of Cubans who practiced Catholicism, from 10% down to 8%. Another 5% claimed membership in a Protestant denomination. Afro-Cuban religions were also popular, but nobody seemed to know exactly how many practiced Santería or to what extent. Recalling the lady in Caibarién with the doll that changed religions depending on her visitors' faith, I could see why reliable statistics might be hard to come by.

A South Coast Beach

Playa Ancón is on a thin peninsula that juts out from the south coast of Cuba the same way the peninsula where Varadero is located juts out from the island's north coast. But Playa Ancón is not as long or as cluttered with resorts. In 1998, Varadero already had a dozen resort complexes, whereas Peninsula Ancón had only two. The nearby town of Trinidad, recently designated as a UNESCO World Heritage Site, attracted many tourists, yet the next fifteen years, which would see almost fifty more resorts built in Varadero, would see only one more built on Playa Ancón.

Ancón is a unique beach by Cuban standards, in that it is strewn with chunks of bone-white coral that are often raked into mounds a metre high. We couldn't know when we trekked across the coral-strewn sand and plunged into the warm Caribbean Sea that this particular beach would remain so little changed in the coming decade. For all we knew, this was our one chance to enjoy the lovely, mostly-empty beach before it was given over to lounge chairs laden with white-bodied sun worshipers from our own country and others. The tent went up, and our own bodies, now well-tanned, went down on the fine white sand.

A breeze came up in mid-afternoon so I decided to take a walk. Heading in one direction, I soon came upon sharp black rocks that the locals call *dente de los perros* (dogs' teeth). I retraced my steps and walked a kilometre or so in the other direction, toward the two big hotels near the end of the peninsula.

However, before I got to the hotels I came to a campismo. It was closed but a dozen teenagers were hanging about getting it ready, they said, to open for spring break. As far as I could see they were not really doing anything. The beach-front patio/dance floor hadn't even been swept clean of dead palm fronds. Windows had been blown out, exposing the inside of the building to the weather.

The teenagers said the damage had been done by Hurricane Lili, which had hit that coast hard five months earlier. I wondered why it had not been repaired or at least those broken windows boarded up. The answer would come a year later when this campismo, like the one in Varadero, would be demolished to make way for another hotel. It would be the third and last to be built on Playa Ancón for years to come.

The kids were full of questions about where I was from and what it was like there. They lived in a big public housing complex about ten kilometres away, near what had once been the port of Casilda. (The port is still there but has been silted in so no longer functions as such. Major shipping off Cuba's south coast had long since moved 100 kilometres west, to Cienfuegos.)

Earlier, when Dianne and I were in Trinidad, I had been approached by museum guides asking for soap, which was in short supply due to the fact that Cuba had only two soap factories and most of that output was needed for the tourism industry. But the only thing these teens asked for was an exchange of addresses and a promise that I would write. They were bored, impatient for the campismo to open, waiting for something to happen. They reminded me of teenagers in the small Canadian town near my home, sitting for hours on the steps of the bank because it offered the best vantage point from which to see and socialize with other teens, waiting for the town's single patrolman to go off duty so they could skateboard on the sidewalk, waiting for the town council to decide that teens needed a skateboard park, waiting for something—anything—to happen.

Surely, in Cuba as in Canada, there were young people doing all sorts of interesting things: studying for exams, holding down jobs, playing sports, or making music. But those would not be the kids you'd see lounging on the bank steps in my home town and they were not the kids I saw hanging out around the closed campismo on Playa Ancón.

Even during the Special Period, the Cuban government gave youth its highest priority. Education to and beyond university was free for those who made the grades. There were plenty of sports facilities and every school and community had its teams. The Young Pioneers, a nation-wide youth group comparable to Scouts, organized camping trips and other outings. Voluntarism was encouraged and applauded. Yet in every community we visited, there were kids like these, languid as fish, floating in the torpor of their own boredom.

The Bay of Pigs

We left Trinidad's Playa Ancón for the Bahía de Cochinos (Bay of Pigs), two hours to the west. The bay extends about thirty kilometres inland, and is surrounded by the 4,230 square kilometre Parque Montemar, most of which is covered by the Zapata swamp. In some ways this swamp resembles the Florida Everglades but it is far less damaged. Around the fringes of the swamp are sugar cane fields and orange groves such as one sees in Florida, but not the huge residential sub-divisions and massive man-made drainage systems that have disrupted water flow to the Everglades. The natural flow of water feeding the plants and animals of the Zapata remains largely intact.

Once in Parque Montemar we passed through two small towns—Playa Larga at the head of the Bahía de Cochinos and Playa Girón at the mouth of the bay. Midway between them was a rustic compound used by Fidel when he wanted to dive there. The bay is a prime spot for snorkelling and scuba diving, and the wild Zapata region had always appealed to Fidel. He probably felt even more affection for the area after the locals, who were among the poorest people in Cuba, turned out in force to repel the US-organized invasion of 1961. Later Celia Sánchez proposed that the area be developed for tourism, partly to provide jobs in an area that did not lend itself to agriculture and partly to create vacation possibilities in a location that would give other Cubans a chance to see where their nation's most remarkable victory had taken place.

For those reasons, the government turned most of the Zapata swamp into a national park and built three modest resorts—one at Playa Larga, one at Playa Girón, and one called Villa Guamá, with individual cottages situated on little bridge-connected islands in the Laguna de Tesores (Treasure Lake). Villa Guamá, which includes a crocodile farm and restaurant serving crocodile meat, would become a popular honeymoon destination for Cubans, and as intended, would provide jobs for the area's 7000 or so inhabitants. But tourism in Parque Montemar remains low-key, geared mainly to Cubans and foreigners with a particular interest in scuba diving, bird-watching, or Revolutionary history.

Dianne and I had no trouble finding an isolated beach just east of Playa Girón on which to pitch our tent—a situation which I would find little changed a decade later. We had hoped to do some snorkelling, and would have liked to see some of the barnacle-encrusted landing craft that had been sunk in the bay during what Americans call the Bay of Pigs invasion and Cubans call *La Victoria* (The Victory). But the day was so windy that neither snorkelling nor sunbathing was appealing. We decided to add to our knowledge of the area's history instead.

At the entrance to the little town of Playa Girón, an enormous billboard proclaimed this to be the site of the *Primera Gran Derrota del Imperialismo en America Latina* (First Great Defeat of Imperialism in Latin America). Given that half a century later it would still be the *only* defeat, Cubans had a right to be proud. And proud of what that victory had achieved. Cuba retained its independence and most of the 1,197 invaders captured on the beach or in the swamp that day were ransomed back to the US for $53 million in food and medical aid for the Cuban people.

At the small Museo Girón we saw weaponry captured during the invasion and a room with pictures of the 119 Cubans killed. Beneath the photos was a glass cabinet that held personal artefacts, touching in their simplicity: a plastic comb, a high school ID card, battered photos of family members. On the wall at the far end of this display was another list. It gave the names of many of the invaders, along with a list of what each family had owned prior to the Revolution—prime urban real estate, sugar plantations, banks, hotels, large companies, and much more. No political commentary accompanied either display. The contrast said it all. It had been a war not of brother against brother, but of a few affluent Cubans against an island full of very poor ones.

Unsentimental as I am, one photograph made me inexpressibly sad. It was of a young Cuban soldier lying next to a wall with the half-finished name of Fidel which he was writing with his own blood at the moment of his death. The fact that this particular photograph is displayed in many places around Cuba for propaganda purposes does not discredit a truth about that young man's life, what he cared about, and how he died. The photograph remains a symbol of the sacrifice so many Cubans are still willing to make for a Revolution that they are ready to defend but will not live to see finished.

That night the wind blew so hard that at times Dianne and I thought our tent was going to become airborne with us inside. But by morning it had died down and the water was smooth as glass. We would have liked to spend days snorkelling in the Bahía de Cochinos and sunbathing on little cove beaches east of the bay, but the date of our homebound flight was at hand. Reluctantly, we packed up our sandy selves into the car and headed for the Varadero airport on the opposite side of the island.

That final day's drive took us along the eastern shore of the bay, through the sugar mill town of Australia, and along many kilometres of perfectly flat highway lined with orange groves. As we motored along, passing Cubans on foot, horseback, and bike, I was reminded that if I really wanted to get to know Cuba, insulating myself in an air-conditioned car was not the best way to do it. How most local people were travelling by necessity was how I should travel by choice. Next time.

PART 3

WINDS OF CHANGE

Anyone who travels east or west from Havana for, say, fifty kilometres, could get the impression that cycling in Cuba is as easy as it gets. The coastal area is nearly flat and the sparkling ocean is almost always in view. The Vía Monumental leading east out of the city and the Habana-Mariel freeway leading west each has a right-hand lane designated for slow traffic, which in Cuba means horse-drawn conveyances, tractors, and bicycles. If you are in downtown Havana and want to cross the harbour in order to cycle east, you can, for a few centavos, push your bike onto the ferry that runs back and forth across the harbour, or take the bicycle bus that runs through the tunnel under the harbour. Both run often and are no different from any other bus or ferry except that you board by ramp and make the short ride not seated but standing next to your bike.

Details like this convinced me that even though I had not even owned a bike since college, I could handle cycling there. Derek, my wise and supportive Canadian partner, has never protested my going anywhere, alone or with whomever I wished to travel. However, when I announced that I thought I would like to ride the entire coastline of Cuba, a distance of roughly 5000 kilometres, he looked dubious.

I cutely pointed out that that was *only* 1000 times further than from our house in rural British Columbia to the nearest town. Borrowing Derek's bike, I demonstrated that I could easily ride those five kilometres and, after a cappuccino break at the village bookstore, be back home again in one morning. I reasoned that it would just take more mornings (and more coffee) to do the coast of Cuba.

In a tiny "sports museum" in Matanzas, I learned that the bicycle was introduced to Cuba about 1900. Beginning in 1972, an international bicycle race modelled on the Tour de France was run every February, from one end of the island to the other. Even before I was aware of those historic facts, I observed that millions of Cubans were relying on bikes as their primary source of transportation. When the US embargo combined with an end to Soviet aid made it impossible for Cuba to get enough petroleum to keep more than a few vehicles running, bicycles were imported from China and distributed throughout the country.

By the time of my first visit to Cuba in the mid-1990s there were more bicycle wheels in Cuba than any other kind. Whole families traveled by bike: dad pedaling, mom on the back, often with a child in her arms and another perched on the handlebars. It was commonplace to see a hog, a goat, or a load of lumber carried on a bike. One even saw bicycles for handicapped people, specially modified so they could be pedaled by hand. This helped convince me that the best way to see "the real Cuba" (the part away from popular tourist destinations) would be to cycle around the island. This could take me to every province, through cities, villages, and rural areas, through orange groves, rice paddies, sugar cane fields, mangrove swamps, and (gulp) mountains. It would be my graduate seminar on Cuba.

At the last minute, Derek, who rightly suspected I knew even less about bike mechanics than I did about the place I was proposing to travel, decided to come along.

Cycling West

In January 1998, Derek and I flew to Cuba, bringing with us my new mountain bike and his old ten-speed road bike. We also brought along two guide books. One was Lonely Planet's *Cuba*, written by a Canadian, David Stanley, who had lived in Cuba on several different occasions and traveled the island end to end by bus, bike, jeep, and train. The other was Moon's *Cuba Handbook* by British travel writer Christopher Baker, who had spent several months touring Cuba by motorcycle. Both writers knew the island well and had a penchant for off-the-beaten path places. The only problem was that I intended to get further off the beaten path than either of them had (or further than either had written about). I had done that kind of travel in other Latin American and Caribbean countries, but Cuba was not like any of them. There was only so much homework I could do in advance. At some point I'd have to start flying—or pedaling—by the seat of my pants.

Derek and I cycled along Havana's Malecón just as the sun was rising and the clouds beginning to blush. Waves were hitting the seawall and splashing over into the bike lane, so that by the time we reached Río Almendares (Almond River), we were as drenched as if we had been riding in the rain. Bikes are not allowed in the tunnel under the river so we detoured a couple of blocks to the pedestrian bridge. Once across the river, rather than following Avenida 5, we rode along Avenida 1 which runs closer to the shore. My plan, or the nearest thing I had to a plan, was to stay as close as possible to the ocean, following Cuba's 5,746 kilometre (3,570-mile) coast wherever there were roads to follow.

We were still in the city, passing embassies and other Havana landmarks. One of these was Hotel Copacabana, which has more stories attached to it than I have space to tell—including ones told to me by the girls at Villa El Salado who agreed that the Copacabana's Disco Ipanema was the best place to pick up "fat foreign men."

We cycled on, past the Russian embassy, a tall brown building bristling with antennae and already looking like the Cold War relic it was. Past the baroque façades of what in pre-Revolutionary days were beach clubs for the wealthy but are now open to everyone for an entrance fee of one peso (about four cents). Past Punto Cero (Point Zero), the compound where Fidel lives with his wife Dalia, and nearby La Rinconada where Raúl lives.

We detoured through Marina Hemingway where hundreds of yachts from all over the world were docked—this so we could buy snack foods at the marina's convenience store to carry in our panniers. We stopped again in Santa Fe where Deisy, now the mother of a beautiful baby, fixed us a big breakfast before sending us on our way.

West of Santa Fe we got on the Habana-Mariel freeway, and soon pedaled past the ocean-front campus of Escuela Latina America de Medicina (ELAM). Here my mind created a fantasy encounter with Argentina-born Alberto Granado, Che Guevara's companion on that famous motorcycle trip through South America. In 1961, Granado moved to Cuba to teach at the Havana medical school. He helped create a Faculty of Medicine at the University of Santiago de Cuba, and later founded the Cuban Genetics Society and the Institute for Basic and Pre-Clinical Studies. It is unlikely that Dr. Granado was on the campus of the medical school as we cycled past, since he was by then 75 years old and had retired about five years earlier. But it would have been fascinating to talk with him, especially at that time, which was several years before he became a celebrity through his involvement with *The Motorcycle Diaries*. That movie was based less on Che's diary of their youthful travels than on Granado's, which had been published earlier under the English title, *Travelling with Che Guevara: The Making of a Revolutionary.*

Che lives in our collective memory, but until the movie came out Alberto Granado was little known outside scientific circles. His forty-plus years of contributions to Cuba vastly outweighed those of Che, but Granado did not do what Guevara did: did not die young, a martyr's death. He merely continued to the end of the century and beyond (he died in 2011, at the age of 88), promoting the humanitarian causes they both believed in.

The Whys of Leaving

The freeway was lightly trafficked, the day sunny, and the ocean in view almost all the way to Mariel. We stopped at Mariel's small municipal museum, hoping it might have a map of the area. The interior of the museum was so dim that at first we wondered if it was even open. A bespectacled man with a receding hairline looked up from an ill-lighted desk. He asked, with the air of one who was quite sure we had come to the wrong place, if he could help us. When we told him what we wanted he looked dubious. What kind of maps exactly did we want?

"Any kind," I said. "We only have one road map, and it's not very good. As this is a natural history museum, we thought you might have, you know, a topographical map or something like that." Even as I asked, I registered the meagre displays and felt that the curator was right to assume we had come to the wrong place.

By then he had taken in our cycling costumes and bikes

parked at the door and must have decided that while we might be crazy foreigners, we were not necessarily dangerous ones. "I'll see what I can find," he offered, and disappeared into a back room. He returned with a large dusty topo map that he unrolled across his desk. When I pointed out our intended route along the coast, he said we shouldn't find it too difficult.

"The Circuito Norte runs along here," he explained. "Five to fifteen kilometres from the coast. It is hilly in places but you won't get into real mountains unless you turn inland." He ran his finger along the middle of the island, from where we were to near the western end. "This is the Cordillera de Guaniguanico. They are not the highest mountains in Cuba but..." He glanced at Derek's well-muscled legs, then at my much shorter ones, and said to Derek, "Your compañera might find them challenging."

We thanked him for his help and asked if we could look at the museum's exhibits. He seemed pleased to show us around.

"I am sorry the labels are not more explanatory," he said lamely. "But I am a historian, not a scientist. That is, a history professor," he quickly amended. "I have only worked here since my retirement, as a service to the people. Something to keep me busy."

As far as I could see, it wasn't much of a service because he didn't have much to work with. Clearly the impulse that had led the Cuban government to establish museums in every town of any size was a good one, but just as clearly, financial support was lacking. Such support probably had been intended but who could worry about museums when the economy had just been flattened for the second time in forty years?

Thinking of the hardships Cubans had been enduring during the past seven years reminded me that Mariel had been the embarkation point of two great exoduses. "Are there any exhibits about the Mariel embarkations of 1980 and 1994?" I asked.

"No." He abruptly walked back to his desk and started rolling up the map. Clearly he did not want to discuss the departure of those thousands of Cubans to the US, but I wanted to get at least one local person's perspective. Leaving Derek to rely on his high school Latin to decipher scientific names on the various plant and animal exhibits, I followed the curator to his desk, sat down across from him, and looked expectant. "But you were here then?"

"I was," he said tightly. "And I am still here."

"You did not want to leave?"

He hesitated, just enough to suggest that maybe he *had* wanted to go. Instead of answering, he only sighed. "It is very complicated. I doubt anyone who does not know Cuban history could understand."

"You mean how President Carter promised that any Cubans who came to the US would be 'welcomed with open arms'?" I shook my head sympathetically. "I was in California at that time. I can just imagine what an influx of Latin Americans or Asians there would have been if the president of the United States had told *them* that!"

"Of course. All over the world there are people who want to move to a country less poor than their own." His brown eyes, magnified by his spectacles, flashed with outrage. "What a barbarity, to promise poor people such a welcome and then betray them!"

I wasn't entirely familiar with US-Cuban immigration issues, but I did recall how, when Floridians saw 125,000 Cubans headed for their shores, they howled with anxiety. And how, in an eye-blink, US policy had changed. Rather than passing out all the perks bestowed on previous Cubans émigrés—permanent status, a relocation allowance, and the right to seek work—the US set up concentration camps where it interned almost all of those who left Cuba in the Mariel exodus of 1980. When Reagan replaced Carter a few months later, the new president found himself stuck with thousands of Cubans whom the US had explicitly invited and then locked up in legally-questionable camps. Negotiations followed, wherein the US government succeeded in persuading the Cuban government to go back to restricting emigration, as it had in the past.

If the man I was speaking with had considered leaving, I doubted he would admit it to a foreigner he had only met ten minutes ago. But didn't he say he was a professor—or used to be? I had yet to meet a teacher who could resist lecturing to an interested student. "What I don't understand," I said carefully, "was why after *that* fiasco, so many Cubans rushed to go in 1994, when Castro again said those who wanted to leave could."

He shrugged impatiently. "That was only four years ago! With the collapse of the USSR and the US tightening the blockade, we were in economic agony! It was all I could do to keep my own family from becoming *balseros*. And I can tell you, nobody supports the Revolution more than we do!"

"Was that your family's only choice? To stay or become balseros? Were there no safer options?"

His laugh was so scornful he almost choked. "By formally applying, you mean? What is the point, when Washington ignores those who apply through legal channels and still gives preference to balseros? And why? Because when people put their lives at risk like that, it makes good propaganda. It can be held up as proof of our desperation!"

It seemed to me that those who made that dangerous sea voyage probably *were* desperate to leave Cuba, but I didn't say that. Instead I pursued my original question. "If a Cuban wants to go abroad and doesn't want to do it that way, can he? Is it allowed?"

"Well, of course. Cubans travel all the time, both for temporary stays abroad and permanent ones. Documentation is required, of course. And money. Isn't it the same in your country?"

"More or less. Canadians need a passport to travel abroad. And usually a visa issued by the country they want to enter."

He nodded. "Our government requires those things, too, plus an exit visa. Men must fulfill their military obligation before they can get an exit visa. Those who have received a university education at government expense, say, doctors, also have to provide some years of service to the nation before they can get one." He paused, and admitted, "So there is more red tape here, and money is much harder for us to come by. But the real difficulty is getting a visa from the host country. When it is the US that one hopes to visit that is an insurmountable difficulty. To my knowledge, the United States does not permit Cubans to come for short-term visits."

"But it does accept up to 20,000 a year who want to move there permanently," I reminded him.

"Yes but as I said, it accepts only a handful who apply through legal channels. It prefers those who will swear that they are fleeing political oppression, and it has an absolute preference for Cubans who 'prove' it by risking their lives to reach US soil. 'Wet-foot-dry-foot' they call that policy. Cubans who manages to set one foot on US territory can stay." He smiled thinly. "Wouldn't it be interesting if all Mexicans and Haitians had to do to get permanent residency was to set foot on US soil?"

A young man had entered the room while we talked, and with only a nod to the curator and a curious glance at me, had taken a chair against the wall. He listened intently to the conversation, but said nothing.

"Still, Cubans don't *have* to take to the sea?" I was still trying to get clear on that. "The Cuban government does give permission for its citizens to leave the country in some normal, safe way?"

"As I explained," the curator said impatiently, "there are thousands like my son." He motioned toward the young man. "Cubans who have fulfilled their military obligation and made application but cannot get an exit visa because they cannot get an entry visa to the US."

"Which takes—?"

"Luck in the lottery," the young man said softly, speaking for the first time.

"Lottery?" I though he meant the usual money kind, which Cuba outlawed decades ago but which still exists illegally. I gave the curator a questioning look. He went into lecture mode again.

"For the few visas the US does issue each year for Cubans seeking to immigrate through legal channels, there is a lottery to decide who will receive them. I often tell my son that he would do better to apply to a country that is more even-handed in the way it treats us, but like most Cubans, we have relatives in the US. If you are going to leave your homeland forever, you naturally want to go where you have *some* family."

I looked at the young man, who stared at his worn ration-store shoes. "I don't want to move to the US forever. I just want to go there, to see for myself what it's like." He looked up quickly, reassuringly, at his father. "But not enough to become a balsero!"

The older man nodded with what seemed to be a mixture of relief and sadness. Sadness, perhaps, that he was unable to offer his son a journey he himself might wish to have taken.

I wanted to pose other, more personal questions, but the curator seemed to feel that enough, or perhaps too much, had been said already.

He shoved back his chair and looked toward Derek. While not understanding the conversation conducted in Spanish, Derek had picked up on the heightened emotions and was heading our way.

"And you, compañero?" the curator asked, switching to heavily-accented English. "Did you learn anything about our flora and fauna?"

"A little," Derek replied, and gave me a look suggesting that it was time to leave.

As we shook hands and thanked the curator for his help, I decided that like Derek, all I had learned in this place was "a little."

I nodded to the young man on the way out and said, "Good luck."

Behind me I heard his father say, "It is not luck. It is our history."

Whatever that meant.

We spent that night in a rundown but nicely located place on a point overlooking the harbour. As we settled into our room at Motel La Puntilla, I tried again to wrap my mind around the issue of Cuba-US immigration. My first lesson in that subject had come from the Cuban émigrés to whom I had served coffee back in Florida in 1960. They left Cuba not because of political oppression but because they were afraid that their wealth might be seized—which in fact much of it was.

However, their conversations, which I listened to for the better part of two years, revealed something else. Cubans had *always* traveled back and forth. Two-way travel was common as long ago as the mid-16th century, when Cuba and Florida were both newly-claimed Spanish colonies. It continued for 400 years, reaching its peak in the 1950s, when planes joined ferries and pleasure boats in moving individuals of both nationalities in both directions.

The easy back-and-forth flow of entrepreneurs, government officials, vacationers, and families with relatives in both countries was brought to a screeching halt in 1962 by President Kennedy's decision to terminate direct flights, ferry services, private boats, and indeed, *all* normal travel between the two nations. Thus a 400-year-old tradition was ended by the stroke of a president's pen.

To me it seemed sad and stupid that the whole affair should have become so politicized, when for Cubans wanting to go to the US—or for that matter, Americans wanting to go to Cuba—economics and politics were probably only part of the reason for such travel, and not the main one at that.

It had not taken political pressure or economic necessity for me to pull up stakes in Florida and move to California, and then leave there for Canada. The almost free higher education then offered in California had been a blessing, as was Canada's health care system, but those weren't my underlying motivations. The driving force was a desire for new horizons. Where in the world do the young and restless *not* feel the need for that?

Where would young people on an island so close to Florida think of going except where generations of Cubans before them had gone? In those earlier times, it hadn't been necessary to decide in advance whether the move would be permanent.

Wasn't it possible that the driving force behind Cubans' desire to leave the island was the same one that led me to make this cycling trip; the same one that fuels any non-essential trip? Namely, an urge to explore the world beyond where we were born?

The Whys of Staying

We left Mariel early next morning, before the motel's restaurant had opened. I am seriously addicted to my morning cup of coffee but our map showed three towns that we could expect to reach within the next couple of hours, and I thought I could make it that far. However, as we passed through one after the other, we discovered that in Cuba a town does not guarantee a commercial centre where one can buy, say, a cup of coffee. By noon I was feeling pretty shaky.

After cycling all around the crowded centre of Quebra Hache (Broken Axe), I leaned my bike against a lamp post and sat down on the curb. Low blood sugar and caffeine withdrawal had me on the verge of tears. Derek hovered, being without fluency in Spanish and not knowing what to do. We both found it incredible that a town of 15,000 or so inhabitants wouldn't have some kind of restaurant open at midday.

The reason for this was because three decades before, the Cuban government had rather absurdly prohibited small private enterprises. Although it was beginning to see the error of its ways and allow little cafes and casa room rentals, licenses for such micro-businesses were so costly that few Cubans outside major cities found it worthwhile to become self-employed. Not until 2011 would the Cuban government give up trying to micro-manage the economy and seriously encourage Cubans to go into business for themselves. It took Cuban planners and legislators that long to agree that the nation did not have to embrace capitalism, with its undesirable tendency for enormous wealth to be concentrated in the hands of a few, in order to benefit from the energies that citizens were willing to invest in small-scale enterprises. A somewhat equitable distribution of wealth could be obtained (if that was a social goal, and in Cuba it was) simply by progressive taxation. But that awareness would be years in coming. At the time of our first cycling trip—1998— Cubans had not paid *any* taxes in decades. Most worked for the government, and if they ran a private business at all, it was *very* private, as in, under the table, often selling merchandise stolen from a state enterprise.

A man crossing the street glanced at me, took a second look, and stopped. "Is there a problem?" he asked. "Can I help you find something?"

"Yes," I said with the whine of a hungry child. "A cup of coffee!"

He looked startled, then smiled. "Come to my house. My wife will make you coffee."

We pushed our bikes along beside him for about ten blocks, to a large housing complex consisting of a dozen four-story apartment buildings. I had seen similar ones all over Cuba, functional cement-block structures that had not been designed with an eye to aesthetics and had only grown more dismal looking as their original coat of paint weathered away. All units had balconies except those on the ground floor which had small patios. On balmy evenings these would be filled with families taking their ease, and children shouting from one balcony to the next or to friends down on the ground. But now most were filled with laundry flapping in the midday sun.

Our new friend—anybody who promised coffee at this point I counted as a friend—told us to park our bikes by the steps, and called to two boys to watch them. We were reluctant to leave the bikes like that, but there didn't seem to be a polite way of even locking them, let alone dragging them indoors and up the stairs to his apartment. So we left the bikes and followed him up chipped tile steps, one, two, and then a third flight, until we reached the apartment where his unsuspecting wife waited.

The apartment was not as dilapidated as the outside of the building. I guessed that was because, although individual apartments belonged to the tenants who had helped build them, overall maintenance of the building required more resources than they had. But from what we glimpsed through open doors on the way up, it was obvious that families took pride in their own apartments. They were very clean, alike in being simply furnished, decorated with the family photographs and plastic flower arrangements Cubans love. But few had been recently painted. Even having dollars did not mean that one could find paint in Cuba at that time.

As soon as our new friend, Jorge, told his wife Lydia that we had not had breakfast (which I had admitted on the walk over), she began scrambling eggs, frying plantains, and making coffee, oh yes, that blessed cup of coffee!

It was a tiny kitchen, with a two-burner stove, sink, and refrigerator along one wall, plus the four-chair table where we sat. While Lydia cooked, Jorge brought out the family photo album, something he seemed to think was the most interesting thing they had to share with visitors. It was, as it gave a larger picture on their life than a mere conversation might have. With his six-year-old daughter's heart-shaped face hanging over his shoulder, he showed us his and Lydia's wedding pictures, pictures of their parents, pictures of the little girl as a baby, and, most numerous, pictures from his brother's family in Homestead, Florida.

"My brother is only an automobile mechanic," he enthused. "And look at all the things they have." (Pointing to a backyard patio shot showing lounge chairs, barbecue, and a bicycle.) "And the car! He got a car the first year he moved there!" On and on the pages flipped, allowing us to see, through their eyes, the benefits that accrued to Cubans who left their country in order to start anew "over there."

It was not until I asked if he and his family had considered moving to the US that there was a subtle shift in the conversation, casting the issue in a different light.

"Emigration is for young men," Jorge explained without anything I could identify as regret. "I would never put my family at that kind of risk, not when we are perfectly comfortable here."

"Perfectly comfortable," Lydia echoed, waving her spatula to take in the small apartment. "There is nothing on earth I want bad enough to see Jorge become a balsero. So many die at sea!"

Lydia sent the little girl to another room to fetch a table cloth. While she was out, Jorge lowered his voice and said, "That's not all. Our Yolani was born with a club foot. You almost don't notice it now, but they say she will need one more operation to make it altogether right. How could we afford that over there?"

"Jorge's brother's wife has diabetes," Lydia put in. "The medicine costs a fortune. And when their little boy was hit by a car while riding his bike, the driver disappeared and they were stuck with hospital costs that will take them two years to pay. Marcus said some employers provide insurance but at small garages like where he works the owners often don't have health insurance themselves. Marcus doesn't even get paid when he is out sick."

The child returned and with her mother's help arranged a cloth on the table. Lydia placed heaping plates of food in front of us, flanked by doll-sized cups of strong black coffee. We happily dug in, Jorge, Lydia and their little girl to lunch, and we to a wonderful mid-afternoon breakfast.

We would hear other immigration stories as we went along. In fact, I had already heard one from Deisy's brother-in-law, Efrain, who had wanted to emigrate to the US but was prevented, first by his mother who thought he was too young, then by the Cuban government because he had not fulfilled his two-year military service, then by his wife who did not want him taking off when they had young children to raise, and then again by the government. That last had happened after the US agreed to discourage dangerous crossings by having the Coast Guard apprehend any it sighted if Cuba would do the same. Nevertheless, Efrain had gone the illegal balsero route, only to be picked up by the Cuban coast guard and given a two-year prison sentence.

When I met him in 1996 he was very bitter, but when I saw him two years later, just before we set off on this cycling trip, his attitude had changed. When I mentioned what a nice home he had, he explained that since the government had started allowing small business, many homeowners were adding on rooms to rent to foreign visitors. Efrain had learned carpentry skills during his two years in jail, and now had a brisk home-based business in doors, window frames, and furniture.

Of all the different perspectives we heard on emigration, I think the one that summed it up best came from Liliana Soto Serrano, a slender, quick-moving young woman of about thirty, from whom Dianne and I had rented a room in Playas del Este. The room displayed two striking photos, one of Che and one of Fidel. I tried to buy the one of Fidel, which was a wonderful close-up of him without a shirt, fishing off a boat. Liliana said it had been taken by her brother, and I could have the one of Che if I wanted it, but she would not part with the one of Fidel for love or money. And indeed, I could not induce her to sell it.

I asked Liliana about her brother, and she said she had two, the one who had taken the pictures and another one who had moved to Miami. "The one in Miami comes home twice a year, for his birthday and Christmas," she said. "He always tries to get my older brother, the photographer, to apply for a visa to leave, but he won't consider it."

"Who do you think made the right decision?" I asked. "The one who stayed or the one who went?"

She said, without hesitation, "They both made the right decision. The one who went loves business, and everyone knows that the US is the best place in the world to do business. The one who stayed, he only wants to do his photography. He cares nothing for money as long as he has the basic necessities of life."

"And you? If you could easily emigrate, would you go?"

Liliana shook her head. "I'm an accountant at a local *organicoponico* (organic garden). I like my job and I like living a block from the beach. But the main thing is freedom. My brother in Miami keeps telling us we're not free, but he also says his wife never goes out alone at night because it is too dangerous. He even worries about his kids at school because other kids carry guns and knives. Here my children can play out in the street long after dark, and if I want, I can sit in the park with my friends till midnight. So, I tell him, 'You are happy there, I am happy here. You have your freedoms and I have mine.'"

Campismo Hospitality

Most of those who held high positions in the Cuban government immediately after the victory of the Revolution had spent the previous two years living in primitive camp conditions in the Sierra Maestra and the Sierra Cristal. They had come to appreciate the personal qualities developed in such rugged outdoor environments. Comandante Celia Sánchez in particular was deeply attuned to nature. She as well as Fidel, Raúl, Vilma, and other Revolutionary leaders believed that Cuban children would benefit from outings that allowed them to get out of cities and cane fields to places where they could enjoy the beauty and diversity of nature. Thus campismos like the one where Dianne and I stayed at in Varadero were built on the beaches of every province and in all the island's mountain ranges.

The first campismo where Derek and I stopped on our westward ride was Playa San Pedro, about 100 kilometres west of Havana. There we fell in with a group of young teachers whose school was closed for spring break. It was in the middle of a sweltering afternoon and our cycling shirts were drenched in sweat. I was dying for a swim, and Derek urged me to go in, but I said I didn't relish cycling with sand in my shorts on to Bahía Hondo where we planned to spend the night.

"No problem," said one of the teachers, a beautiful black man with the even more beautiful name of Bienvenido (Welcome). "You can shower in our cabaña."

Derek, having spent his formative years in the mountains, does not have the same inclination I do to jump into the nearest body of salt water. He was content to wait with Bienvenido and the others while I plunged in. When I came out, Bienvenido tossed me a key and pointed out the hut he and his friends had rented.

Rather than little A-frames like those at the campismo in Varadero, the huts at this campismo were of cinderblock construction. I entered to find a cement-floored room furnished with two iron bunk beds, and an adjoining bathroom with flush toilet and cold-water shower. There was no toilet paper, soap, or towel. No matter. Fresh water was all I needed. I jumped under the single-spout "shower," as grateful for it as I had been a few minutes earlier for that swim in the salty sea.

In Bahía Hondo (Deep Bay) we enjoyed the comfort of an ordinary motel, something we would discover was rare in Cuba. Our next stop was at another campismo, this one called La Altura (The Top). Here as in San Pedro the cottages were full. This time the occupants were fourth, fifth, and sixth grade kids. They and their teachers were spending the whole spring break week at the beach.

The teacher-student ratio was quite high in Cuba at that time, with a minimum of one adult and often as many as three for every twenty elementary school children. Still, wasn't spring break meant to be a break for the teachers, too? I asked a few of them how they felt about spending their holiday at the beach with the kids they had been teaching all year. They said, with smiles that made it impossible to doubt their sincerity, that they loved it. The two reasons they offered were that, "In this different, more relaxed setting, we can teach them different things than what they'd learn in the classroom," and "Vacations like this make for a better relationship between teachers and students."

It was not until we reached Playa El Copey, west of Santa Lucía, that we found a campismo that, although crowded with lively teenagers, did have an empty cabaña where we could stay. The food on offer, costing mere pennies, was quite tasty (not, we would learn later, something you could count on at a campismo). However, something had gone haywire with the water system so there was no running water. Rather than close the campismo during spring break when Cubans all over the island were flocking to the beach, a tractor had towed in a huge tank of potable water. Later, biking through ever-more remote areas, we would often see tractors hauling tanks to fill cisterns in areas that did not have potable water. Elsewhere on the campismo grounds there were places one could fill buckets with non-potable water for flushing the toilet. It was basic but not uncomfortable. There were few lodgings for travellers on this part of the Cuban coast. Without the campismo we would have been sleeping in a tent with no toilet at all.

We did, however, learn two critical lessons. The first was that the Varadero campismo was not the only one with an outdoor amplifier the size of a Volkswagen. They all have them, and when they fill up with teenagers on the weekend, they blast disco music virtually around the clock. Maybe cabanas *aren't* built of cinderblock to withstand hurricanes. Maybe it is to withstand the sound waves from those monster speakers.

The music lasted until nearly dawn. It was like trying to catch a little shut-eye at an all-night rave. That night we learned another valuable lesson. The windows on most campismo cabanas are of the jalousie variety, and since mosquitoes can get in through the cracks whether they are open or closed, we left ours open to catch the ocean breeze. At some wee hour, fingers slipped through the slats and ran along the cement window ledge where Derek had laid his passport bag. By sheer good fortune, those fingers did not close on the bag but knocked it to the floor. Later, in another campismo on the south coast, the person in charge warned us about leaving valuables on window ledges. That incident was a wake-up call to the fact that although Cuba's crime rate is low and rural areas are usually safer than cities, no place in the world is one hundred percent safe.

Our next campismo experience, if it could be called that,

was entirely different. We had just passed the town of Dimas and, rather than cycle on to Mantua, we decided to follow a road that by our calculations would lead to the beach in about eight kilometres. The dirt road was dusty except for low places between hills, where recent rains had left puddles deep enough to soak the bottom of our panniers. We were on the verge of turning back when we were passed by a tractor towing a flatbed trailer. On the trailer was a family—mom, dad, and six children.

"How far to the beach?" I called out in Spanish.

The tractor driver replied with a big grin that it wasn't much further, and all the children squealed in delight, *"Muy cerca!"* (Very close!)

So we rode on, and indeed, a splendid seaweed-strewn beach soon appeared. To our surprise there was also a campismo there—although in ruins. It had once consisted of a long line of cement slabs sheltered by thatched A-frame roofs. The roofs had been largely destroyed by hurricane winds but the slabs remained. We had a tent, but wondered about the family. What they carried with them was plainly visible on the flatbed trailer, and as far as I could see, that was only some plastic containers of water, a large aluminium cooking pot, and a sack full of something that, whatever it was, didn't look like enough to feed a party of nine. By the time we arrived they had already off-loaded their few possessions at the ruins of what may have been the campismo office. The children were frolicking in the sea like dolphins, and the adults were scouring the beach for driftwood to build a fire.

We pushed our bikes further down the beach until we found a wrecked campismo hut we fancied. What was left of the thatch wouldn't have offered much shelter from rain, but it did provide some protection from the wind, which I knew from my earlier trip with Dianne tended to pick up at night.

After setting up our tent we went for a swim. Then we explored the beach which stretched beyond a distant curve in both directions. We stopped briefly to chat with the two men and six children who were now busily capturing big grey crabs. The woman had gone back to their camp. She had built a fire and begun to boil what they had brought in the sack. I recognized it as *yuca* (elsewhere called cassava or manioc). During the Special Period, when flour was in short supply, Cubans often used yuca as a not-very-satisfactory substitute. In Deisy's Santa Fe neighbourhood I had even eaten pizza from a front-yard kiosk that had a crust of yuca. It was okay, but tasted more like mashed potatoes than anything that could properly be described as crusty.

Derek and I went back to our own camp where, with a growing sense of hunger, we considered how difficult it would be to slake our appetite with the food we had with us. We hadn't been able to buy as much as we had expected in towns along the way. Of the pannier food we had bought back in Havana, all we had left was a handful of trail mix and two packages of cookies.

Then one of the men approached and introduced himself as Luis Ramos Lago. His wife Marianna had sent him to ask if we would like to join them for supper. We said yes. He then went back to help his brother José and the children, who were still engaged in capturing big grey *congrejos* (crabs).

He had not said when the meal would be ready so after a while I wandered down to their camp. Marianna had by this time boiled the yucca and removed it from the big kettle. Luis came up from the beach and dumped in a sack full of live crabs. A few minutes later their corpses were fished out and Marianna set to work cracking legs and removing the meat. I watched her for a few minutes then tried to imitate her. I was exceedingly clumsy, managing to clean only one leg to her four. Marianna said little and replied to my questions in monosyllables. But I saw her covert smile of amusement as I struggled to crack the legs and get the meat out without getting bits of shell mixed in. Soon a daughter of about nine came running up. Without being asked, she sat down and began de-shelling crab legs. Even the little girl was able to clean two to my one, and showed consternation when she noticed that I had cut the tips of several fingers on the sharp shell fragments. The job of cleaning all those crabs seemed to take forever. I was fairly sure I would have to be a lot hungrier than I was to voluntarily undertake such a task for any reason other than good manners. It was nearing dark when, finally, chipped enamel plates were passed around, heaped with boiled yuca and crab meat. It was all very simple and yet plentiful. No one would go to sleep hungry.

I once lived on a popular Southern California beach, in a location that allowed me to observe a steady flow of families hauling armloads of supplies from their car to the beach: boxes of food, coolers of cold drinks, paper plates, plastic utensils, big towels and bigger umbrellas, folding chairs, changes of clothing, boom boxes, and kids' toys. There were trash barrels in the parking lot, yet the amount of garbage left strewn across the sand afterwards often made it seem as if they had left behind more than they had carried in. With all that stuff, were they happier than this Cuban family? Maybe. But as evening closed in and the children lounged about pillowing their curly heads in the lap of the nearest adult, the family's quiet contentment made me doubt it. Derek would tell me later that the thing that impressed him most about Cuba was how rarely he had heard a child whine or cry.

After a while I walked back to our camp and got the two packages of cookies. A stingy feeling squeezed my heart. We had been carrying them in case hunger struck on the road when we were far from anyplace we could get food. We did not know how much further we would have to cycle before we found something we could buy. But after the generosity shown by the lovely Ramos family, what could we do but share what we had?

The ugly stingy feeling went away when I saw the delight on the children's faces, and watched as small fingers reached in, and each took only one cookie. The packets had to be passed around again and again. When there were only three remaining, no one would take those until I broke them in half so that there was a final bite for each child.

Cuba's Wildest West

No part of Cuba is quite as surreal as the Peninsula Guanaha-cabibes at the far western end of the island. Most foreigners know it, if they know it at all, only for the fine scuba diving in the Bahía de Corrientes, accessed from Villa María la Gorda. The beach, with white hammocks strung between palm trees growing out of white sand, is dazzling, and the story of how this isolated villa came to be is amusing.

Depending on which legend you prefer, María was either an aboriginal beauty from Venezuela captured by pirates or she was herself a Portuguese pirate, taken prisoner by other pirates in the early 19th century. Whatever her nationality and reason for being at sea in the first place, she ended up stranded on Cuba's western coast. She dwelt there for nobody seems to know how long, at what came to be known as La Casa de las Tetas de María la Gorda (the House of Fat María's Tits). The name would seem to hint at the services she is said to have provided to buccaneers and others in order to earn a livelihood on this beautiful but barren coast.

If one has not been hijacked by pirates, the only way to

reach María La Gorda is via a road leading from the town of La Bajada (The Low Place). We biked into La Bajada late in the day. Rather than continuing the remaining fifteen kilometres to Villa María la Gorda, we stayed the night at El Radar—a radar station. The station, as a means of garnering a little income to supplement its operating budget, rented out simple rooms furnished with bunk beds. In the dining room we were served the same meal of beans, rice, and fresh fish as the radar technicians who manned the place—they being the only ones there other than ourselves.

Next morning we rode on to María la Gorda, then returned to La Bajada to visit the Estación Ecológico, across the highway from El Radar. The young men working there were very enthusiastic about their job as protectors of the Parque Nacional de Guanahacabibes; 110,500 hectares that had been designated a UNESCO biosphere reserve in 1987. The reserve has 150 species of birds. On our guided hike through the low jungle that covers the peninsula we saw a *zunzuncito* (bee hummingbird), barely bigger than a grasshopper, and a *tocororo* (trogon) named Cuba's national bird for its flag-coloured red, white and blue feathers.

The guides also showed us—didn't need to show us because they were everywhere—large *colorados* that scuttled in and out of crevices in the limestone. We thought they were weird, these crabs with their bulging eyes, red claws, and brilliantly marked orange, yellow, and black shells. But, weirdly speaking, we hadn't seen anything yet.

We rode out at first light, not toward María la Gorda this time but in the opposite direction along the coast. There was almost no human habitation between La Bajada and Faro Roncali, a lighthouse at Cabo San Antonio sixty kilometres away. That first hour just before and after sunrise was splendid. The tangled vegetation on both sides of the unpaved track was alive with birds. We even glimpsed the occasional *juita* (tree rat).

There were many saucer-sized crabs on the road, increasing in number as the sun rose. They had just emerged from moist underground tunnels and were racing about in search of a mate. Soon pregnant females would migrate down to the ocean and try to lay their eggs in the water without getting washed out to sea. And without getting squashed on the road before ever reaching the waterfront. Soon we were riding like drunken sailors, jerking our bikes from side to side to avoid them. I'd almost dump the bike swerving to miss one, only to have it, at the very last second, look up in panic, reverse its course, and fling itself directly under the tire—a tire that would soon go flat, punctured by a piece of the creature's shell. As their numbers increased to carpet-like density, it became impossible to avoid hitting them.

"It's like an invasion of alien robots," muttered Derek, who reads a lot of science fiction and had a notion of how an alien robot army might behave. "Sentient beings aren't normally so suicidal."

They *were* suicidal, and had large pincers that they did not hesitate to use. When I tried to kick one away to prevent it from running into my path, I'd end up with the little monster hanging by its claws to the toe of my shoe.

This went on for many kilometres, broken only by stops to repair flat tires, Derek patching and muttering curses while I tried to keep pointy-footed members of the seething orange, black, and yellow mob from scrambling over him.

Finally palms and scrub gave way to a wasteland of sharp black limestone rock, beyond which was a view of startlingly blue water. Although there were still some crabs on the road, it was no longer the shifting mass of gaudily-coloured shells with bulging panic-stricken eyes that we had just ridden through. What lay on the road in this area were iguanas a metre long or more, narrowly watching us as we watched them. It was a relief to discover that they were more traffic-savvy than the crabs. When we approached to within a few metres, they moved with astonishing swiftness into rocky crevices.

At last we reached the western-most tip of Cuba, and there stopped to visit Faro Roncali. We were taken up steep winding steps of the lighthouse for a fine view across the Estrecho de Yucatán, a narrow strip of water that is often rough because this is where the Caribbean Current squeezes into the Gulf of Mexico. The lighthouse keeper said that on a clear day and under certain weather conditions it was possible to see Mexico's Yucatán Peninsula almost 200 kilometres away.

Next day we biked a few kilometres beyond the lighthouse to Playa Las Tumbes (Beach of the Tombs). It was probably called that because there was a tiny cemetery nearby. In olden days, they said, ships often went down in the rough waters common to that part of the ocean and drowned sailors occasionally washed up on shore. What we found there was a hurricane-destroyed campismo surrounded by a bird-filled forest and one of the most beautiful beaches in all of Cuba.

Six months later, on June 1, 1998, a 23-year-old Australian named Susan Maroney would stagger onto this beach, having swam 200 kilometres from Mexico's Isla Mujeres to set a world record for an unassisted swim in open water.

She arrived covered in stings, as the cage she swam in protected her from sharks but not from jellyfish. I saw no sharks or jellyfish the day I swam at Las Tumbes, nor did I see any when I frolicked in the surf lapping that perfect beach again a decade later. But then, I didn't stay in the water thirty-eight hours and thirty-three minutes, like the awesome Susie Maroney.

Hurricanes

I thought I knew something about hurricanes. My Texas-born mother had a historic if not personal memory of the 1900 storm that killed 10,000 people in Galveston, a story recounted to me many times. When I was a small child, my parents moved to the Florida Everglades and settled just south of Lake Okeechobee. Why I don't know, since both lived in mortal fear that a hurricane like the one in 1928 that had broken the dike on Lake Okeechobee and drowned more than 1,800 people would blow through again. Whenever a hurricane was predicted, my family drove to land we owned north of the lake, land that was safe from flooding. There was no house there but my father had built a sturdy barn for just such occasions. It was great fun for us kids, no school for a few days and, once there, being bedded down in the windowless barn with stories read to us by the light of a kerosene lantern. It was like a camping trip but more exciting.

Our home in the vulnerable south-of-the-lake location never was destroyed but outbuildings often were, leaving our tiny subsistence farm reeking of dead chickens. Then there was the year when, just as we were driving to safety in the barn up north, a tree blew down across the road. We were forced to go back and wait out the hurricane in the house. We got through the storm okay, and brought the calves and chickens into the house so they survived, too.

It wasn't until a month later that we drove to our place north of the lake and discovered that that year's hurricane had hit hardest there. The barn my parents had believed to be safe was wrecked. As we three kids scrambled awestruck through the debris, I found a doll, left behind on a previous trip. Its head had been crushed by a roof beam that lay across the place I normally slept.

That was why, as Derek and I cycled around the coast of Cuba, I thought I knew something about hurricanes. As we biked past at least two kilometres of destroyed chicken barns, I was surprised only by the scale of it. Continuing along the north coast over potholed roads and through wrecked campismos, I began to get a sense of how inadequate my personal experience of hurricanes was by comparison to what Cuba had endured, and had been enduring, for as long as anyone could remember.

The last mass-killer hurricane to strike Cuba was in 1963. The Castro government had been in power less than five years when Hurricane Flora ripped through across the eastern end of the island, eroding some coastlines as much as a kilometre inland and killing 2000 people. The new, still-disorganized government owed that region much for its strong support of the Revolution, and promised the people, "Never again." A National Civil Defence Plan was put into effect that would soon make Cuba the best-prepared nation in the world for natural disasters.

Over the next forty years, Cuba averaged not even three hurricane-related deaths per year—this while death tolls in the Caribbean, Central America, and the US regularly reach the dozens, hundreds, and sometimes thousands. According to a 2008 NBC News Report, chances of dying in a hurricane are fifteen times higher in the US than in Cuba.

The Cuban government developed procedures to save people and domestic animals, but it could not totally prevent crop damage. Hurricane damage of crops running into the billions of dollars continues to be a near-annual event that seriously undermines Cuba's attempts to become food self-sufficient.

Since Peninsula Guanachabibes is as far west as one can go in Cuba, and we had ridden along the north coast getting there, it was my (bad) idea to follow the south coast going back. Guide books provided scant information about that area but that did not deter me. Like most beach-loving travellers I was on the lookout for a beautiful beach not yet "discovered." Cuba does have a number of those, but trust me when I say that none are along the island's southwest coast. Much of the area is covered with mangrove swamps that swarm with mosquitoes and tiny biting black gnats called no-see-ums in Canada and *jejenes* in Cuba. Several large rivers empty into the ocean, creating muddy shoals and murky water. It was in this unappealing region that we got a close-up look at what the most recent hurricane had wrought.

Besides more washed-out roads and wrecked campismos, there were small seaside communities that were only beginning to rebuild after being reduced to rubble. One of the communities we passed through, called Playa Rosario, was typical. Veranda-fronted houses stretched for about a kilometre along what until recently had been a paved beachfront road protected by a low seawall. Beyond the seawall there had been a white sand beach where men fished, children played, and families cooled down with a swim during the hottest hours of the afternoon. But when we cycled in that afternoon in mid-January 1998, it was a very different place.

Where the beach had been there were only rocks that the waves rattled incessantly against the broken seawall. Without protection of a seawall, the paved waterfront road had been destroyed, leaving behind chunks of asphalt interspersed with huge potholes. It was so difficult to negotiate that we had to get off our bikes and push them through the debris.

Thus far, government reconstruction efforts had gone no further than restoration of power and water and the rebuilding of public facilities like the school and clinic. Materials had been provided to repair homes, but the work itself had been left up to the owners who seldom had the necessary tools. Some houses had survived and had been largely restored, but many families were still living amidst the wreckage of their homes, or in shacks made of whatever could be scrounged from rubble created by the most recent hurricane.

As in most small Cuban communities, there was no commercial centre. When we asked a fisherman (a successful one, judging by the several big fish he carried) if he knew where we might find a meal, he quickly volunteered that his wife would be glad to cook for us. Given the devastated condition of the town, we hesitated, not wanting to take food from people who didn't have enough for themselves. But the man insisted, so we pushed our bikes alongside him until we reached his home.

It was not one of the repaired houses, but a hovel constructed entirely of scrounged wood, with plastic sheeting that make it more or less rainproof. Once inside this sand-floored yet oddly clean dwelling we saw that they did have plenty of beans and rice—20-kilo bags from a government distribution center. And there was all that fresh-from-the-sea fish. The meal took forever to prepare over a driftwood fire, but it was more than edible; it was delicious.

Later, as we were leaving, a bus pulled in and began off-loading people dressed in city clothes. I asked one of the women in the group what had brought them there. She explained that they were all part of a government team evaluating what was still needed and what the priorities should be in terms of restoring the community to pre-hurricane levels. I would have liked to observe the process but they had work to do and seemed a little suspicious of us. Playa Rosario wasn't the sort of town that foreigners visited even before the hurricane. Our being there now that it was in ruins probably made them wonder about motives. So we wished them well and pedaled on.

I have heard many tourists complain about Cuba's "shabbiness." Strolling around Havana, they often remark, "What a few coats of paint could do for this country!" and "These intercity apartments are so slummy!" Some might be aware that sugar prices are down, Cuba's tourism industry is very young, and the US embargo is still in effect. But few seem to be aware of the economic impact of hurricanes—seventeen major ones in the past two decades. And that's not even counting the ones that didn't actually touch the island but managed to do massive damage anyway.

For instance, in October 2005, Hurricane Wilma, without making landfall in Cuba, generated waves so ferocious that chunks were ripped off the famous Malecón seawall that had protected Havana for five centuries. The ocean flooded inland for four blocks, filling first-floor apartments with waist-deep water. The government sent boats to rescue residents and evacuated tourists from hotels by hydrofoil. Only four people died but there was an estimated $700 million in damages.

The US media, by way of explaining why fewer die in hurricanes in Cuba than in the US, claim that it is because Cubans are forced to evacuate, while Americans are free to stay and take their chances with an oncoming storm. In fact, Cubans are *not* forced to evacuate, yet when the order comes, almost all of them do. That is partly because of pressure from local officials, but there are other reasons as well.

First, the Cuban government engages fleets of buses and, where necessary, boats and planes to facilitate evacuations. It assumes the cost of the evacuation and for housing and feeding evacuees who don't have anyplace to go.

Second, the Cuban Civil Defence figured out long ago that people were more willing to follow evacuation warnings if: (a) they were allowed to take family pets; (b) their most expensive items like refrigerators and air conditioners were trucked to higher ground; and (c) whatever was left behind was protected from looters. All three are standard parts of evacuation procedure in Cuba.

The government also helps replace essential goods lost in natural disasters. I was in Centro Havana a month after Hurricane Wilma and saw government trucks blocking traffic on narrow streets while refrigerators, bedding, and other household items were unloaded for residents who, according to a check-off list being followed, had lost things in the flood that occurred when storm-force waves smashed the seawall.

Travelling around Cuba in the aftermath of hurricanes allowed me to comprehend more than I had as a child living through such storms. My understanding of the economic impact increased when I focused on the single aspect of housing. It goes like this:

2001, *Hurricane Michele* damaged 100,000 homes, 10,000 of which were destroyed.

2002, *Hurricane Isidore*, followed eleven days later by *Lily*. Between them, 60,000 homes were damaged, 17,481 of them destroyed.

2004, *Hurricane Charley* damaged 70,000 homes. Of these, 4,177 were demolished.

2005, *Hurricane Dennis* damaged 120,000 homes in July, destroying 15,000. In August came *Hurricane Katrina* which stayed well offshore but put the coastal town of Surgidero de Batabanó 90% underwater and forced evacuation of 8,000 people. *Hurricane Rita* smacked Havana in September, forcing the evacuation of 230,000 people, including 12,000 tourists from beach resorts in Varadero. And in October came *Hurricane Wilma* which did not hit Cuba but generated waves that broke the Malecon seawall, flooded parts of downtown Havana, and required the evacuation of 760,000 people.

2008 was the mother of all weather-disaster years for Cuba, with five "extreme meteorological events," four of which hit in a single three-week period. Two were "only" tropical storms, but the amount of rain they dumped caused extensive flooding that greatly intensified the damage wrought by *Hurricanes Gustav* and *Ike*. More than 444,000 homes were damaged, 63,249 of those fully collapsed. Two months later, *Hurricane Paloma* came ashore at the town of Santa Cruz del Sur with a surge that carried the sea two kilometres inland. Some 8,000 Santa Cruz homes were damaged, the majority of them totally wrecked.

What this means is that between 500,000 and 1.5 million Cubans have to be evacuated from the path of a hurricane almost every year and don't know, when they return, what will be left of their homes. Unless foreigners consider these environmental disasters collectively and imagine what those kinds of blows do to a nation's economy, they are likely to take the simplistic view that all Cuba's economic problems have been caused by the US embargo (leftie view) or by its socialist form of government (rightwing view).

In 2008, ten years after that western Cuba bike trip with Derek, I drove the length of the island with two Canadian friends, Rhonda Walsh and Terri Nash. The roads were in awful shape, and not only the back roads. Some main highways were so bad that by the end of the day we were shell-shocked with exhaustion. Much of the destruction caused by hurricanes two months earlier had not been dealt with yet, as we saw when we left supplies at a small primary school still missing its roof—students were meeting next door in their teacher's living room—and at a boarding school for the deaf still closed for repairs. Yet already reconstruction crews had been pulled away to deal with the disaster of a whole town (Santa Cruz del Sur) wrecked by the fourteen-foot storm surge that Hurricane Paloma had driven ashore.

If Terri, Rhonda, and I had arrived two weeks earlier we would have been smacked by Hurricane Paloma, but what would it have mattered? The rain would have interfered with our beaching, but we might have had the adventure of being airlifted to a different resort or rescued by hydrofoil. I could have gone through that and continued to think of hurricanes as an exciting adventure like those of my childhood.

It was only by noticing how often hurricanes hit Cuba, by taking a close-up look at some of the wreckage left in their wake, and realizing how many homes and schools and clinics and power lines are being smashed each year, that I came to realize this simple truth: Cuba does not have the resources to replace those homes and essential services and at the same time restore all Havana's historic buildings, paint its public housing, and fix the damned potholes on all the highways tourists are likely to travel.

Until nature sees fit to give the island a break, we visitors will just have to put up with a certain amount of shabbiness.

PART 4

THE KINDNESS OF STRANGERS

My attempt to cycle the entire coast of Cuba (not all at once but in sections) resulted in many questions from friends and friends of friends and complete strangers who wanted to do something similar but did not know how to go about it. What was needed, I concluded, was a cycling guide to the island. I pitched the idea to Lonely Planet and was offered the assignment. I would do most of the writing. Derek would do the technical stuff—mapping, cue sheets, altitude charts, and other information useful to cyclists in a country where maps were frequently inadequate and signage often non-existent.

Lonely Planet paid in US dollars, so I asked that it not send the cheque to me in Canada but to mail it to my US bank for deposit. No point in changing it into Canadian dollars, I reasoned, then having to change it back into US dollars to take to Cuba to pay our expenses (Cuba at that time still using the US dollar as its main currency.) What I had not considered was the fact that the US policy regarding Cuba is not reasonable, nor has it ever been. When the cheque arrived in New York, the Chase-Manhattan Bank returned it to Lonely Planet's Melbourne office with a note saying the bank couldn't process it because it carried the notation, *"For Cuba Cycling Guide."*

The problem was solved when Lonely Planet reissued the cheque without the C word on it. To this day I don't know how an Australian company's cheque to be deposited in the US bank account of a Canadian citizen would have violated the US government's "Trading with the Enemy" law that prohibits its citizens from trading with Cuba.

Homestays

Soon after the Revolutionary government came to power, it tried to suppress commerce by making private businesses illegal. This was about as effective as attempting to abolish sex. The urge for commerce, like the urge for sex, simply could not be legislated away. People inclined to do business either left the island or else stayed, resented the restrictions, and found ways to engage in it anyway.

It took the government four decades to wise up. Just before my first trip to Cuba, the law that had kept all businesses in the hands of the state was changed, and citizens were once again allowed to engage in commerce. Countless Cubans jumped on whatever business opportunities were available. Families were soon opening restaurants, selling farm produce, using the family car as a taxi, and renting rooms.

Thus on that first trip I enjoyed a homestay at Anna's house and then in Deisy's apartment. I visited Deisy again when Derek and I returned two years later. Learning that we would be cycling through the town where her mother lived, Deisy insisted that we plan to overnight with her. She gave us the address and phoned to let her mother know we were coming, although we didn't know exactly what day we would arrive.

I have already described the campismos where we stayed on that trip but left out the memorable night we spent— almost spent—at the home of Deisy's mother.

Mrs. Camancho lived on a pleasant street in the town of Puerto Esperanza. When we arrived in late afternoon it was filled with boys playing baseball with a stick and a rock. We knocked on the door and were admitted to a modest one-bedroom house with a cool patio surrounded by a large fenced backyard. In the yard was a cottage where Deisy's sister lived with her husband, a dairyman, and their two sons. Deisy had phoned, we were expected.

We could not have been made to feel more welcome. There was no mention of paying, and I guessed it would be as it had been when I stayed with Deisy. If we asked how much, she would dismiss the notion with a wave of the hand. If I persisted she'd shrug and say, "Whatever you feel like." All my Havana homestays had been like that, which led me to believe that I had finally got the hang of "the Cuban way" of paying for lodging in private homes. We would not mention money to Mrs. Camancho but would leave an appropriate amount in the room to be found after we left.

Kids bounced in and out all afternoon, as excited by our bikes as North American kids would have been by a Formula One racing car. Derek's old ten-speed, with its panniers, navigation kit, under-seat tool pouch, and odometer was as impressive to them as my new mountain bike. After I showed them how the odometer worked and let them experiment with it, Mrs. Comancho's grandsons rushed off and returned with a bucket of water and a rag and proceeded to wash both mud-covered bikes.

Dinner was served in the patio, and I could tell Mrs. Camancho, honestly, that I now knew where Deisy had learned to be such a good cook. After dinner one of the boys whispered into her ear. She nodded, and explained to us, "The neighbourhood children have prepared a show for you."

Someone turned on disco music and ten kids ranging in age from six to twelve danced and pranced in their version of a chorus line. It would have been cute in any case, but one element made it more than that. One of the older children, a girl of eleven, appeared to be autistic. She did not speak but occasionally emitted a high-pitched shriek for no apparent reason. She was unable to maintain the rhythm of the music and often bumped into the children on either side of her. The remarkable thing was the patience of the other kids in dealing with her. They set her straight when she got turned the wrong way. They patted her when she shrieked. They smiled at her. Never had Derek or I seen any group of children spontaneously treat a handicapped child with such sensitivity. As we traveled through Cuba we would see countless other instances of children's kindness toward younger, handicapped, or upset children, but this was the first time we had been exposed to it, making it unforgettable.

We were given a bedroom that appeared to be Mrs. Camancho's own. This made us uneasy but it hardly seemed our place to question arrangements that our hostess had made. She, I noticed, had made up a cot for herself in a tiny room off the kitchen. We went to bed early with the expectation of getting an early start next morning. However, we had not been asleep an hour when the door burst open and the overhead light was flipped on. A strange man stood there, glowering down at us. He stomped through the room as if it belonged to him, got something from the bathroom and, staring hard at us as he left, stomped out again. What was *that* all about?

We drifted back to sleep, only to be awakened a short time later by voices. Our bedroom window opened into the patio. The conversation was taking place at a table just beyond. One voice was male, speaking in low, even tones. The other was that of Mrs. Camancho, high-pitched and bordering on hysterical. I listened for a minute, and said to

Derek, "It seems to have something to do with our being here. I can't tell what." I dressed and went out to investigate.

"He's giving me a *multa* !" Mrs. Comancho cried. "Look!" She pointed to a line on a form the man was filling in. "A four hundred dollar fine!"

"Good grief!" I exclaimed, and asked the official, "What is she being fined for?"

"A license is required to host foreigners," he said quietly. "She doesn't have one."

"I didn't know!" she wailed.

"We didn't know!" I echoed. "Don't give her a fine! We'll go! Tell us who in town is licensed and we'll move there right now!"

"Yes, you should do that," he said, and went on filling out the form.

Mrs. Camancho placed a phone call to a house a few blocks away and within the hour Derek and I were being shown into a comfortable room that really was a guest room, not the temporarily-vacated bedroom of some member of the family.

We didn't need to tell our hostess, Dora, what had happened. She already knew more than we did. "Her ex-husband reported her," she said. "I don't want to discuss her private life. Go back in the morning and she will tell you what it's all about."

When we woke next morning Dora had lovely ice-cold glasses of mango juice waiting for us. That was some consolation, but not much.

"I don't understand about the fine," I told Dora. "Last year I stayed with people in Havana and no one ever said anything about needing a license."

"It is a fairly new law," she explained. "Well, actually not that new, but only now being enforced. Come, let me show you." She opened the front door and pointed to a sticker glued to the outside. "This identifies a casa as being licensed to host visitors—red for Cuban tourists, blue for foreigners. It is very expensive, this license. We have to pay taxes on the income, too."

That made sense. It was just like a B&B business license in Canada. What didn't make sense was that a license was needed for someone like us—a family friend. When I said as much, Dora shrugged.

"It is assumed that any foreigner staying with a Cuban family is going to pay, if not in cash, then with gifts." She did not look at me when she said this, but busied herself refilling our glasses. She knew and I knew that, family friend or not, we would have left something for our night's lodging.

We cycled back to Mrs. Camancho's house where more of the previous evening's mysterious happenings were explained. We had already figured out that the angry man who had marched through our bedroom in the middle of the night was her ex-husband. But if they were divorced what was he doing in the house?

"It is his house, too," wailed Mrs. Camancho. "In the divorce settlement we each got half. You are not allowed to sell your house in Cuba, only to trade it. But who would want to trade their place for half of an undivided house? Either of us could sign over our half to the other person but he won't give me his half and I can't give him mine because if I did where would I live?"

"Surely they can't force you to go on living here together after you've been granted a divorce?"

"No, we have to divide it. That was the judge's decision."

"Divide it?" I looked around the small living room. "How?"

"It was decided in court that he would get the living

room, that bedroom where you were sleeping, and the bathroom. I will get the back half—the kitchen, that tiny room off the kitchen, the patio and backyard." As she spoke she walked to the doorway between living room and kitchen. "Here," she said, raising her hands to show us. "A wall must be built to make a permanent separation between the two halves." At this she broke into tears. "My pension is so small. I didn't have the money. Deisy thought…"

She didn't say what Deisy thought, but I knew. Deisy thought we would leave $20 or $30 on the dresser, and that would be enough for her mother to buy the materials that her son-in-law could use to build a dividing wall, thereby turning what had been a shared dwelling into two separate ones. That dream was gone now. A more pressing problem, I realized, was the fine. I asked if, after we left, the official had agreed not to fine her.

"No," she said, and brought out the form for me to read. "He only reduced it from $400 to $200." The tears that had stopped began to fall again.

I can't say that we were as upset as she was, but we were very upset. Our travel budget was small and $200 would take a noticeable chunk. Yet if it was enough to be felt by us, how much more would it be felt by a Cuban senior living on a tiny pension?

"Where do I find the official in charge of this business?" I asked. "I don't mean the one who came last night. I mean someone in charge."

"In Viñales," she said, and gave me his name.

Derek and I got on our bikes and rode the twenty kilometres uphill to Viñales. There Derek waited out on the street with our bikes while I tried to convince the head honcho how inappropriate the fine was and how impossible it was for this poor lady to pay it. He brought out a book and showed me the law, which was plain enough. Only houses licensed to rent rooms could put up foreign guests. Certain standards had to be met. There must be a bathroom with a functioning toilet, shower, and wash basin. The room had to have a lockable door.

I thought, ruefully, that if the bedroom door had had a lock it would have been locked, and Mrs. Comancho's ex-husband could not have marched through at midnight to verify that we were there. When I continued to protest that the fine, especially such a large fine, was unfair, he said sharply, "Cuba is a nation of laws. The law applies to Compañera Camancho as much as to anyone else."

"She didn't know the law!" I shot back. "And she hasn't got a lawyer."

He gave me an exasperated look. "You want to see a lawyer? Wait right here." He went out and returned ten minutes later with a woman whom he introduced as a lawyer with a title that I guessed made her something like a district attorney. The official left and the woman, who spoke English, set about demolishing every reason I offered for why Mrs. Camancho should not be fined.

I explained that we were only intending to stay the one night. How could it possibly be against the law to have a foreigner, a *friend*, stay for a single night? That didn't mean she was running a business for which she needed a license!

"Foreign visitors *are* allowed, twice a year," the lawyer explained. "But the homeowner has to notify the authorities that she will be lodging these guests. All Compañera Camancho had to do was call the appropriate office. If she hasn't already had two groups of foreign guests in the year, she could have got permission for you to overnight there."

"She didn't know!" I howled.

"She *did* know. This law has been explained on Cuban

television three times a day for six months. There is no one in Cuba who doesn't know what the law is and that it is now being enforced."

"But she's an old lady, a retiree," I protested. "She didn't understand—"

She interrupted me with a sardonic laugh. "This Compañera Camancho is a friend, you say? Don't you know who she is?"

I was taken aback. "I didn't say I knew her. I'm a friend of her daughter's, in Havana."

"Then here is something you may not know. She is no simple senile senior. She went to university in the Soviet Union. She was trained as a ship's navigator. That was her career, ship's navigator in the Cuban navy, until she retired two years ago. She draws a pension. It's small, yes. But she gets rations like everyone else. She has a television—didn't you see a TV in her house? She is informed on the law."

The lawyer gave me a pitying look and I could see that she was thinking what I was beginning to think: that *I* was the one who had been uninformed.

The woman sat tapping polished fingertips on the desk, watching me struggle with my anger. Finally she said, "There is one other thing you may not know about Compañera Camancho. She has a son who is high in the Pinar del Río Communist Party. By now everyone in the neighbourhood will know she was given a fine. If she was let off it would create a scandal. She will have to pay it."

"She hasn't got that kind of money," I mumbled.

"Not many Cubans do," she admitted. "But I promise you she will not lose her home. There will be a hearing in thirty days. She can challenge the ticket. But in this case that won't do any good. Her ex-husband and the inspector saw you in the house, in bed, in the middle of the night. The best she can hope for is an arrangement to pay over time. This is probably what will happen."

"She can't pay it!" I said angrily. "We'll end up having to pay the fine!"

This, of course, was the crux of the matter, why even after seeing the law in black and white and having an hour's worth of patient explanations, I was still angry.

The lawyer looked genuinely upset. "You shouldn't do that!" she exclaimed. "As a tourist you are not expected to know Cuban laws on these matters. Driving, now that is different. If you drive here, you have a responsibility to know and follow the law. But this law is Compañera Camancho's responsibility. She should pay. It is only just."

Just or not, there was an enormous economic gap between Mrs. Camancho's resources and ours. One day of our shoe-string travel budget was more than her monthly pension. Besides, I really believed that she had opened her home to us at her daughter's request, a spontaneous act of hospitality exactly like what Deisy had demonstrated two years earlier when she invited me to share her tiny apartment in Havana. Furthermore, if Mrs. Camancho had to spend the next year or several trying to pay off that huge fine, she would never get together the few dollars she needed to build a dividing wall to keep her asshole ex-husband out of her part of the house. What could we do?

Nothing really, except what we did do. We went back to her house, left $200, and pedaled west along the coast. We promised ourselves that never again would we stay in an unlicensed casa. Although we felt sure of that at the time, it was a promise we would find ourselves unable to keep.

The Zapata Swamp

Mid-January 1998 found us nearing the Bahía de Cochinos (Bay of Pigs) in Parque Montemar. We stopped for lunch not far from the entrance to the park in the little sugar mill town of Australia. Fidel had made his headquarters here during the Bay of Pigs invasion. The sugar mill office was the only place in the area with a telephone, which he needed to keep in touch with Celia Sánchez in Havana, where bombs had just been dropped in a residential neighbourhood. Later Fidel said that it was a gut feeling that caused him to think that the invasion would happen at the Bahía de Cochinos. The Havana bombing raid, he suspected, was intended as a diversion (something that declassified CIA documents have since shown it was meant to be).

The office of the historic sugar mill was closed, so we presented ourselves at the home of Máximo, a chef at a restaurant in the nearby park. When he offered us a lunch of crocodile I declined, not because I am squeamish but because I am a vegetarian. Derek accepted the challenge, though, and declared crocodile in pineapple sauce to be the best thing he had yet tasted in Cuba.

"Of course," Máximo said complacently. *"Artiste* that I am, I will prepare *cocodrilo* with *salsa de piña,* or in *salsa de vino blanco.* When a tourist at the hotel asks me for crocodile in tomato sauce, I go to the table and tell that barbarian, 'You want ketsup on crocodile, that most delicate of meat, get someone else to cook for you! Me, I am an artiste. I do not prepare the cocodrilo of Cuba with ketsup!'"

"You are surely an artist," I agreed. "But tell me, why would this same meal served in a hotel restaurant not be as good as here at your table?"

He shrugged. "There I prepare one plate after another, like

in a factory. The pay is low, the diners I do not know. Here you are guests in my home. For my guests I cook *con amour!*"

I tactfully refrained from noting that, with or without love, the delicious meal had been prepared not by him but by his wife. Instead I asked, "What about the crocodiles? Aren't they endangered? Do you buy the meat from poachers?"

Máximo put his hand on his chest and bellowed melo-dramatically, "*No! Nunca!* We must protect our Cuban crocodiles! If ever the *Yanquis* are so foolish as to invade us again, Cuban crocodiles will help us defend our homeland!"

His wife indicated Derek's plate. "What you have eaten is a non-endangered species of crocodile raised here in Cuba especially for food. This is what is served in restaurants."

Máximo put his face close to ours and, lowering his voice, confided, "This crocodile I poached from my place of employment."

South of Australia we entered the vast wetland of mangroves and marshes that make up the Zapata swamp, now called Parque Montemar. It is home to at least 160 species of bird, thirty-one types of reptiles, twelve species of mammals, and an uncountable number of fish and mosquitoes. The park is an excellent area for bird-watching if you get out early, and blistering hot if you get a late start. There is a well-paved highway along the eastern side of the Bahía de Cochinos, but the western side, known as the Ciénaga Occidental (West Swamp), is very wild, with controlled access along its one road. Only the military, researchers with special permits, park employees, and tourists accompanied by a park guide are allowed to go into that area, so we rode down the east side of the bay.

Soon after entering the park we passed Laguna de Tesores (Treasure Lake). We did not stop, as we were not planning to stay at one of the honeymoon cottages out in the lake, and had no desire to join the tourists who had been bussed in for boat rides, trinket shopping, and crocodile-ogling. (For anyone seriously interested in crocodiles, a more interesting experience can be had at the breeding farm across the highway where those so inclined can cuddle the baby crocs.)

Our first stop in the park was a few kilometres further on, at the Centro Ecológico (Ecological Centre). Its small museum was interesting enough, but most impressive, and valuable to us as cyclists, was a huge wall map of the area. If we had been able to shrink it down and take it with us we might not have ended up in some of the mucky places we did later on. A number of internationally respected biologists work at this and other Cuban ecological centers. We met one who was researching bats and another who was studying micro-organisms. (Since neither is pettable or what might be called a charismatic species, I did not take notes.)

Centro Ecológico had spruced up four bedrooms to be rented to visitors who wished to overnight. The scientist in charge explained that although the government was keen on environmental research, it had few resources to support stations such as this. Each facility had been advised to look for ways to generate hard currency. Some, like this Centro Ecológico, chose to rent rooms to foreign visitors who wanted to get a bit off the beaten tourist track and learn more about the environmental work going on in Cuba. The rooms were inexpensive and guests dined with the staff and researchers—something that at another time and under other circumstances I would have liked to do.

However, not on this trip. We continued on and soon came to the Bahía de Cochinos. One can swim and snorkel pretty much anywhere along the eastern shore of the bay and the ocean beaches east of the bay, but if you want to go boating or scuba diving that requires a guide. At that time (1998) there wasn't much on the 35-kilometre stretch between Playa Larga at the head of the bay and Playa Girón at the mouth of the bay—just a campismo called La Victoria and, not far from the campismo, the camp where Fidel stayed when he came to dive in the bay.

Over the next decade, each time I traveled this road I would notice something newly built: a much larger campismo, two holiday camps for workers in the citrus industry, and a dive center where tourists could step right off the rocky shore into deep, clear water. There were still small cove beaches tucked between outcroppings of sharp rocks along the way, but other than that, only Fidel's dive camp (state property, not his personally) remains unchanged. Or perhaps, given that Fidel no longer goes there, it has changed most of all.

In Playa Girón, Derek and I did not camp on the beach where Dianne and I had pitched our tent the previous year. Instead, we followed the coast east from the bay along a narrow paved road—paved, that is, for about twelve kilometres. Then the road surface changed to a hard-packed limestone surface called *terraplén*. It was still smooth for cycling, far better than what lay ahead, although we did not yet know that. It ran along the coast just a few yards from the beach but dense scrub prevented us from having a view of the water. The scrub was broken at intervals by sand tracks leading down to the shore. We followed one of these sandy trails at sundown, to a pocket-sized beach perfect for camping.

In the night we heard large animals crashing about in the bushes and had to remind ourselves that this was not Canada, and Cuba does not have bears. Getting up his courage to investigate, Derek's flashlight beam fell on a cow and two goats. Why they would be messing around in the bushes at night we couldn't fathom. Just before dawn we heard footsteps passing nearby but no one bothered us. When we crawled out of our tent we saw, on a nearby rocky point, a lone fisherman.

Naturally all of the area's *cenagueraos* (swamp dwellers) would be fishers, probably as a matter of necessity. The Revolution had brought numerous benefits to this poorest of poor regions—schools, clinics, and jobs at its small tourist facilities. Yet it remained one of the poorest parts of Cuba. One survivalist activity that dated all the way back to the region's indigenous Taíno people—the turning of scrub wood into charcoal—persisted. This we saw when we cycled past several house-sized kilns.

We carried plenty of water but not much food, so we were relieved to reach a small settlement near the charcoal kilns. Not that we expected anything like a café or grocery store, still…hey! Was that—?

The last thing we expected was to see a woman walking along carrying a bag of oranges! I braked to a stop, complimented her on the healthy-looking baby straddling one hip, and asked where we could buy oranges.

She smiled shyly and replied, "They are not sold. These came from the *bodega* (distribution centre). But if you come to my house, I will give you some of these."

It wasn't till we reached her tidy little house and she mentioned that she had two other children, both in school at this hour, that I had a shame attack at having come here with the express purpose of taking some of her, their, food. Of course we would pay, but as had happened before, it occurred to me only belatedly that money does not do a person all that much good in places where there is very little to buy. Here were we, rich (and only temporarily hungry) foreigners, easily able to pay as much for this bag of oranges as her carbonero husband made in a month of charcoal-burning. But then, when would they next see an orange?

The young mom did not make it any easier for us when she upended the bag of oranges on the table and said, "Take as many as you need."

We each took one, it being impossible to take fewer. She tried to persuade us to take several more. We compromised by taking one more, feeling guilty as hell as we did so. And as if the situation could get more embarrassing than that, she flatly refused to let us pay her for them.

However, I had not forgotten everything learned on previous trips about "the Cuban way." I knew what was in short supply and had one pannier stuffed with gifts for just such occasions. As we sipped water and visited in her living room, I queried her about the ages of the other children. When we were ready to go I was able to leave a pair of socks for each of them, a box of band aids, a box of crayons, and shampoo I said was for the kids but suspected, since they were all boys, she would use on her own long hair. She accepted these gifts with pleasure, as they were, after all, for her children. And in Cuba, everyone gives to the children.

We continued to follow the terrapén road. It grew progressively less of a road and more a rocky trail, with thorn bushes on both sides crowding close. Then we came to a division in the road. The route we were intending to follow along the coast was blocked by a barbed wire fence. There was a gate but we were hesitant to trespass on what might be a restricted area, so we took the branch road, which led inland and although dirt, appeared more used.

Having grown up in the Florida Everglades, I am not normally fearful of swamps, especially not this one, since Cuba has no poisonous snakes. However, as the track grew increasingly swampy I became increasingly nervous. As a child I once watched an alligator grab my father's foot and, despite heavy rubber boots, put a fang in so deep that it went completely through Dad's instep and left him limping for a month. My brothers and I were shown the kinds of places 'gators were likely to be, taught to identify the marks on a muddy bank where the beasts slide into the water, and warned never to go near such places. Wandering in the Zapata on a road that was barely a road felt very much like such a place. When we were forced to get off our bikes and ford knee-deep opaque brown puddles, or go around the puddle through swampy undergrowth alongside the track, I was very uneasy. However, the only wildlife we saw was a coven of six buzzards in a dead tree, their wings spread wide to dry in the sun.

Eventually we emerged onto flat grassland with fenced pastures and cows bawling in the distance. We were hungry—the oranges long since gone—and nothing resembling a town in sight. But there was a farm house, and in the yard there were chickens. We must have been a spectacle, covered in mud from hand to foot, but the lady of the house, a middle-aged Afro-Cuban, only chuckled when we told her where we had come from, and nodded agreeably when I asked if she would cook us some eggs. She invited us into the bathroom to wash up but I asked permission to wash at an outdoor hand pump instead. No way would we track across her freshly-mopped floor in our muddy condition!

By the time we had de-mudded ourselves she had emerged from the house with two glasses of lemonade. She waved us to rocking chairs on the porch. (Most homes in Cuba have a porch and on every porch are at least two rocking chairs, so if you find me describing this scene more than once, it's not because I'm at a loss for words. Porches, rocking chairs, and an invitation to sit a spell is Cuba's most commonplace custom, especially in the country.)

The meal took a long time to prepare because of course the lady, whose name was Yadina, wasn't about to serve us only eggs. After all, it was early afternoon, the rice and beans were nearly done, and "the boys" would be in soon. So we sat on the porch sipping warm lemonade while she put the finishing touches on the midday meal.

The scene was so reminiscent of my childhood that I felt as if I had fallen into a time warp. Everything reminded me of the place in South Florida where I had grown up: the way the heat caused perspiration to dampen the skin; the occasional light breeze that wicked it away leaving a fleeting bit of delicious coolness; chickens freely ranging in the yard, cows grazing in the pasture beyond. And beyond all that, the steamy swamp.

Then there was the thud of horses' hooves and "the boys" (actually four men) galloped up from the nearby ranch. They did not dismount at once, but lounged in their saddles as we introduced ourselves and explained our presence. Once they concluded that we were harmless and their horses had cooled enough to be taken to the watering trough, they got down, shook hands, and we all trekked in to share a big midday meal.

Of course we were asked about Canada and whether it was always cold there. Derek said it was cold in winter but in summer it could be as hot as Cuba. One of the men seemed doubtful about this last. He said that on television he had watched a Canada-Cuba baseball game being played in Edmonton. Although it was summertime, some of the people in the grandstands, he observed, had been wearing sweaters and jackets.

When we asked about the road blocked by the barbed wire fence, they told us it would have taken us to Cienfuegos, so, as I still had it in my head that I wanted to cycle the entire coast of Cuba, we later went back and took it the rest of the way. We never did find out if the fenced area was a military zone.

We saw not a soul when we continued along the coast to Cienfuegos, but when the Irish travel writer Dervla Murphy tried to walk that coast route in the opposite direction in 2007 she was told that it was a restricted area and driven back to the main highway. Clearly the officials did not know Murphy for the famously intrepid hiker she is, and saw her only as a 75-year-old woman alone and unfamiliar with the area, setting out to walk to and through the Zapata Swamp. It is possible they only told her that to stop her from attempting a trek they mistakenly believed was more arduous than she could handle.

I later recommended the route to a couple of other cyclists. They were not turned back but both had difficulties. One failed to ensure that his tires had Kevlar linings to protect against the thorns and so spent an exceptional amount of time repairing flats. The other drank water she'd found along the way that turned out to be saline-contaminated and made her sick. Yet both told me that they found the ride along that not-really-a-road between the Zapata Swamp and Cienfuegos to be an unforgettable experience, definitely a part of "the real Cuba."

Trinidad, the Pope, & Other Monuments

We stayed several days in Cienfuegos, not right in the city but ten kilometres to the south near the entrance to the Bahía de Cienfuegos. We got there by popping our bikes onto a small ferryboat at Castillo Jagua and crossing the bay to Pasacaballo (Horse Pass).

Hotel Pasacaballo proved to be inexpensive and comfortable, with all rooms opening onto a long exterior walkway and great views over the bay and surrounding countryside. Ten years later, when the Cuban and Venezuelan governments brought thousands of indigent blind people from all over Latin America for cataract operations, Pasacaballo was one of the hotels used to house both patients and medical teams, with on-site operating theatres and rehab facilities. However, when we were there in 1998 it was just another hotel built in the big, blocky Soviet style, with a pool, restaurant, and bar, plus a dock from whence boats departed regularly to take passengers on tours around the bay. A high-volume television in the bar, carrying continuous coverage of the visit of Pope John Paul II, held the attention of everyone including hotel staff.

Sitting at the bar, I watched an interview with Castro in which he was asked if Cuba had changed its attitude toward the Church. Fidel smartly replied that it was not Cuba that had changed; it was the Church. He said that the Revolution had always worked for social justice, which was why it provided universal health care and did not have children sleeping in the streets as is the case in so many countries in the world. He pointed out that only recently had the Church given priority to such issues, and supported his statement by reeling off from memory pronouncements to that effect from specific Vatican Councils.

I knew this to be true from personal experience. During the 1980s, when I was spending a fair bit of time in Central America recording the horrors of its "little wars," Catholic nuns and priests of the Liberation Theology persuasion were among the bravest people I met, standing with the poor at the cost of imprisonment, torture, and death. Yet the Church was not standing by them. In Guatemala the Church hierarchy allied itself with the vicious ruling class, and the Vatican was largely silent. It deplored the atrocities, of course, but for a very long time it was no more willing to condemn the governments involved than it had been willing to condemn Nazi atrocities before and during World War II.

But as Fidel pointed out, the Church had in recent years become more critical of political and economic systems that facilitated such injustices. Proof of this came a few days later when Pope John, in a televised mass from Havana's Plaza de la Revolución, said, "Capitalist neo-liberalism subjects human beings and nations' development to the blind forces of the market, charging the least developed countries with intolerable costs, thereby making the rich richer and the poor poorer." This statement must have rankled capitalists around the world, but it was said to have garnered more applause there in the Plaza than any other part of his sermon. It was also cheered by the dozen or so people watching it on television in the bar of Hotel Pasacaballo.

I found this nation-wide interest in the Pope's visit surprising since, according to the Church, only eight percent of Cubans are practicing Catholics. When I asked the religion of Cubans glued to their TV sets watching non-stop coverage of the Pope's visit, most told me that they were not Catholic. However, they felt that the visit would be good for Cuba. Many volunteered the opinion that it would help bring about an end to the US embargo. Pope John did call for that but it did no good. A dozen years later the embargo would be tighter than ever. The only difference was that by then Cubans would be putting their faith in President Obama.

From Cienfuegos we rode the eighty-five kilometres to Trinidad, one of the prettiest towns in Cuba. Its charm lies partly in its colonial architecture and partly in the fact that despite being heavily touristed, it is not a resort ghetto. In its well-used parks, small museums, block-long handicrafts market, dance clubs, and music venues, it is as easy to mix with the locals as with other travellers. For visitors, the main downside to Trinidad is the number of jineteros who, especially upon arrival, can drive you crazy trying to persuade you to let them lead you to a licensed casa (for which they stand to earn a commission from the casa owner).

Having been there before, Derek and I did not need a guide. With a minimum of hassle we convinced a crush of eager teenagers that we already had a casa room, knew exactly how to get there, and could manage without their help.

When in Trinidad on another occasion I had stayed with Angelica, a soft-spoken grandmotherly woman as sweet as her name. Her family was an oddity in Cuba in that it owned a number of houses. I had asked her how this had come about. Here is what she told me:

Prior to the Revolution her father had owned one of the largest sugar plantations in the region, and numerous houses in Trinidad and Cienfuegos. The new Revolutionary land reform law (drafted by Che) did more than limit the size of farms; it also limited the ownership of houses to one—the family home. Angelica's father anticipated the change and although he did lose most of his land, he kept most other property in the family by giving one house to each of his twelve grown children. Well, actually, he gave one to each of Angelica's eleven brothers and sisters. As the youngest, she was designated to live with her parents and take care of them in their old age, only inheriting their house when they died. When I met her nearly four decades later, she and several of her siblings had licenses that allowed them to rent rooms to foreigners.

It might seem odd that after forty years, all still owned the house they had inherited, and they or their grown children still lived there. In Cuba that was not unusual, because until

2012, homes could not be sold. Property owners who lost everything in the Revolution were not those who stayed. Had they stayed they would at least have retained the family home. It was only when they left Cuba permanently that the government confiscated the house and assigned it to another family. The same thing happened when the last person in a family died. Angelica's family was large and well entrenched in Trinidad so there was little chance of her family's houses not getting passed on to the next generation.

When we arrived at Angelica's place she greeted me like a long lost soul mate. A grandson took our bikes and rolled them across the centuries-old tile of the big living room and out in the high-walled patio garden where they would be protected. Angelica said that a pregnant granddaughter had recently come to live with her so she no longer rented out her spare bedroom, but her brother could put us up at his place. In the meantime, what about dinner? What would we like to eat and at what hour?

The grandson guided us to the designated house which, as indicated by the sticker on the door, was licensed to rent rooms to foreigners. Regulations governing room rentals require that owners live on the premises, but Angelica's family had its own slightly different system. Whenever someone in the family rented a room in their house, they went to stay at the home of another family member, thus allowing the guest to have not merely one room but the whole house to themselves.

We could have cooked our own meals, but self-catering in Cuba is difficult for foreigners. On a previous visit I had trailed around after Angelica to observe Cuba's convoluted system of grocery shopping. Over dinner, through a series of questions and answers, I got her to explain it to Derek.

"So, Angelica, where did all these fresh veggies come

from?" Cubans are not big vegetable eaters, but Angelica, recalling that I was a vegetarian, had prepared several.

"From the *agromercado*. I could have got the lettuce from there, too, but it's better if you go directly to the organoponico and buy it fresh from the cooperative."

Derek, who was busy stuffing a tiny banana in his mouth, pointed to a cluster hanging from a tree in the patio. "I take it the bananas came from there. They're good! And this yogurt is delicious."

"I make the yogurt myself, just as my mother always did," Angelica told him. "But seniors and children over seven get a daily quota of yogurt on the libreta. We get a bread ration, too. My grandson goes every morning and picks it up fresh."

"And the rice and beans—did you get them with your ration card, too?" I asked.

"Oh, we used up our ration for rice and beans two weeks ago. We have to buy extra to feed our guests," Angelica explained.

"From the *mercado negro*," I clarified for Derek's sake, knowing full well that there was no supermarket this side of Havana that sold such staples; that once the ration was used up, people usually could acquire more only through barter or the black market.

Angelica looked embarrassed, but admitted in low voice, "I get it from a friend who works on a state farm."

I glanced at Derek and saw that he understood that since one doesn't grow rice in a kitchen garden, it would have been stolen from the farm where her friend worked

"And the shrimp? How are they, Derek?"

"Great!" he complimented, and told Angelica, "Living in the interior of British Columbia we don't get much fresh seafood."

"These are very fresh," Angelica assured him. "Caught last night and brought in first thing this morning."

This last was also revealed in a half-whisper, because depleted shrimp and lobster stocks have caused the government to ban non-government fishermen from taking them. Naturally this doesn't stop them. They continue to net shrimp and trap lobsters which they sell on the black market for dollars, usually to people like Angelica who in turn serve them to her foreign guests who likewise pay in dollars.

I do not know what risks she took to ensure that we, her guests, had what we wanted for dinner even though most of what we were served was not to be found in local stores. I do know that a short time later she stopped offering meals to her guests because of the difficulty of getting supplies. That combined with the price of the food license made it not worthwhile. However, most of the casas I stayed in over the next decade did serve meals. Only a fraction of them were licensed to do so.

Trinidad was founded just twenty years after Columbus "discovered" the New World. Declared a UNESCO World Heritage Site in 1988, the town gracefully bears the weight of many old churches. Besides the usual Catholic cathedrals with their centuries-old mysteries, there is a Santaría temple where, for a fee, one can get a blessing or a fortune told. There are also many museums. The only one we visited was El Museo de la Lucha Contra los Bandidos, which displays a shot-down American plane and a one-sided record of the "fight against the bandits" waged in the 1960s in the Escambray mountains above Trinidad.

Initially the Escambray war was a purely Cuban affair waged by locals against the Batista regime. There was a difference, though, between the anti-Batista guerillas in the

Escambray and those in league with Castro. Trinidad was an affluent region and many were of the landed gentry. They wanted the dictator replaced with an elected president, but did not want a social revolution—understandable, since most of them were quite comfortable with the economic status quo. By contrast, Castro's support and guidance came from people like Celia Sánchez, Che Guevara, Vilma Espín, his brother Raúl, and many peasants who didn't care what form the new government took as long as it implemented a real social revolution.

The Castorites won and did launch that socio-economic revolution. Those who had fought against the dictator in the Escambray mountains were cut out of power. The first Agrarian Reform Law added injury to insult by limiting land holdings to 1000 hectares. This cost some Trinadians dearly and turned them against the new regime. Many who had lain down their arms when Batista fell picked them up again, determined to see Castro turfed out, too.

The US, also keen to depose Castro, authorized the CIA to smuggle money, guns, and ammunition to the counter-revolutionaries. This "pouring fire on fire" kept Cuba's contra war raging for five years. Three times as many Cubans died in this conflict as had been killed in the Bay of Pigs invasion.

A particularly sad aspect of this Cubans-against-Cubans war was the fate of many young teachers recruited by the Castro government to go into the countryside as front-line fighters in a different kind of war—one against the island's appalling rural illiteracy. Sending young people into a war zone to teach reading and writing may seem crazy to us, but it was believed by Cuban leaders of the day that peasants were reactionary only because they were ignorant. Once they acquired literacy, knew their own history, understood the root of the injustices that had kept them in poverty, and heard how the Castroites planned to change all that, they would support the Revolution. And indeed, most of them did. This placed them on the winning side of the war but literate or not, it did not necessarily get them or their young teachers through it alive.

The partial history recorded in Trinidad's Museo de la Lucha Contra los Bandidos was so depressing that we decided not to visit other museums, but to bike out to Manaca Iznaga, an old sugar plantation fifteen kilometres east of Trinidad in the Valle de los Ingenios (Valley of the Mills)—a cane-growing area named for the many sugar mills that once operated there. It was a pleasant ride, and we were able to lunch in the former master's house along with tourists who had come out from Trinidad on a little steam train.

The plantation had been developed in 1795 by Pedro Iznaga, but sugar wasn't his only commerce. Iznaga became one of the wealthiest men in Cuba by trading in slaves. However, thanks to a whiff of poetic justice, old Pedro was murdered in 1840, not by the blacks he brutalized but by his physician, Dr. Cantero. They say Cantero gave Pedro poison, then married his widow and inherited his great wealth.

Historical footnote: The importation of African slaves to Cuba became illegal in 1865, but slavery, or something close to it, persisted to the beginning of the 20th century, giving Cuba a full 400 years of that dreadful institution. During the US Civil War, Confederate president Jefferson Davis dreamed of a slave-holding country that would include Cuba. In his vision, this new and bigger nation of the south would, thanks to climate and slave labour, become the world's greatest producer of sugar.

As we and other visitors were gazing at a display of

slave-era artefacts and climbing the 400-foot-high tower built by old Pedro to watch the enslaved at work, it occurred to me that it would be rare to come across such tangible reminders of slavery in the US Deep South. Yet in Cuba there are many, not just in Trinidad but all over the country.

Why? Because the government wants Cubans to remember that it was foreigners who introduced slavery to the island. The lesson visitors are meant to take away is that it the Revolutionary government not only has given blacks equal rights under the law, but has repudiated the capitalist system that made human bondage acceptable for centuries.

Trinidad's architectural charm, scenic setting, and friendly residents have done a remarkable job of repackaging the town's past for tourists. If we had spent more time listening to traditional music or shopping at the block-long crafts market, I might have left Trinidad less haunted by displays at Manaca Iznaga and the Museo de la Lucha Contra los Bandidos. They have remained with me, though, reminders of cruelties inflicted by some residents of the area upon others.

Hard Road to Havana

Beyond Trinidad, the road along Cuba's southern coast doesn't pick up again until 700 kilometres to the east. That roadless coastline was not without interest, for offshore lies the 100-kilometer-long Archipelago Jardines de la Reina (Gardens of the Queen), almost half of which has been designated a marine park. With only a limited number of scuba divers allowed into it each year, it offers some of the best diving in the world—for those willing to pay a premium price to dive from one of the few boats allowed into the area. However, since we were researching a cycling guide and you couldn't get to any of the islands in the archipelago on a bike, we decided to head back to Havana.

Trinidad to Havana is six hours by bus, or six days on a bike by the route we had taken. We had intended to bike back by a different route, over the Escambray Mountains to Santa Clara and west to Havana from there. However Derek wasn't feeling well and I doubted my ability to handle the 800-metre ascent from Trinidad to Topes de Collantes at the crest of the mountains. Considering that we still had a lot of route mapping to do around Havana, we decided to hire someone with one of Cuba's gas-guzzling classic cars—one of the few vehicles big enough to haul both bikes—to drive us back to the capital. We asked Angelica to find someone for us and she did, a little guy named Luis who could barely see over the steering wheel of his big old '58 Chevy.

Although the old clunker was polished to a fine sheen, its slow chug up the steep southern slope of the Escambray Mountains caused us to worry that what was under the hood might not hold together for the journey. But it was only necessary to stop once to refill the radiator. This was at a viewpoint about halfway up. From there we had a last sight of Trinidad nestled in the foothills far below, with the morning sun just touching its church spires. Beyond town we could see the coastal plain, the beaches of Peninsula Ancón, and the Caribbean Sea with its many shades of blue. Then we continued our climb into the Sierra Escambray.

We soon arrived in Topes de Collantes where on a later trip we would spend some time hiking trails in the surrounding cloud forest, enjoying its high-altitude coolness, and air that carried the aroma of locally grown coffee roasting at a nearby plant. But on this trip we were only driving through a little town that for decades has been—well, from time to time has been—a health spa. If you are imagining something like an alpine spa in California or Europe you have got it wrong. The Topes spa, called the Kurhotel, is downright weird; hardly surprising given a chequered history that began nearly eighty years ago.

Batista, the *de facto* dictator of Cuba from 1934 until his overthrow in 1959, had one humanitarian impulse that was quite at odds with that part of his personality that impelled him to arrange to have non-compliant journalists and editors kidnapped and overdosed on castor oil, sometimes to their death. When a younger brother became ill with tuberculosis, Batista cared for him in his own home until the boy died. (Actually, Batista's wife did most of the caretaking, and given the contagious nature of TB, it is a wonder she didn't contract it.) The experience moved Batista to build a sanatorium for those inflicted by the disease, which was then rampant in Cuba.

The Kurhotel was started in 1934 but was not finished until 1954. It operated as a sanatorium only five years before Batista was deposed in January 1959. By the end of 1959 the Castro government was embroiled in fighting counter-revolutionaries in the area, so the Kurhotel was turned into a military barracks. It also housed a teacher training school for young people who had volunteered to bring literacy to the sierra.

Once the Cuban Contras had been defeated and illiteracy pretty much eradicated in the region, the Kurhotel was reborn as a hotel/hospital. In what was being called "clean tourism," it became a destination for foreigners wishing to access Cuba's health care facilities. When recreational tourism took off in Cuba in the 1990s the Kurhotel was renovated into a full-fledged health spa with a multitude of doctors and health care personnel, experts in therapies for respiratory illnesses, cardiac problems, eating disorders, and more. Its hallways are hung with artwork by renowned Cuban painters, making it one of the largest galleries on the island.

Despite its current use and the cosmetic change of the exterior from sinister dark brown to dazzling white, the hulking Kurhotel remains architecturally and proportionately out of place in the little mountain town over which it looms.

From Topes we descended the northern slopes of the Escambray range. Some sections of the road were crowded by vine-covered cliffs spilling small waterfalls. At other points it opened out onto vistas of distant mountains. Luis drove with great care, as do most owners of these classic old cars. Despite the roughness of the road, the three of us were happy and relaxed, not suspecting what a downer awaited us just around the next curve.

Suddenly a police checkpoint loomed into view. Luis muttered *"Pinga!"*

This was slightly shocking because Cubans do not, as many of my Mexican friends do, use swear words in practically every sentence.

"What's wrong?" I asked.

Not bothering to answer, he stopped and reached into the glove box for his car registration and license. The policeman then asked for our passports. We handed them over but he only glanced at the covers to confirm that we were foreigners and handed them back. Then he began writing Luis a ticket.

I couldn't understand what the ticket was for because Luis certainly had not been speeding or driving recklessly. Once the ticket was issued and we were on our way again, he explained. "A special license is required to transport foreigners. Like a taxi. I don't have one." The fine for noncompliance was $75. He said his car would be confiscated if he failed to pay the fine within thirty days.

It was the Casa Camancho situation all over. Several times we had hired cars to transport us and our bikes when we were faced with retracing a part of our route and didn't want to ride it twice. No one had ever mentioned needing a license.

"No car we hired before has ever been stopped," I told Luis. "Is it a new law or an old one just now being enforced?"

"Oh, it has been around a while. They are just being extra strict this week."

"Why this week?"

"The damned Pope. All the foreign journalists are hiring cars to get to wherever he is saying a mass." He added glumly, "I can't drive you to Havana. If they have a checkpoint on this back road they will certainly have them on the autopista."

Luis dropped us at the Santa Clara bus station. He said nothing about the fine, obviously feeling that it was his fault and his responsibility. But he was pathetically grateful when, to the $40 he had asked for bringing us this far, Derek added $75 to cover the fine.

Then we looked around to see what our options were for getting the rest of the way to Havana. Astro buses, which provide very cheap subsidized transport for Cubans, do not take bicycles. The Víazul line, as good as any bus service in North America, did take bikes but there wouldn't be one to Havana until late in the day. There were taxis parked nearby but only one beat-up station wagon was big enough to carry the bikes. We negotiated with the driver to take us to Havana, a straight shot of about three hours up the freeway. As he was in a taxi line-up, I assumed that he was a licensed taxi. However, after we had loaded our bikes into the back of the station wagon, I noticed that he pulled a blanket over them.

"I hope you're licensed to transport foreigners," I said. "Because there are likely to be checkpoints all along the autopista."

"No problem for me!" he said gaily, and hurried us into the back seat of the car.

Unlike Luis, this driver, whose name was Philip, drove at maniacal speed. What made it especially nerve-wracking was the condition of the vehicle, or more particularly, its tires. We hadn't been moving for more than half an hour when one of them blew.

"No problem!" Philip assured us.

He jumped out to replace it with a spare that not only lacked tread, it almost lacked rubber. I could tell by the expression on Derek's face that he didn't believe for a minute that the tire would make it all the way to Havana.

We had been on our way for only a few minutes when a checkpoint loomed. Philip chatted briefly with the inspector. The inspector peered into the back seat at us, grinned, and waved us on.

However, fifty kilometres on when another checkpoint appeared, Philip showed signs of panic. "Quick! Get down!" He grabbed a dirty quilt from the seat beside him and flung it back to us. "Get under the blanket!"

We slunk down in the seat and covered ourselves with the blanket. The inspector, seeing a car driven by what appeared to be a Cuban alone, waved us on.

"No license?" Derek surmised.

"Only to transport Cubans," Philip admitted.

"Why didn't the cop at the first checkpoint give you a ticket?"

Philip shrugged. "How could he? He was my cousin."

We were halfway to Havana when a second tire blew. The car swerved sickeningly to the right and came to a stop in the tall grass.

"Now what?" Derek muttered.

"Doesn't look good," I admitted. "Luis said the reason

they started licensing taxis is to be sure cars are roadworthy. I'm beginning to see why."

Philip got out and stood next to the station wagon, seemingly unconcerned. Another old car passed, slowed, and stopped. Philip went to talk to the driver. A few minutes later he came back rolling the spare from the other car. When the flat tire had been replaced with the other man's spare, the other car drove on. Philip followed.

Derek frowned after the stranger's car. "His tires are as bald as ours. What happens if *he* has a flat?"

"Was that another cousin?" I asked Philip.

"No, he's a stranger."

"A *stranger* lent you his spare tire?" Derek asked, disbelieving.

Philip seemed surprised by our surprise. "Why not? He's not using it. Anyway," he added, "it's only to the Primer Anillo."

We knew approximately where the freeway coming from Santa Clara intersected with the freeway called Primer Anillo (First Ring) that circled Havana to the south and east, because like many freeway intersections it was unmarked and we had missed it more than once.

"What happens there?" Derek asked.

"I have to give him back his tire, because he goes south, and you want to go north to the city, right?"

"Which leaves this car with five tires," Derek muttered. "Two of which are blown to shreds."

"Yeah," I said. "But it could be worse. We've got two bikes with no flat tires. Any idea how far it is from that intersection on to Havana?"

Derek took out the map and studied it. "Hard to tell from this map."

"There is an up side," I said. "We don't have to ride all the way into the city. We can stay on this side of the bay, in Cojímar."

"The downside," Derek said quietly, "is that it's getting dark. And raining."

By the time we reached the intersection it was pouring. The Good Samaritan stopped under an overpass. Philip pulled in behind him, jacked up the car, and returned the man's spare tire to him. With a quick thanks and a farewell handshake, the stranger drove away. Philip stared morosely at his jacked-up, three-tired car. We paid him for having brought us this far and wished him luck. Then we took our bikes out of the station wagon and rode off along the freeway in the rain.

We had ridden on Havana freeways before and found it easy, as traffic was normally light and the right lane was designated for cyclists. But that black night was as hard a ride as we would ever endure in Cuba. The rain hammered us like hail and traffic was unusually heavy. Poor freeway drainage caused deep puddles to form on the pavement. Some we rode through and others were thrown at us in great sheets by passing vehicles. The diffused glare of headlights through the rain made visibility terrible. Vehicles with one or no headlights added to the danger. We could barely see them and only hoped they could see us.

We finally merged onto the Vía Monumental. This put us within fifteen kilometres of Cojímar, the first place I knew of where we might find lodging. But traffic was heavier than ever, causing us to be splashed almost continuously by waves of puddle water. We passed exits but hesitated to take them because they seemed to disappear into darkness—probably because the storm had caused power outages in some areas. At last we came to an exit with what looked like a lighted café nearby where we could take shelter.

The café was an open-air affair with six tables under an awning that sagged with the weight of the rainwater, even as water poured off in curtains on all sides. I pushed my bike over to the woman at the take-out window and asked if she knew of a hotel or villa or campismo or casa in this area where we could spend the night.

She shook her head. "No, Compañera. Nada."

I just stood there. The woman turned and called to the cook. He came out of the kitchen and looked us over. I suspect half-drowned puppies could not have looked more pathetic than we did. The cook and the woman moved out of earshot and conferred. I saw him wave his arm in a gesture that seemed to be telling her that we could wait there in the dining area at one of the metal tables. She shook her head and pointed to a wall clock. It was nearly eight. Closing time? Then she held her hands close to her chest and shook. I realized that she was imitating me, showing the cook how cold I was. I was shivering, even though the temperatures weren't that low. This happens in the tropics. Your body temperature drops and you can get hypothermia even when it's nowhere near freezing.

The discussion continued until something was said that they seemed to agree on. She went out the back door. We waited, with no idea whether she had left for the night, if the place was closing, or what. Ten minutes later she returned and motioned for us to follow. We left the circle of light cast by a bare bulb in the dining area and, pushing our bikes, plunged into the darkness behind the building. I could just make out a tall hedge. The woman walked along it till she came to an opening and ducked through. We followed close on her heels.

We emerged into a small backyard. There was a hutch on stilts and the smell of a chicken coop. She climbed the steps to the house and knocked. The door opened immediately. A man peered out, then opened the door wide and motioned us in. We hesitated, not wanting to bring our streaming bikes in the house or leave them in a strange backyard. The woman who had brought us ran down the steps and helped me push my bike up. Then, as Derek followed, she slipped back through the hole in the hedge, not to be seen again.

We and our bikes stood in the kitchen. An old woman brought two thin towels and the old man put down rags to soak up the puddles we were making on a worn linoleum floor that until our arrival had been perfectly clean. He took our rain jackets and hung them on the back porch. She asked if we had dry clothes. We pulled the rain covers off our panniers and, miracle of miracles, we did.

Eventually we got around to introductions. The couple, Salvador and Josefa, were elderly. Until our arrival they had been watching television. I could hear it still, blaring something about the Pope's motorcade. As Josefa led me through the living room she paused to switch it off. I noticed that there was a Jehovah Witness brochure on the coffee table but had no way of knowing if it was their religion or reading material dropped off by one of the many proselytizers bent on converting Cubans to their particular brand of Christianity.

Josefa left me in the bathroom to change, and when I came out, she sent Derek in. She offered to make something for us to eat but we pretended we had eaten already. Few Cubans have the kind of well-stocked cupboards and refrigerators you find in most North American homes. Electrical blackouts are so common that it is not a good idea to have on hand food that might spoil when the power goes off. Anything they did have was likely to be in the nature of rice, beans, or yuca and would take a long time to cook.

They were astonished to learn that we had left that morning from Trinidad and been on the road all day; many nods of sympathy (but no surprise) as we explained about all the flat tires, and how that led to our trying to get to Havana by bicycle in the pouring rain. Having heard the story of what a day it had been, they understood our weariness and soon showed us into a bedroom. The mattress was hard, the sheets tissue paper thin, and the pillows barely an inch thick, but none of that mattered in the slightest. The rain hammered on the roof and against the window of the little room. We were safe and dry and slept like contented children.

The crowing of a rooster woke us at dawn. We got up immediately, wanting to leave as soon as possible because this home certainly was not licensed to host foreigners and we did not want to cause these kind people any problems. But Josefa must have heard us moving about because by the time we came out she had coffee on and would not hear of our leaving without breakfast. There were eggs, fresh from the chickens she kept out back, and a small dish of yogurt that was probably part of their daily ration as elders.

We were just getting ready to leave when a man on a bicycle rode up. He pounded on the door, and I think my heart pounded just as hard. *Please let it not be a casa inspector who is going to fine them for having let us stay overnight!*

Salvador opened the door and the young man greeted him with a hug. *"Buenos días, Papi."* Then he bounded into the kitchen to hug and kiss Josefa. She introduced him as their son Hector, and excitedly told him how we had been trying to get to the city on our bikes and had got caught in the rain on the Vía Monumental.

"You never could have made it," he told us. "Not with the traffic jams caused by the Pope's motorcade and journalists trying to get out of town. It was chaos!"

"Journalists? Trying to get out of town? Why? Because the Pope is leaving?"

"No, he will be here a few more days," Hector said. "Because of what's happening in Washington. You never saw such a mad rush!"

All sorts of scenarios flashed through my head as to what might have caused a media stampede to Washington. Most Cuban hotels have CNN but the only hotel we had stayed in during the past week was Pasacaballo. We had not bothered to turn on the TV in our room there, and the one in the bar had been tuned to the Cuban national channel with its continuous coverage of the Pope's visit.

"What's going on in Washington?" I asked.

"President Clinton..." Hector began. "I don't know if it's true but—"

"It is not the sort of thing that is discussed in the Cuban media," Salvador interrupted with tight lips that indicated distaste for the whole topic.

I turned to Josefa. She sighed. "There is this woman, Monica somebody..."

Hemingway Drank Here

With the rain stopped and traffic no longer snarled, it would have taken us less than an hour to get to the harbour and there catch a bicycle bus to carry us through the tunnel to Habana Vieja. But we were in no hurry. The previous day had not helped Derek's gastro distress, and a couple of kick-back days in Cojímar, a pleasant town just across the harbour entrance from Habana Vieja, sounded inviting.

The history of Cojímar is intimately connected with that of Earnest Hemingway, not because he ever lived there, but because during the two decades he resided in Cuba he kept his boat, *El Pilar*, docked in Cojímar Bay. The little fishing village is also the setting for *The Old Man and the Sea*, a novel that won him the 1954 Nobel Prize for literature.

Folks wishing to follow the "Hemingway Trail" usually

begin at what were his favourite bars in Habana Vieja: La Bodequita for mojitos and La Floridita for daiquiris. They go to Hotel Ambos Mundos (Both Worlds), where he lived when he first arrived in Cuba and where he began writing *For Whom the Bell Tolls*. From there they might go fifteen kilometres south to San Francisco de Paula to visit Finca la Vigía (Lookout Ranch), which was his home from 1939 to 1960. Finally they'd cross the harbour to Cojímar for drinks at La Terraza (The Terrace), where he and his fisher friends socialized, their boats bobbing in the bay below.

Tourists visit Cojímar daily but few stay the night, probably because in the old part of town there are no hotels or casas licensed to rent rooms to foreigners. Walking from La Terraza around the bay front to the Torreón de Cojímar (a 1649 Spanish fort now occupied by the Cuban coast guard) one passes buildings that Hemingway would have strolled by in the 1940s and 1950s. The little bay, made picturesque by small fishing boats, hasn't changed much either. However, a stone's throw from the Torreón de Cojímar is something that wasn't here in Hemingway's day: a bust of the writer cast in bronze that came from boat fittings donated by Cojímar fishermen.

Not far from Papa's bronze bust is Castillo del Morro, the great fort that for more than 400 years has guarded the entrance to Havana Harbour (not always successfully, for more than once the city was sacked and burned, both by pirates and by hostile European forces). Hemingway would have visited the fort and, as most visitors do today, stuck around to drink *mojitos,* watch the sunset, and listen to the nine p.m. *cañonazo* boom from nearby Fortaleza de la Cabaña—a nightly ritual that has been going on for several hundred years.

The Old Man and the Sea is set mainly in the ocean

where an old man spends long hours struggling with and talking to the biggest, bravest fish he has ever hooked. In the scenes that do take place in Cojímar, Hemingway describes in a few sentences but with chilling clarity the poverty in which most Cubans lived and died prior to the Revolution. That Cojímar no longer exists.

Today's Cojímar is a suburb of modest post-war homes that reflect neither the extreme poverty that characterized the area during Hemingway's time nor anything that smacks of wealth. (Wealth is rare in Cuba, and where it does exist it certainly is not flaunted.) Other changes, dramatic ones, have taken place all around the Cojímar of Hemingway's day.

What Hemingway did not see and today's visitor cannot fail to see is what lies between Cojímar and the forts: an enormous housing estate of five-story apartment buildings. The complex was constructed in the 1960s by *microbrigadas* —volunteer teams consisting largely of unskilled labourers from the slums working under the supervision of more knowledgeable builders. Upon completion, the apartments provided those very same slum dwellers with decent housing that included indoor plumbing, electricity, and clean drinking water.

In the 1970s, an even larger housing complex called Alamar was built on the east side of Cojímar. First Worlders tend to sneer at the boxy design of these units and ill-maintained exteriors that make them seem as down at the heels as any public housing project in the US. Overlooked is the fact that these two public housing developments are built on what in Los Angeles or Miami would be prime oceanfront real estate. In addition to ocean views and easy access to the shore, they have schools, daycare and eldercare centres, sports facilities, a modern hospital, and large organic community gardens. Crime in these neighbourhoods is almost non-existent.

An entirely different kind of development came to the south side of Cojímar in 1990. There the huge José Martí Sports Arena and Veledromo were built to host the 1991 Pan American games. (Cuba came first that year with 140 gold medals, an achievement it has not matched since. The US came second with 130 golds.) These sports facilities are now used for training Cuban athletes and for international events.

Hemingway probably would have liked the jock atmosphere created by the sports facilities. I can imagine him befriending athletes, taking them deep-sea fishing on *El Pilar,* and introducing them to his favourite bars. But by 1991 he was long gone. In 1960, US Ambassador Bonsal went to Finca la Vigía, where Hemingway had lived and worked for twenty-one years. The ambassador informed him that President Kennedy was about to break ties with Cuba, and that he, Hemingway, should leave Cuba to "demonstrate his patriotism." According to Valerie Hemingway, who was then the writer's secretary and later married one of his sons, Hemingway did not cotton to the idea of leaving Cuba. However, he was about to visit Spain, which he did. From there went to the US. That same year (1961), he committed suicide in Ketchum, Idaho.

Near the sports facilities the government had constructed a hotel, the Panamericano, and Villa Panamericana, an Olympic village complex of two-story apartments covering several square blocks. After the games these became available to foreign visitors on a nightly basis. We found it convenient to rent a ground floor apartment when we were cycling because we could ride right up to the door and take the bikes inside; whereas when we stayed at the hotel we had to push our bikes across the lobby and squeeze them into the elevator to get up to whatever floor our room was on. However, the hotel had a pool and good coffee at the lobby bar, and there were always athletes staying there, many of them from Third World countries, recipients of free training provided by Cuban coaches.

As mentioned earlier, few Cuban towns have much by way of a shopping district. Old Cojímar was no exception. But new Cojímar, the part around Hotel Panamericano and Villa Panamericana, does have a farmers' market and a big urban garden where I sometimes bought fresh vegetables. New Cojímar also has a three-block-long section with shops on both sides of the street. One of these was, amazingly, a bicycle parts shop. When we noticed the sign we immediately went there because Derek needed a valve cap to replace one he had lost.

To his disappointment, the shop was pathetically stocked with parts that might have been useful for one of the Chinese-made bikes most Cubans rode, but nothing that resembled any part of our bikes. He came stomping out of the shop to where I waited on the sidewalk with our bikes. "I can't believe it!" he grumbled. "How can a bicycle parts shop not carry a simple thing like a valve cap?"

A boy of about fourteen came along on a crappy Chinese bicycle. Like other Cuban kids we had met, he stopped to admire our bikes. I asked if he knew where we might buy a valve cap, pointing to the valve stem on Derek's tire because I did not know that word in Spanish.

"There?" He indicated the shop Derek had tried.

"No, they don't have any."

Without a word, he reached down, unscrewed the cap from his own valve stem and screwed it onto Derek's. Then, before we could offer anything in return, he flashed us a proud grin and zoomed off down the street.

Los Militares

Unless you happen to be near a military base you don't see many soldiers in Cuba—this despite the fact that Cuba has a well-trained professional force of about 60,000. All able-bodied males (except gays) are inducted at the age of eighteen for a two-year stint, with deferments being granted for higher education up to the age of twenty-eight. Many women volunteer for the military, and twenty percent of its officers are women.

We probably had more close encounters with military personnel than most visitors because of our several trips along the coast. It is only natural for Cuba to put resources into guarding the coast, given that the island has been invaded repeatedly for exactly 500 years. Except for two instances of bombing by US planes just before the Bay of Pigs invasion, every attack came from the sea.

This was true not only of conquistadors, pirates, and the Bay of Pigs invasion. During the 1990s, a group of Miami-based terrorists landed on the causeway leading to Cayo Santa María and murdered a Cuban. Another group arriving by boat from the US attacked Varadero's Melia Hotel. The Guitart Hotel on Cayo Coco was attacked twice. On April 26, 2001, three members of the Alpha 66 terrorist organization made landfall on the north coast of Villa Clara province. They were spotted and captured by Cuban coast guard troops, who relieved them of their M-3 and AKM rifles, hand guns, night vision equipment, and other weaponry.

In 1998, seven Havana hotels were bombed—this the work of Luis Posada Carilles. As of 2012, Posada, wanted by three countries for his terrorist activities (which included the 1976 bombing of a plane carrying the Cuban national fencing team) was living openly and comfortably in Miami while vowing to continue his attacks on Cuba. In short, Cubans have ample reason to guard their coast and pay close attention to strangers who show up on their beaches.

Naturally Derek and I didn't think *we* looked like terrorists, but then, what do terrorists look like? When we first started pedaling around the coast, Cubans had barely adjusted to foreigners bound for Varadero and other tourist enclaves. Independent travellers like ourselves were not only rare; we were puzzling. Why on earth were we cycling like a Cuban when we could be seeing the country through the window of an air-conditioned bus? And why were we choosing some of the roads we did, which plainly had nothing of tourist value on them?

I had my reasons. We were cycling because I wanted to meet Cubans at helmet level. We picked the roads we did because of the map we had. The *Guia de Carreteras* (Guide to Highways), which was the best road map available in Cuba, showed freeways in green, principal highways in yellow, and other paved roads in red. Many red roads led from a main highway to the waterfront and—what? Some lovely unnamed beach, perhaps? Since I wanted to explore the whole coastline, we followed these roads to see where they led. That was how we learned what the map didn't tell us.

Over the rolling hills we would ride until, from the top of one, we would glimpse the ocean and begin to pedal with new energy, refreshed by the very sight of all that cool water. Sometimes we would be within a stone's throw of the beach when we would be brought up short by a young man in uniform. Looking as surprised to see us as we were to see him, he would ask where we thought we were going. When we replied, "To the beach," he would ask to see our passports. After carefully examining every page, he would curtly inform us that this was a military installation and we would have to go back the way we came.

The first few times this happened we were intimidated, perhaps even frightened. But on one occasion I asked if we could refill our water bottles at their station. Of course we could. After that we often stopped to rest at these small coast guard stations, replenished our water, and chatted with the young man (only once or twice was it a woman) who had prevented us from continuing to the beach.

One afternoon we took a beach break at Playa Mayabeque—this on the south coast a little east of Suergidero de Batabanó. Nearby was a small military installation. We stayed on the beach a bit too long, first talking with some kids who had come from a nearby farm, then chatting with a soldier who may or may not have been sent down to the beach to find out what we were doing there. Only after he and the kids had left did we notice that the sun, although still blazing hot, was quite low in the sky. Given how quickly darkness descends in the tropics, we decided we had better camp right there.

We anxiously checked our water, which was running low, and picked a place to set up the tent. As soon as our intent was obvious, the soldier reappeared and told us we couldn't camp there. Although it was a good thirty metres back from the water, he said that the tide would come in later that night and wash us away. I looked at the thick thorn bushes lining the beach, which didn't seem inviting, and back at the sand, which did. But the soldier insisted it was unsafe (and in the morning we would see he had been right). He pointed to the fenced military compound, situated on a small rise, and said, "You can put your tent there on the grass."

We did as he suggested, then I asked if we might refill

our water bottles. He said yes and motioned for us to follow him indoors. The barracks was small, with only four bunks, one rough-hewn wooden table, and a bathroom off to the side that he said we were welcome to use. He invited us to sit down at the table, and we did. For an hour or more we sipped our water and listened to him talk about the hardships (mainly boredom) of being at such a small station. But there was pride, too, as he spoke of Cuba's readiness to repel invaders, and God help any who might try to sneak ashore on that part of the homeland coast he was entrusted to guard.

Besides *los militares,* Cuba also has a defence force called *los vigilantes.* Most have received some weapons training but I have never seen one armed. As the name suggests, their job is to be vigilant. In urban areas they have been called upon to help the police spot street crime and "antisocial elements." In small communities, especially on the coast, their main responsibility is to watch out for strangers who cannot be readily identified as area residents or tourists.

That's why, when I was biking the east coast with two women friends in 2000, and we wanted to camp at a little cove, Ensenada Juan González, we did not set up our tents on the beach as if the place belonged to us. I looked for a local person to ask permission. When I saw a woman scrubbing clothes outside a *bohio* (thatch roofed hut,) I asked her if it would be okay to overnight there. She did not give us an immediate answer but sent for the Capitán de los Vigilantes.

In due time the captain showed up, a diminutive man barely my height (and I am only five feet tall). He listened gravely as we made our request, then gave an order to some teenaged boys who had come with him to get a glimpse of the strangers. They ran off and returned a few minutes later with rakes and machetes. Before we knew it, they had cleared a path through the thorn bushes that might puncture our bike tires as we brought them down from the highway to the beach and raked the sand clean all around the area that the captain thought would make the best campsite.

It was a lovely night, one of the nicest I ever spent in Cuba. We asked the woman in the bohio if she would make supper for us, and two hours later her husband brought it to us in three small plastic pails, each containing a sautéed fish he had caught while she was cooking the rice and beans. We ate the delicious meal there on the beach while gazing out at a Spanish ship (the *Admirante Oquendo)* sunk in this little cove in 1898. Its prow was still visible, cannon pointed skyward, silhouetted against the rising moon.

We repaid the locals as best we could with cash for the couple who made our supper, baseball caps for the boys and the captain, plus pencils, crayons, and erasers for the local primary school. As we tucked in for the night, I reminded Brenda and Terri that unless they wanted to ride in the heat of the day, we would have to rise early and be on our way before the villagers woke up and delayed us with more hospitality.

So there we were in five a.m. blackness, taking down tents by the light of our battery-powered headlamps and re-packing panniers. Suddenly two figures appeared on the beach. It was the vigilante captain and his wife, carrying a thermos and three tiny china cups. They filled the cups with strong hot coffee to speed us on our way.

How, I wonder, does one repay that kind of hospitality? And how is it that Cubans have figured out, better than anyone else in the world, how to combine security precautions with hospitality?

PART 5

CUBA BY SUNRISE

I am not by nature an early riser, but I have long since learned that in any hot climate sunrise is a golden time, not to be squandered on sleep. This is true in Cuba and especially true at the eastern end of the island. There one can count on invigorating coolness only for the first few hours after the sun rises out of the Atlantic and spills its dazzling light across the land. After that daytime temperatures soar to some of the hottest on the island, reducing local folks and foreigners alike to puddles of sweat.

I learned this when, in 2000, I set out to cycle what Cubans call *El Oriente* (The East). Derek wasn't able to go on that trip so I persuaded a photographer friend, Larry Doell, to ride a portion of Cuba's eastern coastline with me. The plan was to start in Baracoa and, following the coast, cycle to Guantánamo and on to Santiago de Cuba. From there we'd return to Havana by train. I would come back later to cycle the rest of the east coast and the intimidating mountains of the Sierra Maestra.

A Night in the Jungle

I had fond memories of Playa Maguana from an earlier visit with Dianne, so I suggested to Larry that before heading into the unknown of Cuba's Oriente we should ride from Baracoa to Playa Maguana—only 21 kilometres west—and spend a day on the beach.

We were almost at the turnoff to Villa Maguana when Larry got distracted by an ox cart and insisted on stopping to take pictures. I chatted with the driver, an amiable young man named Felix, while Larry framed his photos. Felix looked bemused when Larry lay down on the road in front of the massive creatures and aimed his camera (so it seemed) right up their noses.

"Do you plan to overnight at Playa Maguana?" the ox cart driver inquired.

"Yes, at Villa Maguana if it has a vacancy."

"Why don't you stay at my house?" he invited. "It is on the beach, not a kilometre from the villa."

"Is your casa licensed?"

"Yes, of course," he replied without hesitation.

"Well," I looked at Larry, who was now so close to the beasts' noses that if one of them snorted, his lens would have been covered in ox snot. "You want to stay in a *casa particular* tonight?"

"Sure," he said. "Whatever."

Villa Maguana, where Dianne and I had stayed, was near Felix's house, but a limestone bluff and dense vegetation made it impossible to see one from the other. The simple frame house Felix led us to was on a small promontory just a few yards from a lovely beach. It had a veranda facing the sea, and in the clearing out back were several outbuildings. Beyond that was real, picturesque jungle. I was delighted to think that we had lucked onto the perfect "undiscovered" guest house.

I hesitated as we entered. "Where is the little sticker that shows you're licensed to rent rooms?"

"It hasn't come yet," Felix replied quickly. "We got the permit but they were out of stickers."

I accepted his explanation and thought no more about

it. We tossed our things in the bedroom and went down to the beach for a lovely late-afternoon swim.

On the beach we ran into Chris and Kate, a Canadian couple whom we had met earlier in Baracoa. They had been planning to overnight at Villa Maguana, too, but said its four rooms were occupied so they would have to go back to town.

"We're staying in a casa particular," I said, pointing to the house. "I don't know if it's licensed to rent a second bedroom, but you could ask."

Chris loped off to ask about a room. Kate and I tried to do a bit of exploring in the forest but it was very wild and the vegetation was dense so we returned to the beach. Chris soon came back with the news that yes, there was another room available, so they'd stay there, too. They had to go get their things from the rental car which was parked over at the villa, but they would be back in time for dinner.

They returned half an hour later, and said they had met two German backpackers who were also looking for a room to rent. "I knew both the bedrooms were taken here," Kate said. "But we told them where the house was in case they wanted to stop by to ask Felix if he knows of another place."

Around dusk, Felix's wife Nadia called us in to supper—a meal of fresh fish, *congri* (a mixture of rice and beans), and grated cabbage salad. By the time we had finished eating it was quite dark and a slight drizzle was falling. Felix had gone out and Nadia was not very talkative. Two children, a boy of six and a girl of eight, flitted in and out, but they were as shy as their mother. When I asked if they were hers, she said yes but not by Felix. Their father, she said, had gone off with another woman.

"So this is *your* house?" I asked uneasily, recalling the problem we had with the ex-husband when we stayed with Mrs. Camancho.

She said yes, the house was hers. Felix had only moved in with her and the children a few months earlier. She then went to put the children to bed, so I learned no more about her life before or with Felix.

Chris, Kate, Larry and I soon went to bed. We were all hoping to be up and about early the next morning, mornings being when Cuban beaches are at their most beautiful. Our room was a large one with two beds and plenty of space to bring in the bikes. This was a great convenience as it put all our belongings within easy reach and we did not have to go to the trouble of removing panniers, locking the bikes, and so on.

We had been asleep an indeterminate amount of time— one, two, or maybe three hours, when the light suddenly went on. Nadia, Felix, and two men we had never seen burst into the room and began grabbing our stuff.

"Hey!" Larry yelled. "What the hell are you doing?"

"Wait!" I cried. "Come back with our stuff!"

"Come, come!" Nadia cried, grasping us by the hands and dragging us along behind the men—a direction we were willing to go since they were making off with the bikes and everything else. They ran down the back steps and were swallowed up—as we ourselves were—by utter blackness.

As Nadia dragged us across the farmyard and into what I knew to be the jungle we heard voices—two in German and others I recognized as belonging to Kate and Chris. They also were demanding what was going on and where we were being taken.

"*No problema! Calmate! Shhh!*" Nadia whispered.

"Wait here!" Felix hissed. "*Pase la policia!*"

Then our hosts and their helpers disappeared.

"Does anybody know where we are?" Kate asked in a small voice.

"Or *why* we're here?" Chris added.

I sighed. "Felix said something about the police. I think he lied about his casa being licensed to rent rooms."

"What is this license thing?" asked one of the Germans. I explained.

"*Mein Gott!*" exclaimed the other German. "All is our fault!"

"How so?" Chris asked.

"Well, after you said you are staying here, we talk to this Felix. He said he have no more room, but we could stay in the shed behind the house. Hans and me, we got sleeping bags. We was sleeping in there."

"You think somebody saw you go in and told the police?" I asked.

"No," Hans clarified. "*We* told the police. After we decide to spend the night in the shed, we go back to the bar at the villa. Along come two police. One ask if we stay at the villa. I say no, we stay at a house up the beach. We do not know this will make a problem."

"It's not your fault. You didn't know the law," Chris said.

"Does anybody know where we are?" Kate asked again.

"I don't care where *we* are," Larry mumbled. "I'd just like to know where my cameras are."

"The cameras are in your pannier, which is on your bike," I reminded him. "The question is, where are our bikes?"

"What about our passports?" Chris asked. "Mine was on the dresser. And now…"

Now, with all our worldly travel possessions having vanished into the night, the situation was almost too frightening to contemplate. I avoided it by answering the easy question. "Kate, we are somewhere in that jungle just east of the house, you know, the one we went just a little way into, and were saying how it was the first real rainforest we had seen in Cuba."

"I guess that's why it's raining," Larry observed morosely. "I hope my panniers are waterproof."

"It's only misting," I tried to reassure him. "If it doesn't rain too hard, the cameras should stay dry."

Without moonlight or starlight it was impossible to see anything, therefore pointless, I reasoned, to search for our stuff. I walked a few metres and stumbled over a large log. Rubbing my bruised shins, I suggested, "Why don't we sit down and wait till daylight? Then go look for our things?"

The others took a few steps in various directions, but after being whacked in the face by wet lianas and getting stabbed by spiky palm fronds they came to the same conclusion. One by one they sank down on the sand. There we sat, six drizzle-dampened, semi-strangers with our backs against a log and our shoulders soaking up what little warmth we could from the person next to us.

"Tropical rainforests have poisonous snakes, don't they?" Kate asked nervously.

"In the Florida Everglades where I grew up, at least three species," I told her. "And dozens in the Amazon rainforest. But not a single venomous species in Cuba."

"That's right," Chris confirmed. "According to the guide book the only thing you have to watch out for in Cuba are scorpions. And they're not deadly," he added helpfully.

For the next several hours we traded stories as travellers do the world over when they've got time on their hands: where we were from, which parts of Cuba we had already visited, and where we were going from here. Or where we would go from here if, come daylight, we managed to recover our travel documents, cash, and other essentials.

It was around four a.m. when we heard the approach of

people speaking quietly in Spanish. I guessed it to be Nadia and Felix, and it was.

"Police gone," Felix said cheerfully. "Now okay to come back."

"What about our bikes?" I asked.

"Already in your room. Everything like before."

When we reached our room we saw that this was true. Our bikes were as damp as we were but not a thing was missing. Exhausted, and grateful to be back in a soft dry bed, I immediately fell asleep.

In what seemed like five minutes but it was probably an hour, we were again shaken awake. Nadia was explaining to me in Spanish, and Felix to Larry in broken English, that it was morning and we must be gone before sunrise. We dressed and pushed our bikes out onto the porch. Chris, Kate, and the Germans came stumbling out, all looking as sleep-deprived and irritable as I felt.

I faced Felix and said, "You *lied* to me. You said this casa was licensed and it is not. If you had told the truth and I took the risk willingly I would have paid. But you didn't; you lied. I don't pay for lies."

He hung his head like a scolded child. "Sorry."

I turned to Nadia intending to make the same assertion, then remembered what she had told me the evening before about the house belonging to her and how Felix had only moved in a short time ago. It seemed pretty clear who the instigator had been.

"Nadia, if the police had found us in your house last night you would have been fined what—$400 for each occupied room? That's $800, $1200 if they counted the shed. Could you have paid that?"

She shook her head, looking wretched.

"You know if you could not pay the fine they would

have confiscated the house?" At her almost imperceptible nod, I pressed the point. "How can you let Felix put your lovely home at risk? If the government confiscates it because you broke the law, where will you and your children go?"

She put up a hand to wipe away a trickle of tears. The hand trembled, reminding me that she probably had got even less sleep than we did. However stressed we had been, however much we each feared that we might have lost, she had been close to losing far more and therefore would have been far more frightened.

I thought about how just three years earlier, in this very community, Dianne and I had celebrated International Women's Day. Nadia might have been one of the women at that fiesta, although I did not remember having met her. In any case she would have been to other fiestas, yearly ones, celebrating women. Yet here she was, near-victim of a jackass boyfriend whose greed could have cost her their home. What were the high-minded speeches of International Women's Day teaching her, or failing to teach her, about her rights and responsibilities as a woman and mother?

More tears slid down her cheeks. "I didn't know it would be like this," she said.

I felt like crying, too. All the anger generated by stress and lack of sleep was replaced by a little sympathy and a lot of sadness.

"Here is what we owe you for dinner," I said. "We're paying for that because it was a good honest meal. But for the room, no. That wasn't good for us and it wasn't good for you. Don't let Felix bring foreigners here again. You have too much to lose."

Her fingers closed over the money, more money for our two dinners than Felix likely made in a month of hauling lumber in his ox cart. The others followed my lead, paying for dinner but not for their room. Even so, I could tell by the way she looked at the money that it might well be more than she had ever held in her hand at one time.

As we climbed on our bikes and rode east toward the rising sun, I wondered if she would keep it for herself and her children or give it to him. And would she, given the chance, do it all over again?

Cuba's Far East

Baracoa lies on Cuba's northern coast about sixty kilometres from the island's eastern tip. Most of the town is tucked into a stubby thumb of land bounded on one side by the Bahía de Baracoa and on the other side by the Bahía de Miel (Honey Bay). West of that core, across the Bahía de Baracoa, there is an airport, a nice hotel, and some public housing. More town sprawls inland along the highway called La Farola (The Lantern), until it spirals upward and disappears into rugged mountains. The part of Baracoa between the two bays was virtually destroyed by a hurricane in 2008. But when Larry and I were there in 2000, it was a just a funky old town with lots of charm.

When I say old I mean *really* old, and that's not even counting the centuries Baracoa was a native village—one that is believed to have Columbus visited in October of 1492. Nineteen years later another ship from Europe arrived. The Spanish commander, Diego Velázquez de Cuélla, brought along his secretary, 27-year-old Hernán Cortéz who later made a name for himself by slaughtering Aztecs in Mexico. But first Cortéz and Velázquez de Cuélla made names for themselves by murdering the Taíno people around Baracoa and establishing the first European settlement in Cuba.

In the past 500 years, Baracoa's population has increased

to its present 50,000, and everyone of pure Taíno blood, or pure Spanish blood for that matter, is long dead. The streets are paved and cars have replaced boats that were once the only contact with the outside world. But surrounding mountains, the palm-fringed beaches, and the sea itself are all ageless. This little-changed landscape is what gives Baracoa its special charm.

After our unrestful night at Playa Maguana, Larry and I took a day of recovery in Baracoa, staying at Casa Atlantis, the bayfront home of Fermin Pita, a mechanical engineer, and his wife Ziedy, a paediatrician at the local hospital. Their two rental rooms at the back of the house opened into a walled courtyard where we could safely park the bikes. From beyond the courtyard we could hear the gentle slosh of wavelets from the Bahía de Miel. In the 2008 hurricane, those wavelets turned into monsters that pounded the courtyard, the rooms where we had stayed, and the house itself into fragments of broken cement. But that was yet six years off and would have been impossible to imagine during the tranquil time we spent there. Over breakfast prepared by Fermin (Dr. Ziedy being too involved with work to cook for guests), Larry and I discussed our route out of Baracoa.

The snaky highway over La Farola would have been the logical route, and tackling it from the Baracoa side would have given us a feel for what racers face at the outset of the annual *Vuelta de Cuba* (Cuba's version of the Tour de France). But we had come in over La Farola and I was still fixated on cycling the coast. The map showed what might be a road along the coast as far as the mouth of the Boma River. It appeared that we would have to cut inland there, continue east to the Yumurí River, and at that point, cross the Maisí Plateau to a road that ran along the coast as far as Guantánamo Bay. The first section of that route was designated in green on the map, not the red of paved highway. But there was a red line over the Maisí Plateau and I reasoned that cycling something called a "plateau" would be easier than the mountainous route over La Farola. (The only positive to come out of *that* miscalculation was that, after cycling the Maisí Plateau, never again would I lack the confidence to tackle any terrain in Cuba.)

Although we knew we would be doing the first part of the ride on unpaved road, we thought we knew what we were getting into because we had already done some exploring out that way in the newly-designated Parque Majayara. We had spent half a day tromping through its rough terrain with Professor Ordoñez, a local archaeologist who pointed out various pre-Columbian ruins. I was fascinated by the *balcons*, natural semi-caves carved into cliffs high above the beach, along which one could walk for a considerable distance. The Taínos had used these "balconies" to observe the ocean. We were shown pre-Columbian drawings that Professor Ordoñez believed depicted the natives' first sighting of Columbus' ships. To me they looked like squiggles that might as well have been glyphs from some as-yet undiscovered language that translated as, "Here comes doom!"

Parque Majayara was quite wild except for the occasional bohio. These rural huts, commonplace in Cuba, are built of local materials scrounged from the surrounding bush. Here they were surrounded by banana, avocado, and mango trees, coconut palms, *cacao* (chocolate) bushes, pineapple plants, and other tropical vegetation. I guessed that the area was not very changed from how it was when Columbus arrived, except for the wagon tracks which would not have been there then, since the Taínos had neither horses nor wheels.

It was along one of these wagon tracks that we began our sunrise ride. The route was not all that difficult, only occasionally becoming so rough that we were forced to get off and push the bikes up a rock-strewn slope or through a washout. After awhile we came to a straight section with quite a few cottages lining the track. There was also a one-room school, identifiable by a white bust of the poet-philosopher José Martí such as sits in front of every primary school in Cuba.

Children dressed in red-and-white uniforms had just been called into class. When they saw us they stopped to stare, smile, wave, and giggle. Larry, who had long wanted to get inside a Cuban school to take pictures, asked if I would put the request to the teacher, a thin man of about thirty-five, wearing a white shirt, polyester trousers, and the cheap black shoes provided by state rations store for those who have no access to dollars to buy better ones.

The teacher greeted us warmly, but when I asked if we could come into the classroom to take pictures, he hesitated. I hastily added, "We wouldn't want to disrupt your class. What we would really like to do is watch you teach for a little while, to see what the children are studying."

"Oh, that would be fine," he said, but still looked uneasily at the camera Larry was already digging out of his pannier.

"Leave it," I told Larry. "He's not comfortable with the idea—yet."

The teacher, who might have understood a bit of English, said, "I don't mean to be inhospitable, but you know Cuba has just weathered some very hard times. Some come from over there," he waved his hand vaguely toward the north, "and take pictures that show how few school supplies we have, then publish them in America to make Cuba look bad."

"We're from Canada," I quickly clarified. "We know that, supplies or no supplies, Cuba's literacy level is the same as in our country. From what I have seen, Cuba's success is based mainly on the dedication of its teachers."

He beamed. "Yes, United Nations reports compare us very favourably with other countries."

"How far do these students walk to school?" I asked.

"The ones farthest away, perhaps a kilometre. But most live closer. I myself come from Baracoa."

"Surely not every day!" It had taken us nearly two hours to get this far. Although a person could probably walk the track almost as fast as we had biked it, that was still a long way to hike to and from on a daily basis.

"Every day," he confirmed. "I leave town at six in order to be here by eight. Class ends at noon, but I stay until three, to help the children with their homework. Some have parents who can help them, but others don't."

A schoolteacher's peso salary, like just about everybody else's salary in Cuba, would be in the neighbourhood of US$20 a month. Free health care, plus whatever his food, clothing, housing, utilities, and recreation subsidies were worth, would bring that to a bare subsistence wage in Cuba. But for a day that began at six a.m. with a two-hour hike through the hills and ended with another two-hour hike that would get him home just before dark? *That* was teacher dedication.

The hour we spent in the classroom was really fun. The teacher's rapport with his students was great and the kids did him proud, showing off reading, arithmetic, and reciting skills. When I expressed my respect for their level of learning (although what really impressed me was their apparent *love* of learning) the teacher said, simply, "Thank you. It is my life."

The most striking difference between this classroom and the average North American classroom was the absence of artwork or other decorations. Each child did have a cheap lined-paper notebook of a type that is sold for pennies and used in schools all over the island. As far as I could see, all the children had by way of materials were the little blue-books and one yellow pencil each. There were some books, but certainly not one for every child. A number of children sat two to a desk, sharing. The teacher asked if I would tell them about Canada. I said I would if they would promise not to laugh at my Spanish—which naturally made them all laugh.

The teacher laughed, too. "Tell your friend he may take pictures if he wishes."

While Larry was snapping pictures, I asked if we could leave a small gift for the students. The teacher asked what it might be, probably realizing that if I was carrying it in my pannier it must be very small indeed. Together we walked out to my bike, where I retrieved a bag of animal-shaped erasers.

When I handed it to him, he carefully counted the erasers, twice, then said regretfully, "I cannot accept them. You see, there are only nineteen in this package, and I have twenty students. What could I tell the one who didn't get one?"

For a minute I was stumped. Then I pulled the pannier off the bike and dumped its contents on the ground. Larry came out of the school and asked, "What are you doing?"

"Looking for one more eraser. We brought quite a few. Surely there's one more in here somewhere!" And sure enough, just when I had given up and was starting to repack my pannier, I spied one lone pink elephant-shaped eraser.

Then we were off to see what lay ahead in a verdant area not described in any guide book. We soon discovered that what lay ahead was an inlet. It did not show on the map so we had no way of knowing how far inland it went. It was simply not crossable. Or so it seemed until we noticed a boat being rowed toward us from the opposite shore. An old man, grinning broadly, pulled up next to us and without saying a word, steadied his boat while we loaded our bikes into it. Upon reaching the other side I held out some money in several denominations for him to take what we owed him. He selected two pesos, total value, eight cents. I was never sure what to do when someone asked so little (often nothing at all) for a service that was so valuable to us. But I knew that I would have handed any airport redcap at least a dollar tip for carrying my bags a few metres. Did the old man's poverty make it fair to tip him less? That didn't compute for me, so we added a dollar to the pesos, which so widened his smile that I thought his face would split in two.

We had not gone far before we came to another inlet. This time there was no old man in a boat to ferry us across but there was a dirt track leading inland. We followed it and in a little while found ourselves back on the main highway. After pedaling along it for a several kilometres we came to a pretty white sand beach shaded by coconut palms. I called for a swim break, which I took while Larry tried to find something non-cliché to photograph on a beach that was by its very beauty a travel poster cliché.

When I came out of the water he was being hustled by a woman who wanted us to come to her house, which we could see from where we were, for lunch. "She's the fifth person to hit on me," Larry complained. "So far I have been offered a coconut, homemade candy, seed jewellery, and shells from some of those endangered *polimita* snails."

"It figures," I sighed. "We're probably only half an hour from Baracoa by car. I suppose tourists who want your stereotypical coconut-palm shaded beach come here."

"So shall we have lunch at this lady's house?"

"Might as well. As far as I know, there's nothing by way of traveller facilities beyond here."

Part of the woman's come-on spiel had included lobster, very cheap, so that was what Larry ordered. We sat at an oil-cloth-covered table in her tiny house. Within a few minutes I got my plate of rice and beans, cooked earlier that day and no longer warm. Larry got the same except that his included a lobster tail barely bigger than a prawn.

As we picked disconsolately at our meal—the first bad one we had been served in a casa—we tried to ignore sounds coming from a nearby room. Then a girl of about fifteen emerged, followed by a fat Italian who must have been at least sixty-five. He handed our hostess $10, and without a word to the girl he had just banged, got in his car and drove away. (It will do no good to call me a racist for naming Italians as the most prevalent sex tourists in Cuba, then and now. That's just how it is—speaking of male sex tourists anyway. With women, the ones I have met were usually Canadian or British.)

Larry and I paid for lunch and left, upset by the sleaze, our contribution to it, and the irony of the situation. The woman had illegally sold a meal of lobster that had been illegally trapped, and an undersized one at that. She had also illegally rented a room to a man to have illicit sex with a girl so young it would have been considered rape in North America, and for which, if apprehended in Cuba, the man could have ended up in jail and the girl in detention.

"That's free enterprise for you," Larry said glumly.

"Brought to this backwater by us," I added.

"By us?"

"Well, you can bet she wasn't breaking all those laws before foreigners started hanging out on the beach in front of her house."

We crossed the bridge over the Yumurí River and began climbing up to the Maisí Plateau—an ascent of about 200 metres in two kilometres.

"I can't do it," I huffed, pulling into a turnout to catch my breath.

Larry motioned to a tractor with a trailer chugging up the incline. "Shall we hitch a ride?"

"Yes!"

Smiling sheepishly at a grinning Cuban who sailed up the hill past us on a single-speed bicycle, we hoisted our bikes and ourselves onto the trailer. The tractor puttered off, stopping occasionally to pick up other passengers, men and women workers from the coffee orchards lining the highway. We rode until the tractor turned off to a farm.

According to the map this was a paved highway, but it must have been an old map because the amount of asphalt left on the road was minimal. Even more challenging were the deep gullies that cut across the plateau. Going down into them you couldn't get up any speed because of the potholes. Besides, in the bottom of each gully there was often water coursing across the road and you couldn't tell how deep it was until you got there. You would splash through and face an arduous climb up the other side, followed by a brief level ride, then another treacherous descent into the next gully and another climb up the other side. I later came back with Derek to map both this route and the one over the Farola for our Lonely Planet cycling guide. I did not mention in the book that the Farola route over the mountains was for jocks while the one over the Maisí Plateau was for masochists.

By sunset we were not across the Maisí Plateau yet. We weren't even to its 400-metre summit that the map showed to be beyond La Máquina, a town we hoped to reach by dark—and almost did.

We arrived in La Máquina simultaneously with a drenching downpour and were welcomed at the town's only hotel with the news that it was full. Really? It was a pretty shabby place, what was called a peso hotel because the prices were in pesos and thus affordable for Cubans.

I offered dollars for a room, any room, but the man shook his head. "We're full," he insisted. "It's all the truckers. They can't go on in this weather."

With that he shut the door and left us standing in the downpour.

We rode back to the middle of town, which like most small towns in Cuba had nothing resembling a commercial center. The only place showing signs of life was a bodega (store) where local folks go to get their allotment of rationed goods. A roofed porch ran along the front of the building. A dozen men were standing on the porch watching the rain. And watching us. They were probably wondering where we came from and what we were going to do when we got tired of standing in the street in the pouring rain. I leaned my bike against Larry's and sloshed over to where the men stood.

Trying not to sound as desperate as I felt, I said, "We need a place to spend the night. The hotel is full. What can we do?"

I knew there was no point in asking if there was a licensed casa in this town because there wouldn't be. Whatever the risks of staying in an unlicensed one—and we had been reminded of what they were all too recently—we would have to take the chance.

The men shook their heads, shuffled their feet, spoke quietly among themselves. Then one stepped forward and said, "Come with me."

He led us to a jeep parked nearby and told us to put our bikes in the back. I saw by its logo that it belonged to the

Ministry of Agriculture, and wondered if his official capacity with that ministry would keep him from getting nailed for letting foreigners stay at his house. Later I figured out that what made it a no-risk deal for him was because foreigners rarely passed through La Máquina and never were inclined to stay; thus no one had ever been assigned here to enforce the law that forbade renting unlicensed rooms to foreigners.

His name was Umberto. When we got to his place he introduced us to his wife Felicidad, a slender, energetic woman of about forty, and their son Federico. The boy was eleven, a little on the pudgy side, and shy. He was soon to graduate from primary school and had won a scholarship to a school in Havana for high-performance students. Umberto and Felicidad were enormously proud of him. While Felicidad made dinner Umberto brought out report cards to show his son's high marks. When I asked the boy what he planned to study, he said he wanted to be an *agronomista* like his father, but Felicidad called from the kitchen, "Or maybe he will study engineering or medicine."

It was easy to understand why she spoke with such confidence. Higher education in Cuba is free, and a choice of what to study is up to the students as long as they have the grades required to get into university or their preferred training program. Any kid who excelled in school as this one did certainly had all those options open to him.

Before dinner we were shown to the bathroom. It was outdoors and I do not mean by that an old-fashioned outhouse. It consisted of a ceramic toilet perched on the wooden top of a cesspool, with a bucket of water beside it for flushing down anything that didn't run down of its own accord. There were walls around it but no roof, no shelter from the rain.

Then we were shown to where they expected us to sleep. That was even worse. It was clearly the couple's own bed and there was only one. Larry and I had been friends for twenty years but it was not *that* kind of friendship. Once before on this trip we had been forced to rent a room with only one bed, but upon explaining to our host that we were not a couple, he had dragged a plastic chaise lounge in off the patio for me and provided extra sheets and a pillow. This home had no patio, no chaise lounge, no sofa in the living room. The only other bed was in their son's room. Felicidad assured me that she, her husband, and Federico would be completely comfortable sleeping there together.

Later, in the privacy of our room, Larry and I each made noises about sleeping on the floor but the bed had only a single sheet for covering and no blanket or pillow that the one who took the floor might use to cushion their martyrdom. Finally we both lay down at the furthest edge of our respective side of the bed, fully dressed in what had been dry clothes but after a trip to the outdoor bathroom were only a little less wet than our wet ones. I thought I was too uncomfortable to sleep but I must have drifted off because the next thing I heard was a thud and "Oh, shit!"

The voice was Larry's but he was no longer in the room. A moment later he staggered in and fell on the bed with a groan.

"Larry!" I whispered. "What's wrong?"

"That back door," he moaned. "A Dutch door, I think it's called. I got the bottom half open but couldn't find the latch to the top half in the dark so I ducked under. Coming back from the toilet I didn't duck low enough. I might have a concussion."

Neither of us got much sleep after that, what with Larry's intermittent groans and me worrying how I would get him to the nearest hospital, which was probably in Guantánamo, if he really did have a concussion.

Fortunately, he didn't. We were up at first light, tucking money for our lodging and meal discreetly under a vase of plastic flowers and swearing to pretty Felicidad that we never ate breakfast before riding and had to leave right away. No mention was made of the huge purple goose egg on Larry's forehead. Maybe they thought it was a natural deformity. Or maybe they had heard the crash and were embarrassed, as people often are, when a guest hurts themselves in their home, even if it is through no fault of their own.

They did ask if Larry would take a picture of the three of them before we left. He did, and sent a copy back to them later. I sent along an inexpensive set of flatware because I had noticed at dinner that there were no knives or forks, just a soup spoon for each person even though the meal was rice and beans, not soup. It struck me as one of those Cuban oddities that a family without an indoor bathroom and too poor to own forks knew for a fact that their bright little boy would be able to go to university.

We had planned to ride from La Máquina down to Punto Maisí, that being the furthest east point on Cuba's north coast and I determined to get there. I did, but not on that trip. Umberto said it would take several days to repair the damage that the previous night's heavy rains would have caused to the road leading to Punto Maisí. Until then, only someone on foot or horseback could get through. So it was not until later, when I returned with Derek, that I made it the remaining twelve kilometres to that rocky point from which, on a clear day, one can see Haiti.

Even when Derek and I made the trip months later, the Punto Maisí road was nearly impassable. And we didn't see

Haiti when we got there. What we found was a small village of shabby houses, a lighthouse, and a rocky beach. Between the beach and the village were foundations, abandoned a decade earlier, of what were to have been better residences for local families. From the foundations we could see that they were meant to have been cookie-cutter cement block houses laid out in a grid several blocks square. They would have had piped-in potable water and indoor bathrooms. Unfinished projects such as this clutter the Third World, works normally begun by one government and abandoned by the next, who doesn't want previous politicos to get credit for having initiated anything. But that was not what had caused this project to be abandoned. It was the loss of the Soviet aid, a precipitous drop in sugar prices, and a decision to resuscitate the economy by investing most of Cuba's resources in the development of tourist infrastructure.

This was not the only big project abandoned midstream. In 1990, the USSR had walked away from a nuclear power plant it was helping Cuba build near Cienfuegos. It is now rusting away, as abandoned as this housing project and even less likely to ever be completed. But perhaps that was a backhand blessing. Without nuclear power, Cuba began making widespread use of alternative forms of energy that it probably wouldn't have considered. When petroleum again became readily available from Venezuela, Cuba did resume its reliance on that fossil fuel, but in the meantime, progress had been made. There is hardly a community on the island so small that it does not get at least some of its energy from solar or wind.

As for the folks in Punta Maisí who never got a new government-built house, who is to say that they were not just as proud of the wood-and-stone homes they had built themselves?

Derek and I were about to leave when an army truck loaded with black people passed. We asked a local man who they were and where they were going, as our map showed nothing beyond Punta Maisí.

"Haitians," he said. "Boat people. They come here illegally. If they get caught, like those in that truck, they get sent back to Haiti. They are held down there," he waved in the direction the truck had been headed, "until the next boat sails for Haiti."

"Haiti, horrible!" shuddered a woman.

"Have you been there?" I asked.

"No, but Cuba has hundreds of doctors in Haiti. I have seen them interviewed on television. The stories they tell! What poverty! And the violence, the awful, awful violence! I don't understand how people can live like that. We cannot take them, of course. But it is sad that they have to go back."

As we left I took one last look across the ocean to where Haiti lay just seventy-seven kilometres away. How good life seemed in Punta Maisí probably depended on where one was coming from.

Larry and I cycled the remaining distance across the Maisí Plateau that morning and were rewarded with a smooth glide down to Cuba's south coast. There we got on the well-paved highway to Guantánamo. It was a glorious ride, with a strong tailwind and great waves crashing against the rocky coast below. The only problem was that we could not make it all the way to Guantánamo in a single day, and there were few facilities where foreigners could stay.

We were turned away from the campismo at Cajababo because its cabañas had been reserved for several busloads of Cuban teens soon to arrive from the city. We rode on, another fifteen kilometres or so. It was nearly nightfall. I was beyond exhaustion when we found a holiday camp on the beach. It consisted of cottages for vacationing families and was nicer than a campismo. Being midwinter, it was empty except for the cottage where the camp manager and his wife lived.

When I asked if we might rent a cottage for the night, he said, simply, *"No es possible."*

He said that we must go to a hotel that accepted foreigners because this place was for Cubans only. He knew and I knew that the nearest hotel was in Guantánamo, still eighty-five kilometres away.

"Look," I said desperately. "We have come all the way from La Máquina. I can't ride any further."

He shook his head, as if to say that was not his problem. I started to cry.

His wife, sitting in a rocking chair next to him, spoke sharply, a single word I didn't catch.

"Okay," he said gruffly. "You can have the cabaña at the end."

"Great," I sniffled. "How much?"

He looked at his wife. She said, *"Catorce."*

She might have meant fourteen pesos but I handed him fourteen dollars, and gave Larry, who had been waiting out on the road, a thumbs up. We had a comfortable cottage on the beach all to ourselves. We had no food to prepare in the little kitchenette so would go without supper, but with two beds and an indoor toilet, the place seemed absolutely luxurious.

We reached Guantánamo next day. I knew it was a highly militarized area and didn't expect to like it, but I did. Despite bunkers hacked into hillsides all around the city, despite all the ugly things that went on (and would only get worse) at the US naval base on the other side of the bay, despite the military college we passed on our way into town and a display of military weaponry in a grassy field near our hotel, the city was *tranquilo*.

There were a few licensed casas near the city's pretty central park but we opted for a night in Hotel Guantánamo. The hotel manager offered to take us next day to a place where we could look through a telescope to see the American base. I declined. Just thinking about the greed that leads a nation the size of the US to grab and squat like a mean dog on a chunk of land belonging to a country as small as Cuba was upsetting enough. I didn't need to see it.

Parque El Weird

I wanted to cycle right around Guantánamo Bay and along the coast to Santiago de Cuba, but thanks to all those fierce American dogfaces barricaded at the naval base, that was not possible. We followed an inland route to Santiago, then doubled back to a road through Parque Baconao in order to cycle a portion of the coast we had missed.

Parque Baconao is an 800-square-kilometre UNESCO biosphere reserve. The name derives from indigenous accounts of a magic tree called the *bacona* that, according to legend, once cast a spell on a young Indian, enabling him to play music with the lagoon's shells, a gift that was passed to the trees when the boy died. But that is not what makes Bacanao weird. You can find that kind of weird in California. You can also find the same dry cactus-pricked landscape in California. Maybe you could even find a similar assortment of slightly askew artistic visions scattered across the American West. But Parque Baconao's *atracciónes turisticas* are as weird as anything you will come across in Cuba.

Part of the weirdness comes from the fact that there even *are* "tourist attractions" in a place that feels so isolated and unpopulated. However, Parque Baconao is not as empty or cut off from the outside world as it seems. There are several resorts on the park's thirty-kilometre coastline. Los Corales, El Carisol, Costa Morena, and El Bucanero are pretty typical three-star-all-inclusive resorts. What fills them winter after winter are Canadians who can get a full week at any one of them, air fare, buffet meals, and unlimited rum drinks included, for as little as $500. Each resort has a not-especially-nice beach, swimming pool, mopeds for the adventurous, and taxis waiting to schlep the bored to Santiago to escape a sense of being stuck in the absolute middle of nowhere.

Well off the main road through the park there is also the little-known Villa Colibrí (Hummingbird Villa) with individual cottages for vacationing Cuban families. While following a dirt track through the scrub to Villa Colibrí we discovered one more "holiday spot"—a lodge called Casa del Indio (House of the Indian). We also discovered something you do not want to know when you are travelling through wild countryside on a bike: We learned that this particular part of the park was a hunting reserve. It was our good fortune, I guess, that none of the Cuban military brass that frequent such places were out and about just then.

Not long after we were there, part of the fence around the hunting reserve collapsed under heavy rains. Deer, antelope, and other wildlife with a whit of survival instinct fled to more remote regions of Parque Baconao. For a time it was a rehab center for drug-addicted Venezuelans. Then, in an attempt to attract the eco-tourist crowd, it was renamed Reserva del Indio, which is what it is now.

Not far away is Playa Daiquirí, a resort with a rather different history. This was where Teddy Roosevelt and his

Rough Riders landed in 1898 when they came to "save" Cuba from Spain. It is also where the US Marines landed in 1912, and again 1917, on those occasions to "save" Cuba by putting down a series of strikes. And yes, it is where the rum cocktail that was to become a favourite of Hemingway and JFK was invented. Playa Daiquirí now has a hotel and a fine grey sand beach, but it is not, never has been, your typical all-inclusive.

The Cuban government operates various classes of holiday facilities. There are the basic campismos already described, where foreigners may be allowed to stay but were really built to provide almost free beach accommodations for Cubans.

There are also holiday camps for the employees of particular companies like the Cuban-owned citrus industry or the jointly owned (Canada-Cuba) nickel industry. There are resort hotels which until recently were mostly (but never entirely) for foreigners. And then there are special resorts for the armed forces where no civilians are allowed. Playa Daiquirí has always been such an exclusive resort, except for a few years after certain members of the Cuban military were caught playing naughty.

That was in 1987, when the Cuban military was implicated in the transhipment of drugs. Trials were swift and retribution harsh. A general and two other high-ranking officers, plus a colonel in the Interior Ministry, received the death penalty. Ten lower-level officers got sentences in the thirty-year range. To make sure that both high and low-ranking military personnel got the message, Playa Daiquirí, which was involved in the drug transhipments, lost its status as a military resort. Or so I was told by civilians who claimed to have stayed there around 2002 and drank its daiquirís. However, Playa Daquirí later reverted to the exclusive use of the Cuban military, and civilians are again turned away.

Narco-trafficking is not common in Cuba, but common enough worldwide that it may be unfair to characterize a place as weird just because several drug shipments passed through one of its resorts on the way north, especially since that is now old history. So let me back up a bit, to the point where Larry and I began our ride through Parque Baconao. First we came to El Jardín de la Esculturas, which for a small fee we were able to cycle through, to view sculptures that would surely tickle anyone who is more into the bizarre than beauty.

Next we passed the *granijita* (farmhouse) where Fidel and 120 others prepared their 1953 attack on the Moncada barracks. Half of the participants were soon dead. The rest, including Fidel and Raúl, were captured, tried, and sentenced to fifteen years (but served less than two). The farm is now a museum, its road lined with boulders that bear the names of those who did not survive the assault on Moncada.

Another atracción turistica in the park is the Museo Nacional de Transportes. It displays about fifty classic cars, including the one Raúl Castro drove in that ill-fated Moncada attack. There is also a collection of over 2000 toy cars. An adjacent room holds a smaller collection of dolls to entertain female visitors who are not as thrilled by cars and toy cars as large and small boys are.

You ride on a bit and see, perched on a hilltop among the scrub, metal sculptures—an antlered stag, perhaps, or a rearing horse. Who put them there, and why?

A little farther on, as the road climbs, you look down across a valley that stretches for a kilometre or so. And what do your wondering eyes behold? A stampede of *dinosaurs*. Not real ones, of course, although at a distance they could pass for that. This is the Valle de la Prehistoria, with 242 life-sized (or what we assume was their actual size) prehistoric monsters cast (sculpted?) from concrete. Some of the woolly mammoths are being pursued by spear-wielding savages. A brontosaurus is wallowing in the mud. Two tyrannosauruses are fighting, sending splashes of red paint down their opponents' necks. Grazing placidly amongst this prehistoric drama are some real goats. All of the critters except the goats were created by inmates of a prison across the road. So too were the metal sculptures mentioned earlier.

Sightseers not satisfied with cement animals made by imprisoned men may want to stop further on at an *acuario* where imprisoned dolphins are held for the pleasure of cement-minded tourists. Or one can continue to the far end of the park where boat rides are available on Laguna Baconao. The lagoon also has dolphins but you wouldn't want to swim there on account of the crocodiles. Some of the crocs are prisoners at the nearby breeding farm while some, I suspect, maintain their independence in the lagoon's weedy shallows.

Larry and I biked a kilometre beyond Laguna Baconao, stopping only when we came to a barricade manned by a young soldier. He said we could not ride up into the barren hills beyond. When I persisted, pointing out that my mountain bike could easily handle the road and terrain, he reached across the rifle slung on his belly, laid his hand on mine, and said with sweet concern, "Compañera, you really do not want to go there. There are land mines everywhere."

Land mines to prevent Cubans from getting to that part of their island called Guantánamo Naval Station? Or to prevent US military personnel or US-based terrorists from crossing this no-man's-land to infiltrate the rest of Cuba? I don't know. What I was told was that the mines had been planted by both sides at different times.

What I was not told, what no one was being told at that

time, was that each year the US and Cuban military conducted *joint* manoeuvres in the area. It wasn't until the summer of 2009 that the general public was allowed to know that these joint Cuban-US military manoeuvres had been going on for a decade! Why the secrecy? I contend that what both armies were *really* afraid of was not each other but the reaction of Miami-Cuban hardliners.

In case you are wondering why I have spent so much space describing an area of Cuba that few foreigners will ever visit and even fewer will feel was worth their while, it's because in its weird way Parque Baconao expresses a range of Revolutionary values. It was designated as a biosphere reserve to indicate a dedication to conservation, but it was also intended as a recreational area where Cubans could do day trips or take longer holidays. The small-scale facilities developed there would, like those located around the Bay of Pigs, also provide a few jobs for people living in the area. The entertainment on offer is kind of kitchy, but it was meant to be, and is, a blend of the natural, the historic, and the artistic.

A few months later I returned to Parque Baconao with Derek and visited two places that Larry and I had missed, both more interesting and less bizarre than the stuff described above. One was the tiny community of Los Mamoncillos. Tucked in among the big trees that gave the place its name were small houses built by the government specifically for artists—sort of an art commune but not exactly. Each family has its own home and each home its own studio where the artist works and can, if s/he chooses, invite the public to observe. The only communal aspect is a central gallery where all the artists exhibit their work, with an English-speaking attendant whose salary is paid by the government.

It was once believed that Baconao's resorts and "tourist attractions" would bring a steady stream of potential customers to the gallery, but they didn't. Residents told us that we were the first visitors in a week. The art on display was not great but it wasn't all bad. Some of the more successful painters and sculptors had moved away to flog their work in Santiago or Havana. However, one or two who might have made it in the city had chosen to stay in Los Mamoncillos for the *tranquilidad*. I liked the tranquility, too. It might not be a good place to sell but for an artist or a writer working from an inner vision, the peace of the woods, the beach, and few distractions made it a perfect work environment.

The most beautiful place in Parque Baconao is not down on the beach. It is La Gran Piedra (The Big Rock), up in the mountains at an elevation of more than a thousand metres. The contrast between the hot cactus-dry coast and La Gran Piedra's cool alpine atmosphere could hardly be greater, and it's hard to believe that chaotic Santiago is less than an hour away. Up on La Gran Piedra, one's senses are caressed by soft breezes that whisper through the pines, the quiet whirr of hummingbird wings in the Jardín Ave de Paraíso (Bird of Paradise Garden), and the perfect silence in a little museum at Finca Isabelica, a ruined coffee plantation named after a French planter's slave lover. We did not stay at La Gran Piedra in one of the rental cottages tucked in among the trees, but it remains on my list of things to do in Cuba.

Troubles with Trains

On my first train trip at age five I concluded that trains were the most civilized mode of travel, vastly preferable to my parents' pickup truck, the back seat of our neighbour's Buick, or my tricycle, which were the extent of my experience at that time. This certainty as to the civility of trains was reinforced during an autumn I spent making the most of a

Eurail Pass. Sadly, by the time I started doing cross-continent trips in North America, both Canada and the US had allowed their passenger rail service to deteriorate to the point that almost any alternative was preferable. But what about Cuba's trains?

After finishing our tour of Parque Baconao, Larry and I rode to the Santiago train station, put the bikes into the *bagon* (baggage car) of the overnight train to Havana, and went off to find our assigned seats. It wasn't the nicest train I had ever seen but it was not that bad, except for the windows which were opaque with filth (and later, the toilet).

A bevy of smartly-uniformed attendants boarded with the aplomb of stewardesses preparing to pamper passengers on the Concord. However, they plopped themselves together in the back row and provided zero service for the entire twenty-hour trip. I couldn't even get one to intervene when the only other foreign passenger, an Italian woman, allowed her rambunctious six-year-old to run screaming up and down the aisle, deliberately kicking his soccer ball into people's faces. Other than that, it was an uneventful trip.

Only after we had reached our destination and ridden away did we discover that our panniers, which we had left on our bikes in the bagon, had been riffled. A pair of Larry's cycling shorts had disappeared, and my under-seat tool kit. Since we had been told that only the two guards were allowed in the bagon, and their names would be known to the train's administration, we reported the theft. A female functionary politely took our report but nothing ever came of it. When we complained of this to other Cubans they only shook their heads with grim tolerance and the warning that there were always thefts from the bagon. Over and over we were told, "On a Cuban train, never let your stuff out of your sight."

To catch our homebound flight out of the Varadero airport, we might have taken the Hershey electric train from Havana to Matanzas. But I had already done that trip and didn't care to do it twice. Havana to Matanzas is scarcely two hours by car or bus, but it takes four hours on the Hershey train. The best thing about the Hershey train is that although it could be a Disney-type tourist experience, it isn't. The temperature is conditioned only by a hot breeze that blows in off corn and cane fields when the train is moving—moving, I might add, at a speed that wouldn't have seemed that fast even back in horse-and-buggy days. For one who wants to experience rural Cuba at 19th century speed without being distracted by automobile traffic, the Hershey electric train provides that option. However, we chose to cycle from Havana back to Varadero, even though it meant fighting a headwind.

This is a pleasant ride, much of it right along the waterfront. I was dawdling, admiring the view, when Larry spurted ahead. He had sighted a sexy jinetera flaunting her charms in a red and white Lycra outfit. Behind her was a red, white, and blue billboard that read, *Socialismo o Muerte* (Socialism or Death.) She had her thumb out, hitchhiking. Larry was almost close enough to ask if he could take her picture when a car pulled up and offered her a ride. She got in and was gone.

I found him sitting on the side of the road with his head in his hands. Never had I seen him so distressed. "It was *perfect*," he wailed. "That once-in-a-lifetime image that perfectly captures the character of a country."

"Really?" I was puzzled.

"Don't you get it? Prostitution is the most individualistic kind of free enterprise. There she was, the ultimate free-enterpriser, backed up by a socialist slogan! Total contradictions harmonized in one great image! Just like Cuba!"

I saw his point. We were now familiar with how Cubans grabbed opportunities for free enterprise but were unwilling to give up the safety net provided by their socialist system—a system they so took for granted that it was like a part of the scenery.

For Larry, though, it wasn't about philosophy and politics. It was about *art*. I doubt he ever flips through his many stunning Cuba photos without moaning, "But there was this one image, the perfect image…and I missed it!"

Soon after that trip I returned to Cuba with two other Canadian friends, Brenda and Terri, to cycle the rest of the island's southeastern coast. We flew into Varadero but because we wanted to start our ride in Santiago, we cycled to nearby Matanzas and popped our bikes on the train.

Do I make that sound simple? It was not. Getting *on* the train in Matanzas was a big hassle, partly because the station agent didn't know if a train would run that day, and if so, at what time. And partly because—and here is the single ugliest thing about Cuba—anywhere Cubans are in positions of serving other Cubans, that service is pure crap. This is true in hotels, restaurants, shops, public toilets, and government agencies. In more than a decade of travels through Cuba, the only exceptions I have seen are services provided by doctors and teachers. Otherwise it is so rare to see a Cuban employee providing anything like competent courteous service to a fellow Cuban that you want to cry. The level of service does not go up when a foreigner enters such an establishment either, like, for example, to purchase a ticket in a train station. At the main station in Havana, where there is more of a mix of foreign and Cuban customers, service is marginal but usually adequate. Here it took five hours to get ourselves and our bikes on the damned train to

Santiago. And this time we *did* remove panniers, navigator kits, and tool pouches before entrusting our bikes to the bagon guards.

We soon gave up trying to watch the scenery out the dirty windows, and anyway, it was getting dark. I fell into conversation with a Dutchman named Hans who, with his wife, had recently immigrated to Cuba permanently. I knew of First Worlders on the lam from the FBI who had taken up permanent residence in Cuba, including the CIA whistle-blower Philip Agee and the Black Panther, Assata Shakur who, although never convicted of a crime, was labelled by Hoover's FBI as a "cop killer" and held in prison for six years until she managed to escape and was given asylum in Cuba. (Agee died in Cuba in 2008, but as of 2012 Assata still lived there.)

However, Hans, a civil engineer of about sixty, was a thoughtful, well-educated European who didn't look like someone who would have tangled with law enforcement agents in any country. His wife was Dutch, too. He said they had lived in Cuba for eight years and only recently had been granted permanent residency status. I asked if that had been difficult.

"Very. We each had to undergo five separate psychiatric evaluations." He smiled wryly. "I think they thought anyone who chose Cuba over Europe must be crazy."

Having met First World expats in every country in Latin America and knowing that most opt to live in a Third World country because their pensions allow them to live better there than they could back home, I didn't find his decision so unusual. Cuba, though, was different. It almost never grants permanent residence status to foreigners who are not married to Cubans. And in Cuba a foreigner with a mod-est retirement income cannot buy a big house and live with lots of servants and other comforts the way they can in, say, Mexico. So I had to ask Hans, "Why *did* you choose Cuba?"

He replied, very quietly and with no hesitation, "We like the values of this society. Even though they have not been completely realised, still Cubans are trying. They have not given up. We are more comfortable here than in our native country, where even the most sacred things—nature, religious holidays, family relationships—are contaminated and often destroyed by materialism."

He was silent a moment, then added, "Also, we are not so young, my wife and I. It is everywhere known that Cuba has one of the best health care systems in the world." His blue eyes twinkled with sly humour. 'Perhaps the very best in a country with so much sunshine."

"So those were your reasons?" I asked. "Cuba's values, its medical system, and the climate?"

He smiled. "You put it very succinctly. We are not religious, but coming from a climate with many cold dreary days, we worship the sun. All the time we feel good here."

I fell asleep after that and did not wake when Hans got off the train in Camagüey. I did wake up when, with much shrieking of metal against metal, the train ground to a stop in an unidentified rail yard. An attendant made an announcement I didn't catch; then she and the other attendants disappeared. People began pulling their bags down from the overhead rack and getting out.

"What's going on?" I asked a fellow passenger.

"Broke," he told me. "We must change trains."

So at four a.m. Terri, Brenda, and I schlepped all our stuff out onto a poorly-lighted platform and went looking for the bagon to get our bikes. We found it by following other passengers who were trying to claim their luggage, too, before boarding a not-broke train.

It took nearly three hours to get going again, which meant that instead of arriving at Santiago at a cool six in the morning, we arrived at nine. By then it was sweltering hot. We got ourselves organized as quickly as possible and, dodging cars, trucks, pedestrians, bicycles, bici-taxis, and a variety of horse-drawn conveyances, peddled out of Santiago and along the coast.

Because we had got a late start, and because as soon as we reached the beach at Playa Verde we needed a swim and a nap to make up for the sleep we had lost on the train, we only made it as far as Ensenada Juan González that day. What caught our attention about that spot was an old Spanish warship that had been sunk just offshore in about thirty metres of water, its prow still visible above the waterline.

"Let's camp here," I said, and we did, with the kind attentions of helpful local folks described in an earlier chapter called "Los Militares."

Next morning we continued toward the western end of Cuba's "foot," a ride that would take us two or three days and through the Sierra Maestra range. Long stretches of the coast road are within view, and sometimes within splashing distance, of waves crashing against the rocky shoreline below. Storm-driven surf often bites off great chunks of pavement and a hard rain can send landslides crashing down from above, to make the road passable only on foot, horseback, or a bike. If you ever decide to drive that route you'd want a report on road conditions from someone who has recently (like the day before) traveled that way because sometimes the road is simply not there.

There are places to stay along this section of the coast, all in rural settings. The all-inclusive hotels—Sierra Mar and

Marea del Portillo—are similar to those in Parque Baconao in that they offer packages that are relatively inexpensive and might be a good value if what you're looking for is a beach holiday that includes lots of rum and three big (not gourmet) buffet meals a day.

Also along this route are two motels, a rarity in Cuba. Apparently they were built to house technical staff during the construction of the hotels. Brenda, Terri, and I spent a night in each and found them acceptable—although as you might imagine, anyone who has biked over one or more mountains that day is not going to be too fussy.

Then there were the two campismos, La Mula (The Mule) and Las Coloradas, this last named for big bright-coloured land crabs that meander about this end of the island, too, although never in swarms such as what Derek and I had ridden through on Peninsula Guanahacabibes.

Campismo La Mula was better than basic. The sheets were freshly laundered, the windows were screened, and there was a fan in the room. However, the food was awful. One 10-cent plate of mushy pasta tinted pink with tomato sauce sent me looking for alternatives. Because we had dollars to pay, one of the camp employees was able to find someone in the nearby village to fix us a nice chicken-rice-beans-salad meal that was served behind our hut in the shade of a big tree. We all liked La Mula, so much that we stayed an extra day. (This turned out to be a big mistake, because that took us into the weekend, which was *very* noisy.)

The beach at La Mula is rocky but great fun because it's possible to swim back and forth between the open ocean and a shady fresh-water lagoon. It was on the shore of the lagoon that I met a Rastafarian musician from Santiago who called himself Ónice (Onyx). He was exceptionally dark, and without question the most beautiful man I have ever seen in Cuba. He had arrived the day before with a good-looking German woman, very blonde and like him, very tall. She was in the lagoon swimming with a group of young people, mostly guys, who had arrived that morning by bus.

I took Ónice for a jinetero. (And was I guilty of racial stereotyping? Yes I was.) But in the course of our conversation I discovered that was a wrong impression. He said he had been playing at the Casa de la Trova (folk music centre) in Santiago when the German woman came up to him and asked if he would show her around. She said she didn't want to go to the usual tourist places, but to go where "real Cubans" went. He had borrowed a friend's motorbike and took her up into the mountains to see a waterfall. Then they had come here because it was the only place they could stay together that he could afford and he thought she would like it. She had seemed happy with the place but... At this point he fell silent.

As we watched, she shed her swimsuit top, as well-bodied Europeans are wont to do in warm-water environments. She soaked up the attentions of the shocked but awestruck Cuban guys around her, while the few young women in the water looked away uneasily. Ónice looked away, too, seeming more bewildered than angry. I guess he was trying to adjust to the idea that this *chica*, for whom he had borrowed a friend's motor scooter, acquired (with difficulty) two litres of gasoline, and paid for a night's meals and lodgings, had no concept of the near-universal dating etiquette that says you should "dance with them what brung you."

Ónice soon wandered off. A little while later the German girl came out of the water and struck up a conversation. I asked how she had met her musician boyfriend. She confirmed his story that he had not hustled her but rather, she had gone after him at the Casa de la Trova.

"He's not my boyfriend," she clarified. "But he has shown me a good time and so far hasn't asked me for a cent. Not that I'd give him one. I know all about Cuban guys who link up with foreign women to get them to pay for things. I would *never* pay."

"Not even for good music and good sex?" I teased. "Or is the sex not that good?"

"Oh, it's fine," she said blithely. "But I've had enough. Now he's sulking. I'm ready for a change anyway. It's back to Santiago this afternoon and goodbye Ónice."

"He said you had just arrived in Cuba. Are you leaving already?"

"Oh no, I've got another week." She wrung the water out of her long blonde hair and tied it in a twist on top of her head. "But I certainly don't plan to spend my whole vacation with one guy."

She went back into the water and I went back to our cabin. I heard Ónice in the cabin next to ours playing his guitar. He was exceptionally good—not surprising, as most of the musicians who play at Santiago's Casa de la Trova are. However, most of the traditional Cuban music one hears at the Casa de la Trova is not sad, as his most surely was.

I thought about how anyone reading the posts on a website like cuba-love-and-lust could easily get the impression that in Cuban-foreign relationships the foreigner always ends up being used. Maybe that's true. Or maybe it's just that there isn't a website where Cubans can post their side of the story.

Brenda, Terri, and I rolled out before sunrise and pushed on over several more mountains, for along this stretch the Sierra Maestra comes right down to the sea. They, the real athletes in our trio, had to wait for me at each summit. Then we would go whooping together down a long glide into the next valley. At last we crossed through the mountains and came back down to the coast at Niquero. We followed a mango-tree-lined highway until we reached Campismo Las Coloradas, where we took another beach break.

Next day Terri, who was suffering from a cold, recuperated on the beach while Brenda and I rode the twelve kilometres to Cabo Cruz. Along the way we passed the mangrove swamp where Fidel and his compañeros had landed (actually run aground) in the yacht *Granma* when they came from Mexico to start the revolution. Further along we passed a lagoon filled with flamingos. And then we were at land's end in Cabo Cruz.

From the lighthouse we gazed out over white fishing boats bobbing in water of such blue intensity that it seemed like one of those clichéd paintings where the artist has gone a little overboard with the colour. But when you turned around and looked at the town, the feeling was altogether different. Mud-and-stone cottages perched on land that was more jagged rock than soil. The whole place had the same end-of-the-world air of isolation as Punto Maisí. No one came out to greet us—the only place in Cuba I have ever been where that happened. I don't think that was because they were unfriendly. It didn't feel unfriendly. It just felt as if everyone was watching. Perhaps they were waiting for us to indicate why we had come and what we wanted. But we didn't want anything. We left without having spoken to a soul.

We regretted leaving Playa Las Coloradas with its pretty tree-shaded beach and friendly fishermen whose wives prepared us really *good* lobster dinners. But we had another sixty kilometres of cycling to reach Manzanillo. That was the end of the road along the southeast coast of Cuba, so our plan was to take a train from there back to Havana.

The ride to Manzanillo was blazing hot, made longer and hotter by my insistence that we take a "short cut," which resulted in our getting lost in a sugar cane field. We might be there yet had a cane cutter not left off swinging his machete to guide us through a bewildering maze of wagon tracks back to the main road. When we finally reached Manzanillo we were told that the train did not have a bagon and therefore would not take our bikes. The ticket agent said we would have to go another sixty kilometres to Bayamo to find a train with a bagon. That train, he said, left for Havana at four in the afternoon.

It was then around one p.m. We could probably cover sixty kilometres in three hours, providing the terrain was not as rugged as what we had come through on the coast where slowpoke Rosa only averaged ten kilometres an hour. We decided to give it a try, and found the gently rolling hills no great challenge. Had it been a cool morning we might have made it, but it was mid-afternoon and the heat was blistering. We kept stopping to rest in the shade of mango trees until there was no hope of getting to the station in time to catch the train.

That was when, by common accord, we decided to hitch a ride in a truck. It was quite a long time before one stopped. The driver and his companion cheerfully hoisted our bikes into the back. We climbed in after them and quickly secured our bikes with bungee cords to keep them from being thrown from side to side or against the long boxes stacked toward the front.

We had been bumping along for a while when Terri pointed out that the long boxes were coffins. Each had a little window in the top. We considered looking into one, but decided that if the coffins contained bodies, we did *not* want to know.

Just as we reached Bayamo the sky opened and we were deluged by a massive tropical downpour. The truck driver kindly went out of his way to drop us right at the train station. I left Brenda and Terri standing out front in the pouring rain and ran to the ticket window at the back side of the building next to the tracks.

"So glad we made it!" I huffed. "We planned to catch the train in Manzanillo but it didn't have a bagon for our bikes."

"Neither does this one," yawned the ticket seller.

"But—it's raining!" I exclaimed, as if having to yell to be heard over the din of rain on the station's metal roof had not alerted her to that. "Please! We need to get to Havana!"

"No bagon, no bikes," she said, and called a supervisor who repeated the rule.

I considered crying but what good would that do? With so much rain streaming down my face, who would have noticed tears? Then I had a better idea. "We can take our bikes apart," I said. "The pieces will fit up in the overhead rack."

This required consultation with various railway employees, which took half an hour. But finally I was able to race back to where Brenda and Terri were waiting with the bikes and give them the good news. The waiting room through which we had to pass to reach the tracks was so crowded that we had to lift the bikes over our heads to squeeze through.

Once we reached the train, we hunkered down in the rain and began to remove panniers, handlebars, wheels, and such—a process watched with great interest by five or six railway employees. When the bikes were disassembled, one of the men stowed the pieces into the overhead racks. We collapsed into our seats with sighs of relief.

Terri looked around. "Why are we the only ones on this train?" she asked.

Brenda looked at her watch. "I thought it left at four. It's already after five."

"There are mechanical problems," explained one of the men who had helped us. "The train will not leave till eight. But it's okay for you to wait here."

The train didn't leave until nine-thirty, and broke down twice on the way. But at least we didn't have to change to a different one in the middle of the night. We had nothing with us to eat, and did not arrive until two in the afternoon of the following day. By then we were all so whacked that it took two days on a Varadero beach to recover.

That was my last train trip. I was not even tempted when the Tren Frances started running between Havana and Santiago. The Tren Frances, so named because in a former life it made the run between Paris and Brussels, was old but reliable. For a time it was so reliable that passengers got their fare refunded if it was more than an hour late.

But not even a reliable train can travel well on unreliable tracks. By 2010, passengers were reporting that the Tren Frances had become a Tren Cubano, with posted departure and arrival times more hopeful than actual.

Americans in Wonderland

In 2003 I got a call from Earthways Foundation, the Malibu-based non-profit that supports many social justice and environmental projects, including some I was working on in Central and South America. The Earthways office manager said Pond Foundation would send two Earthways project facilitators to Cuba for an international conference on sustainable agriculture. Earthways wanted to send me because I had initiated an organic agriculture project in a Mayan village in Guatemala.

I said I would love to go, and asked her to ask Pond Foundation for enough money to bring along the Guatemalan woman who was the hands-on manager of the organic agriculture program, and the project's nurse. Pond generously agreed and the trip was on.

It was to be different from other trips I had made to Cuba in that it would be a "delegation" sponsored by the San Francisco-based Food First Foundation. The eighty participants would come from all over the US. We were to meet in Cancun and fly from there to Havana. Food First would do the necessary paperwork to get State Department permission for the US citizens so they could make the trip legally.

This was not necessary for me, of course. Being a Canadian citizen, I and my Guatemala co-workers did not need such permission from our respective governments to go to Cuba. I was glad of that, because the US government travel permits required the Americans to leave Cuba within twenty-four hours after the end of the conference. I can think of no reason for this condition other than to prevent the Americans from straying far enough from the conference site to get a sense of what Cuba was really like.

Showing the Americans some of Cuba beyond the conference room was precisely what our group leader, Peter Rosset, had in mind. He managed to do that by including in the licensing application a four-day tour of farms, research stations, bio-pest labs, plant nurseries, agro-markets, and urban gardens *before* the conference, as if it were part of the event.

The group rendezvoused on the designated date in Cancun. There we met Peter Rosset, author of *The Greening of the Revolution*, and extremely knowledgeable about sustainable agriculture in Cuba. Most of the delegates were connected to US universities and land grant colleges, working in the field of sustainable or organic agriculture. I was surprised by how apolitical most of them were. Americans who visit Cuba typically have some interest in politics, but few in that group knew or cared anything about Cuba other than what it was doing in the field of organic agriculture.

When I remarked on this to a woman from Idaho, she said, "You have no idea what it's like to teach a bunch of high-energy college-aged kids. I come home at night exhausted. I can barely stay awake long enough to do the reading I have to do in my field to keep ahead of them. I don't even follow US politics, let alone Cuba's."

Despite being uninformed, she, like most others in the group, believed that Cuba was a police state and we would not be able to go anywhere or talk to anybody without a minder keeping close watch on us and monitoring every exchange.

"And I suppose they'll only show us their best," said another woman. "We've got some nice *models*, too. But what's getting out to the people?"

Apart from Peter Rosset and me, the only person in the group who seemed to have Cuba-sympathetic politics, or any politics at all for that matter, was Goldie Caughlan, a Seattle activist and veteran of leftist causes from way back. I felt blessed that she and I had been assigned as roommates.

One other couple caught my attention. I'll call them Edward and Mary. Edward ran a mail-order organic seed company in Vermont. He was a big guy, over six feet tall. He said little and coloured everything he did say with gruff scepticism. When I asked him what he knew about Cuban agriculture that had convinced him to come on the trip, he said that he *knew* nothing and although he had tried to read up on it, in his view it was all BS because no way could Cuba have accomplished what was being claimed, not in a society where entrepreneurship was practically non-existent.

Mary said she was not interested in organic agriculture at all and had come along only to be with her husband. She was a dancer, and circled the get-acquainted meeting in a long gown that caused the rest of us women in our jeans, tank tops, and sandals to roll our eyes behind her back. I figured that once we reached Cuba and headed into the countryside she would switch to practical clothes but I was wrong. When we boarded the bus for our first farm visit, she floated down the aisle in a white dress, smiling with sweet vagueness, oblivious to the activated eyeballs of other females silently reflecting incredulity to each other.

Peter divided the eighty of us into four groups, twenty on each of the chartered air-conditioned buses. These would take us to places that could be reached from our Havana hotel in an hour or two. For me, being on a tour was more novel than being in Cuba. By now I knew the lay of the land so well that when our bus driver got lost in a rural area, I was able, without a map, to direct him to where he was trying to go. But I was not used to travelling with a bunch of strangers or depending on people I didn't know to handle all the arrangements and set our agenda. I had made my share of dismissive remarks about tourists "seeing" Cuba through the windows of air-conditioned buses, but as we cruised around Havana Province in sweat-free comfort, I had to admit this was *nice*.

Even nicer was having an agenda set by Peter Rosset, whose work in organic agriculture and experience in organizing conferences such as this was legendary, and so appreciated in Cuba that the government bent over backwards to make sure his groups got to see anything and everything Peter thought they should see.

I changed seats often in order to chat with the Americans in the group. They seemed enthusiastic and knowledgeable about organic agriculture, but many complained about how little funding their institution provided for organic agriculture research. This was especially true, they said, in comparison to the amounts being spent by the agro-industry on aspects of agriculture that benefited multinational companies such as those that produced chemical fertilizers or were involved in genetic engineering. All the Americans I spoke to seemed dedicated to their work, but the lack of funding and institutional support seemed to have left many of them feeling hopeless about the future of organic agriculture in the US. Some spoke of their discouragement and a sense that the work they were doing was not very important, or at any rate, would never be seen as such.

Our first excursion was to a small, eight-room laboratory in a rural area about an hour south of Havana. We were greeted by the facility's director, Alberto Fuentes, an Afro-Cuban so big he dwarfed even Edward, and was as upbeat as Edward was dour. Alberto welcomed us enthusiastically and introduced the facility's co-director Margarita Vidal, a grey-haired woman of about forty. Margarita would take half of the group through the lab, explaining the research underway in each room. The other half would follow Alberto to see what was going on in the field. Then we would switch places, giving everyone a chance to see everything, in groups small enough that we could ask questions of the people working there.

After roaming around the fields, Alberto took us into the barn. When we entered its cool dim space his seemingly boundless enthusiasm doubled.

"Here is where I keep my darlings, my little worms," he cooed. He knelt to scoop a handful of fine black soil. "Look at this! Isn't it the most beautiful stuff you ever saw? Vermiculture is our future! Cuban agriculture is now using over half a million tons of worm castings every year!"

His explanations of the work they were doing, and how they were "rolling out" soil-enrichment and bio-pest-control techniques to farmers, were impressively scientific, yet comprehensible even to a lay person like myself. Later, when we toured the lab, we found that the women working there were equally capable of answering technical questions about the nature of their work.

Back on the bus, a man from North Carolina asked if I knew anything about the Cuban education system. I said kids who did well in the lower grades normally spent what we call high school in a university prep program, while the less academic were tracked into a technical school that taught what might be anything from computers to cooking, depending on their interests and what training was available.

He said, "That Fuentes guy seemed pretty well-informed for a tech school graduate."

I laughed. "What makes you think he went to a tech school?"

"Not because he's black," the North Carolina man said quickly. "Just because, well, that's not a very big facility, is it? And out here in the middle of nowhere."

"*Dr.* Fuentes has a PhD in bio-engineering from the University of Moscow," I said. "That's the same university where Alberto Granado, Che Guevara's motorcycle pal, got his PhD in genetic engineering, and Fidel Castro's son got his in nuclear physics."

The North Carolina man stared at me. "How do you know that?"

"I asked him," I said. "He was so knowledgeable it made me wonder if they are teaching all that stuff in Cuban universities now. He said that when he went to grad school in the late 1980s they weren't, but now they are. Incidentally," I added, "Margarita also has a PhD but didn't say where she

earned it. She runs the lab and he handles the field teams—
that is, the teams who get the vermiculture and bio-pest
methods and such that they have developed at their facility
out to the farmers."

The man was silent a minute, then asked, "How much
do you think they earn?"

"Probably the same as other professionals in Cuba—
$20 or $30 a month."

"My god!" gasped the Carolinian. "How can they get
anything done in this country paying wages like that?"

"I think that's a question you'll have to ask a Cuban,"
I said.

The next day's trip was to a 500-acre co-op that grew
vegetables for the domestic market and tobacco for export.
There we were told, most apologetically, that the bilingual
person designated to show us around was sick, but we were
free to wander where we pleased and ask questions of
anyone we found working in the field.

"You mean we can go anywhere? Talk to anybody?"
asked a woman from Iowa.

"That's what they said."

She seemed doubtful that I had understood correctly.
"If we go off by ourselves, who will be monitoring us?"

"What do you mean, monitoring?" I asked.

"Isn't that what they do in Cuba? They don't just let
people wander around willy-nilly, do they?"

I shrugged. "I always have. But I guess there's not much
point in wandering willy-nilly if you don't speak Spanish
and can't ask questions. Why don't half of you go with the
translator from the bus and the rest with me? My Spanish is
not as good as his English, but I'll do the best I can."

By the time we'd roamed the fields and talked to workers

as long as we could without dropping dead from sunstroke, I knew two things about the group with me: that they were unimpressed with the level of "organicness" of the crops, and that they could scarcely believe how knowledgeable the farmers were. It seemed that the roughest farm hand could lecture for ten or fifteen minutes on some aspect of what they were doing, and why doing it that way was better than how it used to be done.

Back at the main building, the kitchen staff had spread a midmorning fruit buffet for us, and the farm manager asked if we had any criticisms of their work, or could offer any advice. This seemed to stump the Americans. One finally said she had seen some bugs. The manager said yes, there were bugs. They didn't aim for total eradication, only at keeping them down to "an acceptable level." Asked what they did if the level grew too high, he said they started with bio-pest control methods and if that didn't work, switched to pesticides.

"So you're not *really* organic?" someone asked.

"Cuba only produces five crops that meet EU standards for organic," explained the spokesperson. "We don't raise any of those crops on this farm."

I wandered into the kitchen to talk to the staff. When I came out, the North Carolina man sidled up to me. "These people," he motioned to the farmers in their work clothes, "must make even less than those we saw at the lab, right?"

"No," I said. "They actually make more. This is a co-op farm, and since 1994 cooperatives have been allowed to sell on the open market. They do have to sell their tobacco to the government because it's an export crop and the government is the only exporter. But at least they are paid for it partly in dollars. Whatever profit the farm makes is divvied up. For the field workers the share is decided by how much they grow on the particular plot they're responsible for. The kitchen staff, bookkeeper and other support people get a percentage of the gross."

"Which adds up to?"

"I guess it varies from year to year. The cook told me that last year she earned less than $40 a month because of hurricane losses, but it could be twice as much this year."

"The *cook* on this farm in a *bad* year earned more than that Dr. What's-his-name we met yesterday?"

"That seems to be the case," I said. "Of course, Dr. Fuentes told me he travels abroad quite a bit, which means the government has to give him a per diem allowance in foreign currency. He probably stays with friends in the countries he travels to, and is able to pocket his per diem."

"That's crazy!" he sputtered, heading for the bus. "Absolutely crazy."

"Yeah," I agreed. "But have you noticed how much people seem to be enjoying their work?"

"Because they're crazy!" he called back over his shoulder.

The next day we visited a huge urban garden, one of the organiponicos which we were told provides over ninety percent of Havana's fresh vegetables. Again we found workers well-informed about what they were doing to reduce pesticide use, conserve water, and enrich the soil. It was a big garden and the project director expressed his concern that the land they were on belonged to the medical school. It was rumoured that the school was going to expand, in which case, "We may have to pack up all this beautiful soil we have created and take it with us to a new location."

A woman employee chuckled to me that her son had recently graduated from medical school and she earned more as a member of this co-op than he did as a doctor. I did not tell the Carolina man that. No reason to provide him with more evidence that Cuba had got everything upside down.

Of all the farms we visited, the most delightful one belonged to a man named Franci. It was a little one-hectare place (slightly over two acres), farmed in the "permaculture" style pioneered in Australia and which I had promoted in my food self-sufficiency project in Guatemala. Permaculture looks messy but is very good for the soil. You might have potatoes growing underground, squash on top of the ground, and corn above that with bean vines climbing the corn; in essence, utilizing different levels of the same space to grow compatible plants—ideal where land is scarce or clearing it is difficult.

Dr. Fuentes' enthusiasm about his worms was downright low-key compared to chubby little Franci's enthusiasm about his "invention." He was famous in Cuban agricultural circles for developing a device that could be stuck in the ground and would automatically turn on a watering system when the soil got too dry for the crop growing there.

A man in our group sniffed that Franci had not invented it; that such devices had been available in the States for at least a decade. I did not mention that due to the embargo, it probably had not reached Cuba; thus might have been necessary for someone like Franci to invent it here.

I noticed that Franci had four big greenhouses. Although he told me he earned the astonishing sum of $90 per month, I felt sure that he wouldn't have been able to afford them. I asked if the greenhouses belonged to him or to the government.

"They are *mine*," he said, bowing out his chest with pride. "They are what the government gave me in exchange for the patent on my moisture-sensing device."

Just then a young man bounded out of the house. He was dressed in tennis whites and had a racquet stuck under his arm. "I'm off, Papí," he said, giving his foot-shorter father a peck on his bald spot.

"Be careful!" Franci called after the boy as he hopped on a moped in the yard and roared away.

"This is a family farm, right?" I asked Franci.

"Yes," he said. "My wife and I and, well, my son, not him so much anymore, we own the land and do all the work ourselves."

"Doesn't your son want to follow in your footsteps?"

Franci's chin drooped sadly. "He wants to be a tennis instructor at one of the resorts."

A few minutes later an American teacher from a Kansas university sidled up to me and said, "You know, sometimes I think all these Cubans are just putting on a show for us."

"What makes you think so?"

"Didn't you see how Franci was hopping around here, running up and down the rows, showing us his 'invention,' and so enthusiastic about the support he got from the government to get this farm up and running?"

"Yeah, so?"

"So look at him now, when everybody has gone around to the patio for a snack and he thinks nobody's watching."

I turned and saw Franci still staring down the street. True, he looked like a terribly sad old man.

"Oh that," I said. "It's because of his son."

"What about his son?

"He's their only kid. He doesn't want to have anything to do with farming. He wants to be a tennis instructor at a resort."

The Kansas man's mouth opened and closed. Finally he said, "Oh my god. Just like kids back home."

He walked over to where Franci stood and with awkward tenderness, dropped an arm around the old man's shoulders. Franci gave him a wan smile, and together, wordlessly, they headed for the patio where juice was being served.

Whenever we stopped at a farm or lab or some other facility for show-and-tell, Edward had a tendency to wander off from the group. He was very observant but he had told me he did not speak Spanish. When I said that we were lucky to have Peter Rosset to interpret for us, he had snapped, "I don't *need* somebody to interpret farming for me." As if any explanation might be propaganda, and he wasn't having any of *that*. So when I saw him off on his own watching workers, I supposed he was trying to figure out what was going on without benefit of language. When the worker he was watching smiled at him, sometimes, tentatively, he smiled back. More than once I saw a farmer use sign language to explain something. Given the language barrier, I couldn't help but wonder what cynical Edward was getting out of it.

Mary, too, wandered about alone, but not out into the fields because her slipper-type shoes weren't suited to that. While the rest of the group trailed around after the translator, and Edward was doing his independent people-watching thing, I often saw Mary observing a bee collecting pollen, or staring out at the bent backs of farmers in the field, or simply standing in the pose of an arrested dancer, letting the breeze ruffle her hair and dress.

I saw very little of those in our delegation who were not assigned to the bus I was on, not even much of my friends from Guatemala because our buses went to different places each day. I saw a bit more of my roommate Goldie, enough to learn that she was a nutrition educator and all-around mover-shaker for one of the largest food co-ops in the US, and that her (now deceased) husband had in his day been a leftist lawyer famous for defending Americans blacklisted during the McCarthy era.

We were busy in the evenings as well. Delegates headed off to events of their choice in the city and came back with different stories; how jineteras in the Copacabana disco had tried to pick them up, or how the Tropicana cabaret was overpriced at $75, but astonishingly, front-row tickets to the National Ballet had cost only $10.

"Ten dollars for us, but for Cubans ten *pesos*," Goldie exclaimed. "Can you imagine? Just forty cents for a performance of the best ballet troupe in Latin America!"

When the conference started we were moved from the Copacabana Hotel over to Hotel Palco, adjacent to the Palacio de los Convenciones, so we would have easy access to whatever seminars we chose to attend. Midway through the conference Peter told us that there would be some members of Witnesses for Peace out in the lobby at lunchtime, if any of us wanted to meet with them. About a dozen of us showed up at the designated spot, including Edward. Two earnest young women talked about the negative impact the US embargo was having on Cuba, and what we could/should be doing to get it repealed. After they had finished their presentation, they asked each of us for our thoughts.

One or two of the organic agriculture instructors said they did not feel they knew enough about it to comment. Another said that since the US traded with China, she didn't see why it couldn't trade with Cuba. Another said Cuba needed American know-how, and the US government could *certainly* learn from Cuba how to roll out organic techniques to small farmers.

Then it was Edward's turn. He said, in his abrupt way, "I don't belong here."

"Why is that?" asked the Witness for Peace girl.

"I think ending the embargo would be the worst thing that could happen to Cuba."

You could practically hear the rest of us sucking wind, then letting our breaths out as we concluded that he couldn't possibly have meant what he said.

"You mean...?" the other young Witnesses for Peace began uncertainly.

"I mean," Ed said grimly, rising and looming over us with his six-foot-plus height, "the people I have seen here are taking more pleasure in their work than people back home who are earning a hundred times more. They are more open. More sharing. More caring. Or—damn it, I don't know what. Just that there is something we've lost and they haven't. You think it's a *good* thing to end the embargo and let our money-obsessed culture flood theirs and wash all that away?"

He turned and lumbered away. The rest of us sat silent for a minute. Then the Witnesses for Peace asked if any of us wanted to sign their petition, or maybe start one back home, to end the embargo.

The seminars were interesting. The Minister of Agriculture told us that to make the progress it has in organic agriculture, Cuba had to overcome *three* blockades: one by the US, one by bureaucrats who stood to lose power when the big state-run farms were broken up for redistribution to individual farmers, and one by the Cuban people who "just don't care that much for vegetables."

I thought that was pretty funny, and later, when I caught up to the minister in another meeting, asked what they were doing about that third "blockade."

The minister sighed and said, "Oh, we've given up on the adults. We're just trying to educate the next generation to eat vegetables."

I told her I had already seen that happening in a kindergarten class across the street from a casa where I stayed on a previous trip. Children sat down to a hot lunch that had an array of vegetables on the plate. Before eating they sang a little song with lyrics about which vitamins were in each vegetable and what it was good for, like Vitamin A for eyes and so on. Those who ate all the veggies on their plate got a gold star pasted on their forehead.

She laughed. "That's good to hear. Come back in ten years and maybe we will have weakened our own people's blockade against vegetables."

At a workshop with the Deputy Minister of Agriculture, one of the Americans asked if he thought Cuba had made a mistake to follow the Soviet model.

"Yes, that was a mistake," the official admitted. "Most of us were young urban professionals with no knowledge of farm life. We believed it would be more efficient to have teams that moved across the country doing the ploughing, planting, harvesting, and so on. We did not understand about a farmer's attachment to the land. Our reliance on big farms worked by transient labour caused that connection to be lost. Production fell like a stone."

He paused, and added wryly, "One thing we do well, and I mean *really* well, is gather statistics. So when a policy fails, we have the stats to prove it."

Everyone laughed. Then someone asked, "Are you moving away from big state farms because they proved inefficient, or because the Soviets cut off aid and you had no choice?"

"We already had plenty of data showing that except for a couple of areas like sugar and citrus, the big farms were steadily declining in efficiency," explained the Deputy Minister. "But so much had been invested in them that we couldn't get anybody to consider a different system."

"Just like with agro-business in the US," murmured someone from California.

The Deputy Minister continued. "It was the loss of Soviet aid that forced even those most resistant to change to re-examine the premise that bigger was better. Once we had no fuel or spare parts for farm equipment, and no money for commercial fertilizers and pesticides, it made sense to go back to animal traction, and that required a return to small-scale farming. This began a decade ago. All our data since show higher yields from small farms." He smiled innocently. "Would that be entirely due to our new market policies, where farmers are allowed to sell what they raise on the open market? Or is it that a man's love of the land and personal pride in what he produces has something to do with it?"

A small chuckle of appreciation went around the table, followed by sympathetic laughter when the Deputy Minister added, "We have yet to figure out how to measure intangibles like personal pride and love of the land, to say how much they contribute to productivity. Cuban statistics do have limitations."

On the last evening of the conference, Peter had all eighty members of our delegation sit in a big circle and each tell the group what we had got out of the conference. Veronica Girón, the facilitator of my organic ag project in Guatemala, said, "The support farmers get from their government, both material and non-material, this is our dream in Guatemala. I don't believe it will happen there in my lifetime, but the fact that it has happened here gives me hope. Sometimes you doubt things will ever get better until you see a place like this where it has actually been achieved."

"I can't believe how self-critical they were," said a woman from Tennessee. "They kept asking us if we had any criticisms or could offer advice on how they're doing thing. Like *we've* got the answers!"

"The weird thing," another said, "is that we *do* have the answers. But *they've* got the method, plus the political will to switch to organic. What good are answers going to do if we're not willing to apply them nationwide, like they claim to be doing here?"

"Like they *are* doing here," Peter corrected him.

Others expressed similarly positive views but with less certainty. Some said they hoped to return because there was still lots they didn't understand. (Most would not make it back because as soon as Bush II took office, Americans could no longer get licenses to attend international conferences in Cuba, regardless of whether the subject was sustainable agriculture, solar energy, medicine, or what.)

When it was Edward's turn, he sat for a moment saying nothing. Then he picked up a small black box next to his chair, cleared his throat, and said, "I'm not very good with words. But I have written some music I would like to play that expresses my feelings about what I've seen."

With that he lifted a silver flute to his lips and began to play, notes that came slow and tentative at first, gradually growing more definite and livelier.

Mary, sitting next to him in one of her floating, veil-like dresses, rose and began to dance. She unfurled herself, welcomed the sun, wilted with heat, was revived by rain, grew and blossomed and danced for the joy of being alive. She was the earth, a plant, a farmer, or perhaps all three.

I can't think of anything harder to put into words than a free-form dance unless it is an unnamed piece of music. But in discussing it later, everyone I spoke to agreed that the emotions expressed in the music and dance of those two Americans captured something of what we all had felt out in the hopeful, heat-drenched fields of Cuba.

Brown Rainbows

After Derek and I were done pedalling around Cuba, and our cycling guide to the island was published in 2002, I resumed writing fiction and did my cycling closer to home. I expected that future travel would be to places I hadn't already visited. But somehow Cuba's complexity wouldn't let me go. The challenge of understanding how and why Cuba is the way it is kept drawing me back.

In 2006 I found myself waking to yet another Cuban sunrise. Foregoing coffee, I stepped out into one of Trinidad's cobblestone streets for a stroll during the sweetest time of day—those first hours just after sunup when the air is cool, the light is soft, and only local people are about. I didn't want to miss my favourite sight, one I had seen countless times in all parts of Cuba, from tiny mountain hamlets to Havana's historic Prado. It was that of primary school children in red-and-white uniforms, themselves ranging in colour from golden tan to darkest brown, skipping, hopping, holding hands, and hanging on each other as they made their way to school. I wished I had brought my camera so like millions of tourists, I could take photos of this little brown rainbow, more representative of Cuba than its red, white and blue flag.

One does not see a lot of older children—gold-and-white uniforms for middle school, tan-and-white for vocational school, navy-and-white for pre-university, and so on—because many of them attend boarding schools located in rural areas. But when I visited such schools I had noticed the same rainbow of skin tones in easy proximity to one another. I never saw Cuban children of any age, including university students, self-segregate into groups according to colour, as is so common in North America. I found myself reflecting on the difference and what its implications are for race relations. (My assumption is that racism exists to some degree in all cultures; it's just a question of how much of it there is and how it reveals itself.)

It is hard to say exactly how many Cubans are black, white, or *mulatto* (mulatto being a mixture of Spanish-African blood). That depends on whether the statistics-taker wants to call people black because they are dark-skinned (how dark?) or because they have some percentage of African blood (what percentage?) The Cuban government doesn't play this game of judging who is or is not "black." It does have race-related statistics, but they are based on how its citizens define themselves. By that criterion, Cuba lists 65% of its 11 million people as white, 24% as mulatto, 10% as black, and 1% as who-knows-what. That of course is not good enough for foreign sociologists and other scholars. Using god-knows-what criteria, or maybe simply by eye-balling the population, they guestimate that over half of Cuba's population is mulatto, with dashes of French, Chinese, Japanese, indigenous Taíno, and European-North American heritage tossed into the mix. If you want a racial description of Cubans less complicated and more reliable than that, you should probably accept Fidel Castro's, which is simply: "We are a Latin-African people."

It is an undeniable fact that Latin and African cultural elements are integrated in Cuban music, dance, painting, sculpture, literature, language, folklore, and fashion. And about a third of all marriages in Cuba are interracial. As I wandered across Trinidad's Plaza Mayor that morning, two interracial couples strolled by, encircled by five pre-schoolers whose skin tones created a rainbow of browns from golden to chocolate—a commonplace sight in Cuba.

According to a 1993 doctoral dissertation on Cuba's interracial marriages by Nadine Fernandez at the University of California, *The Colour of Love: Young Interracial Couples in Cuba*, there has been a steady increase of such marriages since 1959. This naturally has led to a growing number of *mulattos* (mixed-race browns with more African features) and *morenos* (mixed-race browns with more Spanish features), and is further support for Castro's definition of Cubans as "a Latin-African people."

Nobody actually knows how many Cubans are of mixed blood, and what's more, few Cubans care. The national ID card includes skin colour, but only as part of the person's physical description like eye colour. Officially race is considered both irrelevant and indefinable. To quote Fidel again, "Nobody can consider themselves to be of pure race, much less a superior race."

When Fidel made that statement, soon after taking power, there were plenty of light-skinned Cubans who considered themselves superior. The victorious rebels had barely reached Havana when Che Guevara's black body-guard was kicked out of a "whites only" beach club. Che threw a fit and Fidel immediately gave one of his hours-long speeches in which he pleaded for an end to racism.

"Why do we not tackle this problem radically and with love, not in a spirit of division and hate?" he asked in a speech in March 1959. "Why not educate and destroy the prejudice of centuries, the prejudice handed down to us from such an odious institution as slavery?"

The Revolutionary government's efforts to eradicate

racism were facilitated by the fact that so many of Cuba's white elite promptly fled to Florida, where their belief in white superiority fit right in with the hard-core racist attitudes prevalent there at that time. Back in my days as a waitress in South Florida of the 1960s, I recall a Cuban immigrant eliciting jocularity from locals when he said he left the island because, "Castro brought the monkeys down from the trees, cut off their tails, and put them in charge."

Castro and those with whom he shared power blamed race prejudice on colonialism and materialism. They naively thought that to eradicate it all they had to do was make it illegal, and re-educate the population. To this end, all race-based institutions and organizations were banned. Universal free education was instituted, including free university and postgraduate work for those who could handle it academically. Immediately more Afro-Cubans (and women and poor people in general) started preparing for professions to which they could not have aspired before.

Article 41 of Cuba's Socialist Constitution, adopted by the national referendum in February 1976, requires that "the institutions of state educate everyone, from the earliest years, in the principle of equality." And Article 42 states: *"Discrimination because of race, skin colour, sex, national origin, religious beliefs and any other form of discrimination harmful to human dignity is forbidden and punishable by law."*

Despite those anti-racist laws and sentiments, Afro-Cubans were *not* immediately integrated into the government in numbers proportionate to the population. The reason for their exclusion was not colour; it was religion. The Communist party (Cuba's only political party) and the National Assembly (Cuba's law-making body) excluded religious people. This fell disproportionately on Afro-Cubans, some of whom were Christian, some practioners of Santería, and a good many who practiced both religions. This law was abolished in 1991, and in the two decades since, the National Assembly has achieved a racial balance that is approximately the same as in the nation as a whole.

Meanwhile, the flight of doctors, engineers, the managerial class, Catholics, and officers from Batista's army not only removed from Cuba a lot of opposition to the Revolution's new colour-blind policies, but left many more professional positions open for all young people on the island, including Afro-Cubans. Within a few years, a great many blacks (and women) were in university and moved from there into all the professional fields.

An often-cited example of the progress people of colour have made in Cuba in the past five decades is its number of black doctors: 13,500 as of 2006. A Cuban black today is four times more likely to be a physician than an American black. In Cuba, white doctors outnumber black ones six to one. In the US, white doctors outnumber black ones by fifty to one.

In 2006, bussing from Trinidad to Havana, I was seated next to a well-dressed young woman from Paris. She asked a question I did not understand because she spoke neither English nor Spanish and my French is practically non-existent. An Afro-Cuban youth across the aisle answered her question in French. I asked where he had learned his French, which sounded pretty good to me. He replied (in English to me and then in French to her), that he had studied it in university; that it was necessary for his major, which was French literature. In fact, he said, pulling out an airline ticket to show us, he was on his way to Havana to catch a flight to Paris, where he would be working on a PhD in that field. The young woman asked if he was on scholarship and he said yes, again repeating his remarks in French for her and English for me.

"And will you have to work?" she asked.

He looked at her blankly. "To work? No, I am going there to study."

"What will you do for money?" she persisted.

"The government is paying: my tuition, school supplies, food, lodging, all of that."

"But you'll need spending money," she insisted. "You know, to buy things."

"What things? How many 'things' does one need to study?" he shot back, sounding a trifle impatient.

She gave an elaborate shrug, one of those where the shoulder comes up to almost touch the ear, and said, "You'll see when you get there. In France even students have things. Clothes, for example. Otherwise you will not fit in."

He gave a similar shrug, which I took to be a parody of hers, and said, "It seems to me that the study of ideas doesn't require 'fitting in.' Especially since I plan to bring what I learn back to Cuba and put it to use here."

With that he closed his eyes and either fell asleep or pretended to, as elaborate a gesture of dismissal as I have ever seen.

I don't know what the French girl took from the conversation, but what I saw was a young Afro-Cuban who had not only the academic ability but the political savvy to earn one of the most difficult of all scholarships to get in Cuba: one that covers the cost of studying abroad.

His attitude and responses did reveal a type of—well, let's not call it prejudice, call it "selectivity"—that exists in Cuba. It is not racial; it is political. The last thing Cuba wants to do is raise healthy youngsters and educate them to a high level only to have them siphoned off by wealthier nations who could bloody well afford to raise and train their own doctors, athletes, engineers, etc. So when a young Cuban applies for a perk as pricy as study abroad, the selection committee wants to be very sure he or she has a strong attachment to the motherland, a strong belief in the Cuban system, and a strong commitment to the value of service to one's country without regard for monetary incentives.

Only time would tell whether the youth on the bus had all that. But he certainly convinced me, and apparently had convinced the selection committee.

Having met Afro-Cubans like the boy on the bus, having read Cuba's anti-racism laws, and seen statistics on the number of Afro-Cuban doctors, I couldn't help but feel that Cuba has made more progress than the US, which started trying to dig itself out of the mud of racism at about the same time. But steady progress is rare in real life, and racial realities in Cuba are murkier than such examples suggest. Despite tens of thousands of Afro-Cuban professionals who work without discrimination alongside their Latino-Cuban colleagues, the past two decades have seen Latino-Cubans move ahead of Afro-Cubans economically.

Up until about 1990, Cuba's track record on the reduction of racial disparities was just about unbeatable. Then a policy change reversed that trend, causing the economic gap between Latino and Afro-Cubans to widen again. This was the government's decision to allow private citizens to engage in small business activities. It probably didn't occur to policy makers that this would give Latino-Cubans an economic advantage over Afro-Cubans, but I noticed it almost as soon as I began travelling around the island.

Initially I was under the mistaken impression that the government had confiscated all private property, and was surprised to learn from the *Boston Globe* that over 80% of Cuban families own a mortgage-free home. However, houses could not be bought and sold, only traded. So as I traveled about, I was curious as to how each family had acquired their home. I always asked, "How long have you lived here?" or "How did you come to own this house?"

I learned that most houses had been in the family since before the Revolution, and most of those home-owning families were white. Prior to the Revolution, there simply had not been many Afro-Cuban property owners. Rural blacks usually lived in huts on somebody else's land, and most urban blacks lived in shabby rented apartments. Many blacks were given homes by the Revolutionary government, but in most cases this would have been title to a shack on a small patch of land or to the slummy apartment they had been renting.

Even if the government gift of a home had been a new apartment in one of the recently built housing complexes, these units, while vastly better than where the family had lived before, were rarely suitable, three or four decades later, for turning into a *casa particular* (B&B) or a *paladar* (home-based restaurant). White families were the ones most likely to own property suitable for these purposes, and began engaging in such businesses as soon as the law permitted.

Even for Afro-Cubans who happened to own a suitably large house in an area frequented by tourists, fewer of them had relatives abroad who could front the money to fix up their place to meet the standards required for rental, plus pay the (very high) monthly permit fee. Latino-Cubans, more often than Afro-Cubans, had relatives abroad who were financially well-off enough to provide the necessary start-up funds.

The law changed in 2011 to allow the sale of homes,

and also to allow a person to own two houses. This will further increase the disparity, simply because those who have access to resources such as property and seed money are going to move up the economic ladder more quickly than those who do not.

What foreigners will have a hard time wrapping their heads around is—what about all those Afro-Cuban *professionals?* Don't doctors, engineers, plant managers, and government bureaucrats make good money, too?

In Cuba, no, they do not. A typical monthly wage for a professional is about US $20 or $30. Mind-boggling, right? How can anybody, even in a Third World country, get by on so little? In most countries people do it by living at a level of poverty that is almost inconceivable to us. In Cuba, low wages do *not* reduce people to abject poverty because: housing is free or nearly so; utilities are free or nearly so; health care is virtually free, and regular wages are paid when one is unable to work for health reasons, even if it's a long-term illness like AIDS; every family gets a food ration that will cover at least half its nutritional needs, with more available at very low subsidized prices. Thus it is possible to get by on a tiny salary, supplemented by barter. But products that the government does not choose to subsidize are priced beyond the means of the average Cuban *unless* that Cuban has a source of foreign or "hard" currency.

And who in Cuba has a source of hard currency? The list is quite long, but for the reasons mentioned above—the fact that Latino-Cubans are most likely to have relatives living abroad who are affluent enough to send money, and can use some of that remittance money to turn the family home into a casa particular or paladar—there are many more Latino-Cubans with access to foreign currency than Afro-Cubans.

Where Afro-Cubans do have an opportunity to start

their own business, there is no shortage of entrepreneurial spirit. Many take to the streets to sell art and crafts to tourists (as well as other, illegal offerings). And some who have suitable homes situated in areas frequented by foreigners do rent rooms or offer food services, or both. Probably 95% of the casas I have stayed in were owned by Latino-Cuban families, but I have been hosted in a few owned by Afro-Cubans. Two were beachfront homes—one in Siboney, near Santiago, which had been in the lady's family for generations and one in Playas del Este, whose owner, a veteran, told me he had got it through a redistribution program that gave housing priority to veterans.

My favourite Afro-Cuban-owned casa particular was that of Gladys Aponte Rojas. When I asked how she acquired her big colonial house, located a block from the cathedral in downtown Remedios, she explained that during her youth she had been the live-in caretaker for an elderly white widow. The old lady was the last in her line, so when she died the house reverted to the government for redistribution. However, local authorities decided that inasmuch as Gladys the caretaker had lived there for years, it was as much her home as it had been the old lady's. Thus the house was given to her, and when the law changed to allow small businesses, Gladys converted what had been the old woman's huge bedroom with en suite bathroom (and therefore required no renovations) into a nightly rental unit.

One room in the house is set up as a Santería shrine. And a few years back, when Gladys decided to go to college, she wrote a dissertation on Santería as it is currently practiced in Cuba. The last time I stayed at her place, in 2008, it was her daughter's birthday. Both guests and grandchildren present were the usual "brown rainbow" one meets in almost every Cuban social setting. I do not know if either of Gladys' grown children are doctors, but even if they are, she with her regular room rentals earns a great deal more than they do.

The economic disadvantage Afro-Cubans have faced in the past two decades may never disappear as long as home-based businesses are easier for Latino-Cubans to start. However, there is another major source of foreign currency open to all Cubans regardless of ethnicity. This is tourism, where one can earn tips in hard currency rather than in moneda nacional. It is said that the rest room attendants at Hotel Nacional (many of whom are black) earn more in tips than the Minister of Tourism (who is white) earns from a peso salary.

There *is* discrimination related to hiring practices in resorts, both on the part of the Cuban government and on the part of the foreign joint-venture partners. But the bias is not against blacks and mulattos; it is against "ugly." The José Comas Institute of Hotel and Tourism Services, which does most of the training for Varadero's resorts, admits that it does not accept "fat, disfigured, or ugly people." Why not? Because, according to the training institute, big resorts and hotels will only hire people with *buena presencia*. (Literally, "good presence," implying both physical attractiveness and a pleasing personality.)

In 2008, while walking on Varadero beach, I paused to watch a volleyball game between some extremely attractive young Cubans. Two were black, three were blond, and the others had features and skin tones that in Mexico would have caused them to be called *mestizo* (mixed).

Another brown rainbow, I thought, and hung around a while, wanting to know whether they were employees or guests at one of the resorts. It turned out that they were neither.

A pretty Afro-Cuban girl whom I guessed to be about

twenty plopped down on the sand next to me. "Where you from?" she asked.

I said I was from Canada. She tried another couple of questions in English, but it was clear that she didn't understand my answers so we switched to Spanish. She explained that they were all students at the José Smith Comas Institute of Hotel and Tourism Services.

I had heard that there was a racial bias in selecting students for "hospitality training," and after we had talked a bit, I asked her directly, "Do you feel discriminated against at the school?"

She stared at the sand, a little shamed-faced, and nodded her head.

"Because you're black?"

She looked up quickly, shocked. "Oh no! Because my English is not good."

"I thought it was necessary to speak at least one foreign language to get into a hospitality training program," I said.

She looked more embarrassed than ever. "I told them I spoke English. And I did pretty well on the written test. But when it comes to pronouncing those words, or understanding what someone is saying, I'm lost."

The volleyball game ended and the others splashed into the water for a cooling swim. When they came out, several dropped onto the sand next to us. The other Afro-Cuban in the group asked, "Aren't you going to swim, Elvi?"

"I'm working on my tan," she joked. And to me, "Lionel speaks English *and* French,"

"I'm impressed!" I said. "Did you learn them in school, or are you studying them at the Institute?"

"Both," he said. "I decided to study French after I saw a TV documentary about Jacques Cousteau. Do you know who he is?"

"I certainly do!"

"Cousteau said, 'Impossible missions are the only ones that succeed.' I decided my impossible mission would be to become a scuba diver."

"Why did that seem impossible?" I asked.

Elvi answered for him. "Because the only way for one of us to afford that sport would be to work in tourism as a scuba guide."

Lionel qualified that. "I might have been able to get into scuba if I had made a career of the navy but I did my two years and that was enough. Working in tourism will be easier. And it pays better."

"Isn't it sort of like the navy, in that they won't necessarily give you the job you want?" I asked.

"You have to have a plan," he said importantly. "Many French tourists come here to scuba dive. Canadians, too. I figured that if I spoke English *and* French, I could easily get a job as a scuba instructor or guide. So I focused on languages and I'm going to get one of those jobs!"

Elvi looked disconsolate. "If my English doesn't improve, *I'm* going to end up with a kitchen job."

I suspect both of those young Afro-Cubans were correct in these assessments of their job possibilities in tourism. At hotels where I had stayed, it seemed to me that blacks, whites, and mulattos were represented in something approximating their percentage in the population. But I had noticed that there was a tendency for certain ethnic types to hold certain positions, probably reflecting race-based managerial choices. Any resort guest will notice, for example, that Latino-Cubans are most visible at the front desk, car rental agencies, and as waiters, whereas many mulattos seemed to hold jobs as entertainers, tennis instructors, scuba guides, masseuses, and dance instructors. The darkest Cubans are often positioned as gardeners, bellhops, rest room attendants, or kitchen staff.

In North America that would mean that light-skinned employees had the best-paying jobs, but not so in Cuba. In Cuba, the pay scale for all those jobs is equally low. The difference between a tourism job that pays well and one that doesn't lies in its tipping potential. Thus, of the jobs dominated by Latino-Cubans (front desk and waiters), the former has no tip potential, while the latter has excellent possibilities. In areas dominated by mulattos, entertainers are rarely tipped, while scuba guides, tennis instructors, dance teachers, and masseuses often are. Jobs often assigned to Afro-Cubans, bellhops and rest room attendants are normally tipped, while gardeners and kitchen staff are not.

But as the young trainees on the beach knew, language proficiency (plus a perky personality) is the real key to a good job in tourism. Resort managers may have their preferences, but no Latino-Cuban is likely to score a tip-rich job as a waiter if he speaks only Spanish, and no bilingual Afro-Cuban is likely to get stuck on kitchen detail.

What it comes down to is that economic advantage in Cuba doesn't break along race lines *per se*. It depends on who has access to foreign currency and who doesn't. Any Cuban with zero access to foreign currency is *poor*. In certain ways, Cubans are comparable to welfare recipients in the US. Their basic needs are met but there is almost nothing left over for even the smallest non-necessities. The main difference is that in Cuba, the children of people in that lowest economic bracket will get an education that is as good as everybody else's, and if they are academically inclined, they have ready access to university—or to a vocational school that will help them acquire the language skills needed for a job in tourism that has the potential for some hard-currency income.

Those with a source of hard currency from tips, relatives living abroad tips, or a business offering goods or services priced in hard currency have become Cuba's new middle class. They can fix up their homes, acquire electronic toys, vacation at beach resorts, or buy gasoline for that classic old car that has been in the family for forty years.

Does that answer the question of how much racism there is in Cuba today? Probably not—nor does it explain how existing remnants of racism may impact non-white visitors.

This brings us into the subject of *jineteros,* or hustlers. The word includes prostitution but isn't only that. A jinetero might also hustle cigars, guide services, or anything else for which a tourist is willing to pay. Afro-Cubans don't dominate this group, but they are as much a part of it as they are of every other facet of society.

Enforcement of no-hustling laws varies widely depending on location and what is being hustled. In most places cops ignore teenaged boys hustling casa rooms, because that's something tourists need and, given the lack of advertising in Cuba, may have trouble finding without a guide. Casa jineteros are so numerous as to drive a visitor crazy in a couple of towns, particularly Pinar del Río and Trinidad. But in most places they are more helpful than harassing.

Prostitution is a different matter, and the cops can be tough on any Cuban they think is engaged in that particular hustle. The problem (for the cop) is this: if a person who *looks* Cuban approaches a person who *looks* foreign, is that enough to justify asking for ID from the suspected hustler? And how does a Cuban policeperson, whose responsibility is "preventive policing" (that is, preventing crimes from occurring) decide who might be engaged in an illegal activity *without* relying on visual clues?

Once in Santiago I watched from a park bench as about thirty foreigners got off a tour bus and began wandering around the historic Parque Céspedes. Although there was a policeman posted on every corner, several jineteros began discreetly working the crowd. When a Canadian woman wandered down a side street, she was trailed by an Afro-Cuban who I knew, from a previous conversation with him, was a hustler. The hustler had not been speaking to the woman five minutes when a cop approached and asked for his ID. Then, with a gesture (no gun, no handcuffs), took him into custody.

The Canadian woman was outraged. "We were just talking! You can't arrest him for *that!*" As the cop, ignoring her, led the man away, she shouted after him, "You're a racist!"

Almost simultaneously, just a few feet from where I sat, another Canadian woman approached a different cop to complain that she was being harassed by hustlers, and what good did it do to have police all over the place if they didn't prevent tourists from being annoyed by touts?

It seemed that no matter what the police did or didn't do, somebody was going to see it as unfair, incompetent, and possibly racist.

Cuban cops come in for a lot of criticism for using colour as one of their criteria for profiling people, partly because they occasionally mistake Afro-American or Afro-European tourists for a Cuban and question *them*. They do this most often in night clubs where they're on the lookout for prostitutes. The first factor they feed into the prostitution profile is age: whether one person in a couple appears two or three times older than the other. But that detail only has relevance if one half of the couple (usually the older half) is perceived as foreign and the other, younger half looks Cuban. This is where race comes into it. If the younger person has a light complexion, the police will hesitate about asking for ID, since he or she might be a tourist. However, if the younger person is of Afro heritage, he or she is assumed to be Cuban for the simple reason that there are hardly any black tourists in Cuba, so there's a high probability that any black person is Cuban (or else an illegal immigrant from nearby Haiti).

Thus it is not uncommon, in a nightclub or even on the street, for the presumed Cuban half of a couple to be asked to produce ID. If that person *is* Cuban, and strikes the police as a possible prostitute, s/he may be taken down to the station for a computer ID check to see if there has been a previous conviction for prostitution. A first-time conviction will garner a fine, second conviction a larger fine, and the third time, jail time.

These incidents clearly involve racial profiling, but the profiling is not based only or even primarily on race. Several years ago a Canadian couple I know—he a striking blond Nordic type and she an ordinary brown-haired Canadian with a light tan—returned to their casa to find the police waiting for them because a neighbour had reported seeing a foreign man go into the house with a Cuban woman, something which to the nosy neighbour smacked of prostitution. Once the police spoke with the couple it took only a minute to clarify that both were tourists, at which point the cops apologized and left. No harm done—except to the landlady's nerves and the Canadian woman's dignity, the latter somewhat piqued at having been taken for a Cuban prostitute. But how much more offended that couple would have been if the wife had been black!

Casa inspections of this nature no longer occur in Cuba because it is no longer against the law for a Cuban to share a room with a foreigner. The government has found a more effective (and less insulting) way to determine whether prostitution is involved. Just as foreigners have their passport number recorded when they register in a hotel or B&B, Cubans have their ID card number recorded. Periodically the government runs hotel and casa room registrations through a computer, and only when a Cuban's name comes up in the context of having shared a room with three or more different foreigners in a single six-month period does the "probable prostitution" light go off, and that person gets called in for questioning.

In 2008, travelling with two women friends by car, we picked up a young Afro-Cuban hitchhiker on the Habana-Pinar freeway. As we approached Viñales, a town that takes a very pro-active approach to preventing hustling, we were pulled over at a police checkpoint. The young man was asked where he was going, and why. He had already told us that he was going to Viñales just to "hang out," but he lied to the cop, saying he was going to visit family.

"What is your family's name?" inquired the policeman.

"Well, actually, friends," the youth amended.

"And their names are—?"

Instead of answering the question, the young man burst out, "Look, I'm clean! I don't have any kind of record! Check the computer; you'll see."

"Good idea," said the policeman, and motioned the youth out of the car. He then waved us on, and we went. In the forty-five minutes or so the young man had been with us he had not tried to hustle cigars, drugs, unlicensed guide services, or anything else. He was, I believed, just going to

Viñales for the reason he had said—to hang out. Would he have engaged in some kind of illegal activity there? I have no idea. What I was certain of was that the cops had profiled us. We white women driving a rental car fit the tourist profile. The youth, being half our age and black, fit their profile of a Cuban—and after he admitted to going to Viñales for no particular reason, fit their profile of a hustler. If they did not find him in their computer system, they probably let him go—but probably did *not* allow him to continue to Viñales. In short, he likely did end up paying a price for being black (and young, and a bit mouthy with the cops).

All of which is to say, racism does exist in Cuba. It is not quite like racism in North America, yet it is not entirely different either.

The equality in educational opportunities for all Cubans, combined with a growing number of jobs in tourism that give blacks and mulattos a fairly equal shot at earning hard currency obviously helps level the playing field. Politically, too, there have been recent efforts to achieve a better balance. In 2011, Raúl Castro called for an increase in the number of blacks in top positions in the Central Committee of the ruling Communist Party. This resulted in a ten percent increase in the number of black and mestizo members within a year.

On the economic front there are the new laws that went into effect in January 2011, expanding areas where Cubans can operate private businesses. Within three months more than 100,000 had applied for a license to become *trabajadores por cuenta propia*—that is, self-employed. More than half of the applicants had no previous employment status, which strongly hints that the businesses they proposed starting were ones they had already been engaged in under the table. While these "new" entrepreneurs were not predominately

Afro-Cubans, that ethic group was certainly well-represented and so should be well-represented in Cuba's recently permitted commercial enterprises.

But there is still that remittance disparity, the fact that an Afro-Cuban is less likely than a Latino Cuban to have relatives living abroad who are affluent enough to provide start-up funds for new enterprises—most importantly, money to purchase property.

As new businesses pop up all over the island, leading Cuban economists have already pointed out how this factor is increasing economic disparity. President Castro has indicated his concern, but from the government point of view, it's not an easily fixable problem. There is progressive taxation, of course, and it is a tool they are putting to use. But still the economic gap is widening and with it the cultural gap. And in that space, mistrust flourishes.

Equality has always been the Revolution's most cherished value, and while never fully realized (as ideals never are), that value certainly has not gone away. In 2008, the issue of values was introduced by delegates at the Union of Writers and Artists of Cuba (UNEAC) at the National Congress, and a permanent commission was created, dedicated to promoting "deep and fundamental reflection on racism." And in 2009, UNEAC created a group called *Color Cubano,* with the objective of addressing the problem of racism by a more positive representation of Afro-Cubans in the media.

Fidel Castro, in denouncing racial discrimination and prejudice, has said, "What the eternal enemies of Cuba and the enemies of this revolution want is for us to be divided into a thousand pieces, thereby to be able to destroy us."

Thus drawing social distinctions along the lines of colour, class, or anything else is considered worse than politically incorrect. It is considered dangerous. Inclusion and unity are taught to Cubans from a young age, not only as a matter of "playing nice," but as a matter of national survival.

Once in 2005 I drove across Cuba alone in a rental car—alone, that is, except for hitchhikers whom I picked up and dropped off all along the way. In Holguín, near a hospital, I gave a lift to an Afro-Cuban radiologist who had just got off duty. There were three Latina women in the back. She climbed into the front in a seat that had just been vacated by a woman and child. The radiologist was quiet—perhaps she was tired—saying little for the next sixty kilometres. However, just before we reached Bayamo, she pointed to a statue near the highway and said, *"Es Rosa la Bayamesa."*

I glimpsed a statue of what looked like a woman on a horse, so I whipped a U-turn and stopped to get a better look. We all got out and read the plaque. It told us that Rosa la Bayamesa, born a slave, was a nurse in the 19th century war for independence from Spain. She had used her natural medicine skills to treat the sick and wounded. To facilitate her work, she had established a network of hidden hospitals in caves all over this part of the island.

We five women then stood looking up at the statue, our variously-coloured faces dampened by a misting rain that had just begun to fall. The face of Rosa la Bayamesa glistened too, as moisture slid like beads of sweat down her bronze cheeks.

The radiologist said, *"Rosa fue una negra."* (Rosa was a black woman.)

"Yes," I said. "I can see that."

Another said, *"Sí, una negra. Y una Cubana."* (Yes, a black woman. And a Cuban.)

The others in the group echoed, as a kind of soft chorus, *"Una Cubana, sí."*

There was silence. Then the radiologist said, "*Sí, la negra Rosa fue Cubana.*" (Yes, the black Rosa was Cuban.)

It seemed to me that they were agreeing that the radiologist's ethnicity gave her a special connection to the honoured person, and that Rosa la Bayamesa, as one of the nation's heroes, belonged to them all.

So, I believe, do Cuba's children, who are the nation's rainbow and its future.

One Long Day

After our cycling guide had been published, I did a good deal of travelling by car in Cuba. The cycling had been fun but that wasn't the only way to get to know the people. Loading a car with hitchhiking Cubans was in some ways better, as it put me in touch with a cross-section of society and allowed time for long interesting conversations. I could fill an entire book with those if I had been taking notes instead of driving, but I didn't take notes, so here I'll only recount highlights from one very special trip on the *Día de las Madres,* 2005.

On that Mothers' Day I picked up 96 passengers during a 10-hour drive from one side of the island to the other. If you have just done the arithmetic and think that's flatly impossible, let me explain how it came about.

It started on Cayo Saetía which I had wanted to visit for several years. Once I negotiated the rough road leading to the bridge that connected Saetía to the mainland, I found the island totally enchanting. It is impossible not to be captivated by a place when you are greeted in the parking lot by a six-foot-tall free-roaming ostrich, and you discover you have the island all to yourself except the for employees at its one small lodge.

I was put off by the dead animal body parts decorating the restaurant at Villa Saetía, but the waitress assured me that the island no longer served as a private hunting preserve for Cuba's military brass; that it was now a *parque ecológical* and the remaining wildlife, both domestic and African, was protected. I greatly enjoyed my time there, dozing on its little cove beaches and bouncing through the bush on dirt tracks. More than once I was startled to see zebras grazing in a meadow or had to brake for a herd of gazelles. I could happily have stayed on Cayo Saetía for many more days.

However, I wanted to get to the other side of the island, to Manzanillo and Media Luna, in time to be at a celebration honouring Celia Sánchez' 85th birthday. It wasn't that far—six or seven hours, I calculated. I could be there by early afternoon.

Anxious to get an early start, it was not yet sunrise when I reached the parking lot. The ostrich was not around but three men were waiting by my car, lodge employees whom I had met the day before.

"Felíz Día de las Madres," they greeted me, and asked if I could give them a lift off the island. It was Mothers' Day and they wanted to visit their moms.

"Of course," I said, and away we went.

Their families lived in a rural community only a few kilometres from the bridge that connected island to mainland. It wouldn't have been unusual to see people hitchhiking from there because such a small out-of-the-way place surely did not have bus service. In fact, it wasn't surprising to see Cubans hitching anywhere. But one normally didn't see them so early in the morning. Government bureaucrats, medical personnel, teachers, and students usually didn't appear until near seven a.m. Then those without bikes would be walking or thumbing for a ride on anything that rolled. A little later there would be mothers taking small children to the doctor, and whole families journeying to visit other family members. As this was Sunday, I also would have expected people hitchhiking to church. But *not* at six a.m. when I dropped off the young men from Villa Saetía.

As they got out, I motioned for four women with five children between them to get in. They did, each lap layered with a child, and one child holding a baby in hers. They were not going far. Each had the same yet a different destination: her mother's house. As the morning wore on, the number of hitchhikers along the highway increased. As soon as I dropped off one passenger or group it would be replaced by another. They always thanked me as they got into the car and wished me a happy Mothers' Day. This would be followed by an explanation that, being Sunday, there were no buses running, and a sigh, *"La transportación es el problema más grande para nosotros, siempre."* (Transportation is the biggest problem for us, always.)

At a crossroads outside Mayarí, most of my passengers got out and three more women got in with four more kids. One woman scored the front seat for herself and had just settled her little boy in her lap when an old man came hobbling up.

"Excuse me," she said, laying a hand on my arm to stop me from driving off. "El Viejo [the Old One] must ride." With that she got out and helped the old man into what had been her comfortable front seat, closed the door, and pulled her child back so I could drive off.

"There is room for you in the back," I told the woman who had got out, although I could see that would make it uncomfortably tight. She smiled gratefully and squeezed herself and her child into the back seat with the other women and children.

We had only been travelling a short distance when the old man muttered a word I didn't catch, something like *cuarta* or *cuatro*. Cuatro is four, but cuarta I didn't know. In any case, neither word by itself meant anything to me. The old man stared straight ahead. I wasn't even sure he was speaking to me, so I ignored him and began talking with the women in the back seat. I discovered that they included a forty-year-old mother, her twenty-year-old daughter, and two-year-old granddaughter, all off to visit the matriarch of the family at her home in *el campo* (the country).

Meanwhile, the old man kept muttering "four" or something like that, each time louder and more irritably. Finally I glanced back at the women with a look that asked, "What is he saying?"

One of the women leaned forward and said, "He is telling you to put the car in fourth gear."

"Oh!" With embarrassment, I realized that after down-shifting to climb a steep hill I had only gone back to third gear. As I shifted into fourth I couldn't help but wonder how this old geezer, who obviously didn't own a car himself, could possibly know I was in the wrong gear. I had to ask, "Do you drive?"

"For forty-six years I drove a bus," he replied with dignity. "It hurts the engine to drive in the wrong gear. And it hurts my ears."

A short time later, in the middle of nowhere, he indicated a little thatched-roof hut where he wanted out. Slowly and stiffly he got out of the car, then, leaning against the hood, worked his way around to my window. He took out a small change purse and said, "How much do I owe you?"

"Nothing," I said. "It would be wrong to charge for transport on the Día de las Madres."

He nodded gravely, as if this made perfect sense. "Would

you care to come in for coffee?" he asked. "My mother is ninety-two, but she is very alert. She would enjoy your visit."

I would have enjoyed the visit, too; I'm sure of it. But there were three women and four little kids in the back seat all wanting to spend the day with their mothers and grandmothers, so I declined and we went on our way.

A kilometre further on I stopped for a farmer with a machete, who took the seat vacated by the old man. And then, walking alone, was a young woman who carried what seemed to be a heavy bundle so I picked her up, too. She was very slim and could squeeze into the back. She passed the bag forward for the man in the front to put by his feet. It was a little smelly and I asked, "What's in your bag?"

"Cheese," she said. "I'm going to see my mother in Holguín. Some is for her but most I'll sell."

"Where did you get so much cheese?" I asked, thinking that here must be an entrepreneurial-minded young woman who had learned the art of cheese-making and started a home-based business.

"My boyfriend works at a dairy," she said.

The dairy would belong to the government, which meant that the cheese had been stolen and was on its way to the black market. If anyone in the car thought of her activity as a crime, they didn't show it. I recalled how, many years ago when I worked as a secretary, every item in my home office had been pilfered from the company. The same was true of all the other employees except our department head, whose pilfering took the form of padding his expense account. We (clerks and secretaries) justified our thievery on the grounds that we weren't getting paid very well. I don't know how the department head justified his.

"Can I buy some cheese from you?" I asked.

"Sure," the girl said, and told the man with the machete

to reach into the bag and get a chunk for me. He extracted a piece about the size of a softball.

I said to him, "Divide it up, will you? A piece for everybody in the car."

He unwrapped the ball and examined it from several angles. Then, holding it in the palm of his hand, reached for his machete, which he had stuck between the seat and the door.

"Wait!" I told him, not wanting to consider the consequences if the car hit a pothole while he was sectioning the cheese with a machete on the palm of his hand. I fished for my Swiss army knife and handed it to him, then reached under the seat for a package of crackers which I passed back to the women to divide amongst us all.

A little later, having lost some passengers and gained others, I stopped to buy a pineapple from a roadside vendor. This time we all got out of the car and the farmer did use his machete to slice it for us. I could see other pineapples growing in the farmer's front yard, so knew that this was a legitimate home-based business.

I was running low on moneda nacional, a small problem because I hadn't yet paid the woman the twenty pesos she had asked for the cheese. That would be moneda nacional pesos, worth about four cents each. This is the currency in which Cubans are paid. It will purchase farm produce, subsidized goods, and food from street vendors. Anyone who wants unsubsidized goods or services, like, say, a rental car, a hotel room, gasoline, beef, cooking oil, or non-essential consumer goods must pay in "hard" currency. Up until the end of 2004, that would have been US dollars, because Cuba didn't have a hard currency of its own. However, it was now 2005 and the only hard currency in circulation was the peso convertible. A peso convertible was worth roughly one US or Canadian dollar.

Most foreigners had no difficulty understanding that upon arrival they needed to exchange their own currency for Cuban currency. What confused them was the fact that there was this *other* currency in circulation, the moneda nacional that locals could use to get things dirt cheap. Many visitors felt "ripped off" that they had to pay a reasonable price of, say, ten pesos convertibles (about $10) for ticket to the ballet or a concert while a Cuban could get in for ten pesos in moneda nacional (about forty cents). They could not wrap their head around the fact that moneda nacional was the government's way of subsidizing prices for its own citizens, who were earning so little.

This trip in May 2005 was my first one since the change from dollars to pesos convertibles, and I was just getting used to using them, being careful not to mix up a moneda nacional peso worth four cents with a peso convertible worth a dollar. I usually carried a supply of both, because when in a rural area such as where we stopped to buy the pineapple many people lived entirely within the moneda nacional economy and never laid hands on a peso convertible.

Now this farm girl had asked twenty pesos for the cheese. She couldn't mean pesos convertible because that would have been $20. She had to mean twenty pesos in moneda nacional, or about eighty cents. But I was running low on moneda nacional pesos, so I asked if she would take one peso convertible. She looked dubious.

"The price is only twenty pesos. The exchange rate is 22:1, so you would be giving me too much. And I don't have any change."

Concealing my surprise that she knew the exact exchange rate, I said, "That's okay. You can use the extra two pesos to buy ice cream for your mother."

She smiled and took the peso convertible, worth one

dollar. I found it interesting that while the two currencies drove visitors flat crazy, an apparently simple farm girl had no difficult understanding their relative value.

Later on the trip I purchased tangerines, not from a produce stand but from a man standing on the side of the road holding up strings of a dozen tangerines each to tempt passing cars. Seeing I was a foreigner, he said, "Un peso," and we both knew he meant the peso that was worth a dollar. I also knew that had one of my Cuban passengers rolled down her window to buy the fruit, he would have charged her maybe two moneda nacional pesos, or about ten cents. But why shouldn't Cubans pay less? It was their country and their earning power was a fraction of mine. What I would spend on a single tank of gas for this economy car was more than they earned in a month

For quite a distance, both sides of the highway had been lined with orchards too large to be privately owned so I knew that the tangerines, like the cheese, would be from a state-owned farm. And although there was now a policeman in the car, he ignored the illicit sale.

I should say a word about this policeman. I don't often pick up Cuban cops because I don't like the way they dress up in their uniforms and wave tourists down as if it's an official stop when really they're just hitchhiking like every-body else. But this one hadn't tried to use his uniform to get a ride, and in fact, had put a woman and child ahead of himself, only getting into the car when I saw there was room for one more and invited him to come along.

I probably wouldn't have done that if he had been wearing a gun, but few Cuban police are armed. More often, even when they're on duty, they roam about on bicycles, wearing baseball caps and not carrying a weapon. I had noticed that there had recently been a change, and in Havana quite a few cops had begun to wear side arms. I mentioned this to the policeman and asked if he carried one when he was on duty.

"Never," he said. "Havana is different. There is a lot of theft now and the police have started carrying guns. But that's not necessary here. There is very little crime in this area."

"Very little crime here," the others echoed, reinforcing the fact that the theft of the cheese and tangerines from state-owned farms was not regarded as crime by any of them, not even the cop.

The issue of corruption in Cuba is fascinating. Deisy's boyfriend (the father of her child), is a Cuban living in Canada. He owns a manufacturing company that sells pipe all over Latin America. He explained it to me like this: "I never pay bribes in Cuba because it's against the law, same as it is in the US and Canada. And I don't have to bribe people to do business. Whereas in countries like Mexico and Venezuela, if I didn't pay bribes I might as well pack up and go home because that's the only way to do business there."

I had asked him at the time if he was saying there's no corruption in Cuba.

"Oh sure there's corruption here," he confirmed. "But it's what I call 'subsistence corruption.' You know, people ripping off small amounts to help compensate for the damned low wages they get. Like stealing rice or cigars from their place of work. Or giving you back the wrong change."

During my travels in Cuba I would encounter this so-called "subsistence corruption" on a near-daily basis, from the airport where the map vendor, knowing the just-arrived tourist is dealing with unfamiliar currency, often returns less change than is due, to the departure lounge where the price of a doll-sized cup of coffee is CUC $1, but some enterprising coffee-bar tenders charge CUC $1.50. Tourists can be almost certain that their bill in any restaurant or bar will contain a "mistake." If you check it over and ask for a correction, this will be quickly and courteously made. If you don't, well, it's your loss and always, always, their gain.

I once did an informal survey of other travellers to Cuba to find out if my experience was common, and yes, it was. However, it was common only when dealing in pesos convertible. When dealing with moneda nacional, no one I interviewed could remember ever being cheated of so much as a centavo.

Gasoline, however, is not sold for moneda nacional pesos. It is priced in pesos convertibles. I pulled into a station, asked for a fill-up, and handed the attendant two twenty-CUC bills. The cop, in the seat next to me, murmured, "Check your change."

When the pump attendant returned, I did. I saw at once that it was wrong, because the amount had come to $29.25 and he had given me back an even ten, shorting me 75 cents. I could have let it go but this sort of thing annoys me. "This isn't correct," I said.

The pump attendant shrugged and said, "We're out of change."

"Then put in more gas, because I'm not paying for what I didn't get."

He sighed, reached into his pocket, and gave me the correct change. Everyone in the car remained silent. Were they embarrassed?

I said to my passengers, "You know, this only happens with things priced in pesos convertibles. I have never been cheated by anyone selling anything for pesos in moneda nacional."

"Es un problema," sighed one woman, and the others echoed, *"Sí, un problema."*

But what kind of problem was it for them? If they were outside the hard currency economy, dependant entirely on pesos and ration coupons, such minor rip-offs of tourists didn't affect them at all. On the other hand, if they or someone in their family worked in a job where a little skimming was possible, it would be to their economic benefit. I guessed that only the policeman got the bigger picture, because he said, "It hurts Cuba's reputation. It makes foreigners think we are not honest people."

This Mothers' Day was the only time I ever kept track of how many hitchhikers I picked up. It was also the day I had my worst hitchhiker experience ever. It was a conservatively-dressed lady with a large purse. I hated crowding the back seat because it caused the compact I was driving to ride low, and that made for slow going where the pavement was bad. But there was a light rain falling and I didn't have the heart to pass her by, so I stopped. She greeted us all with "Felíz Día de las Madres." The mothers in the back piled kids in their laps and squeezed over to make room. The instant the car started moving there was a blood-curdling scream that nearly put all of us through the roof of the car. It came not from the lady but from a tiny pink piglet in her handbag. It was a Mothers' Day gift for her old *mamí*, and I suppose the little pig must have feared, with good reason, that it would never see its own mother again. It screamed continuously for the entire hour that it and the lady were in the car, making this—no question about it—the worst hitchhiker decision I ever made.

What with the dozens of hitchhikers I picked up that day and dozens of stops to let them out, plus stops for gas and food, the drive to Manzanillo took much longer than I had anticipated. Even so, I was there by mid-afternoon and had time to hang out with some hundreds of others gathered on the steps of the Celia Sánchez memorial, Calle Caridad, and help celebrate her birthday, or what would have been her birthday had she still been alive.

I had intended to stay there on Calle Caridad (Charity Street) at the casa of Adrián and Tonia, but they had no vacancy. I didn't want to go to the big hotel on the outskirts of Manzanillo, having stayed there before and not liked it very much, so I drove downtown to see if I could find another licensed casa. Manzanillo has a lovely downtown core, its big tree-shaded park surrounded by old buildings in the Andalusian style. But there was almost nothing for a foreigner to do, and oh my god, was it hot!

Finding no place to stay, I got back in the car and sat there trying to decide what to do. Spying two pleasant-looking young women chatting on the sidewalk, I called to them, "I wonder if you know of anyplace where I might spend the night?"

They burst out laughing. One said, "We're just trying to figure that out ourselves. We're not from here; we're from Bayamo. We thought we would be able to get home this afternoon but there are no buses running on account of it being Día de las Madres. We don't know a soul in town."

And just like that I said, "I'm going to Bayamo. Get in and I'll take you home."

If that sounds a little crazy, it was, but just a *little*. It was only an hour back to Bayamo, and there were several hotels and many good casas there. True, I had been driving the better part of the day, but what difference did one more hour make?

Their names were Laura and Isabel. Both were in their early twenties, not especially pretty but with perky personalities that made them seem so. Neither had wanted to go to college or had any interest in training to work in the tourist industry. Isabel had worked in a bakery since high school and Laura at a daycare center. They had come to Manzanillo for the same reason I had, to enjoy the celebration at the Celia Sánchez memorial. It wasn't until they were ready to start home that they realized that they would either have to hitch or spend the night in the bus station.

By the time we left Manzanillo it was already five in the afternoon. I wanted to get to Bayamo and find a room before dark, so decided not to pick up any more hitchhikers. But in the town of Yara there was one I could not pass up. She was an old lady with massively swollen legs whom I thought had no business being out of her house, let alone on the highway, hitchhiking.

She was dubious about getting in, and kept repeating, "This is a very elegant car. How much will you charge?"

Only when I, with Laura and Isabel's help, convinced her that it wouldn't cost anything did she finally allow them to help her into the back seat.

She told us she had been to the doctor and was on her way home in the next town, about five kilometres up the road.

"Did you see the doctor?" Isabel asked.

"Yes. There was only one at the clinic today. She gave me more pills for the swelling in my legs." The old woman sighed. "I don't like taking them. They make me pee too much."

Upon reaching the next town she indicated a bus stop where she wanted out, but I wasn't about to put someone in her condition down anywhere except at her own front door. "Show us where you live," I told her. "I'm taking you to your casa."

I followed the directions she gave, which took us to a barrio about a kilometre from the highway. It was as bad a neighbourhood as I had ever seen in Cuba, with tumbled down shacks and pigs wallowing in mud-holes in the middle of the unpaved street. I realized that it must have been places such as this that Cuban leaders were referring to when they said that between population growth, hurricanes, and the embargo, the nation hadn't been able to keep up with housing needs; conditions had deteriorated to the point that 40% of Cuba's housing was in "mediocre to poor shape." Decent housing has been, and continues to be, as great a problem for Cubans as transportation, if not more so.

As Laura began to help the old lady out of the car, a middle-aged woman came running out of the house.

"Mamí!" Her shriek of relief was followed by a string of incredulous questions as to how her mother came to be with us.

Laura explained where we had found the old lady. Putting her hands on her pretty little hips, she proceeded to lecture the woman, who was at least twice her age. "Look at the condition of your mother's legs! How could you let her go all the way to Yara alone?"

The woman turned up her hands in a gesture of helpless embarrassment. "I told her it was Día de las Madres and there wouldn't be many buses running. But she kept insisting she had to see the doctor and finally I said, 'So go!' I didn't think she really would. I didn't even know she could get that far!"

Laura, with the self-righteousness of youth, was unimpressed by the excuse. "At her age she needs attention. Think of all she must have sacrificed for you. Now it's your turn to look after her. We must honour our *abuelas*. On this of all days!"

"Yes, of course!" the woman agreed, and seemed immensely relieved when I called Laura into the car and we bumped our way out of their slum and back to the main road.

Side note: A short time later, after Cuba's Parliament Speaker Ricardo Alarcón told a UN conference that housing was his government's most serious challenge, a Swiss NGO, Habítat-Cuba, organized local families in this area and they worked together to build new homes for about 10,000 people.

When we arrived in Bayamo, I took the girls home, met their parents, and we chatted briefly. But I was tired and anxious to get to a casa where I could spend the night. I had previously stayed in one I liked in Bayamo, owned by a coach of the national fencing team, but Laura and Isabel said they knew someone with a very nice house and wanted to take me there, so I agreed.

I parted from them reluctantly—they were truly lovely young women—leaving each with a pair of black Victoria's Secret bikinis by way of thanks for their kindness and company. The panties were more frivolous than the gifties I usually take to Cuba, but I had rationalized that they didn't take up much space and I would surely find someone who would appreciate them. I had not known who that some-one would be, and was as tickled as Laura and Isabel that it turned out to be them.

The two-storey casa where they left me was as nice as promised, but if I had not been so tired I would have gone elsewhere because the lady of the house said she didn't cook for guests because it was "too much work."

We sat down at the dining table of her nicely-furnished home to fill in the guest registration form required by law. I saw that there was a bowl of fruit on the table and asked if

I could have a banana. She said yes. That would have to do me till morning.

A white-haired old man, slender and erect, came into the room. The woman introduced him as her father. "Papí fought in the Revolution," she said proudly.

"Really!" I exclaimed, and rose to shake his hand, delighted to meet someone who had been a participant in that historic event.

"Sit, sit," he said. *"Mi casa es su casa."* (My home is your home.) "But my daughter exaggerates. I didn't actually fight, because I wasn't up in the sierra. I was only sixteen years old at the time. Along with some other boys, we were assigned to guard the mouth of Santiago Harbour. It was known that the US was allowing Batista's planes to use the air field at Guantánamo, and there was a fear that *los Yanquis* would send ships to help Batista hold Santiago. But that didn't happen so we never saw combat."

He sat down at the table and I began to pepper him with questions. His daughter, who had heard it all before, soon became bored and wandered off. She returned several times to suggest to her father that it was getting late and he should go to bed. Her husband, a bulky guy with a blustery manner, did the same.

But I found the old man to be a fascinating conversationalist, careful as to detail and not given to exaggeration. Each time he started to rise I held him with another question. Our conversation lasted over an hour, but finally the urgings of his daughter and son-in-law prevailed and he toddled off to bed. Then *they* sat down with me and I discovered the real reason they wanted the old man out of earshot.

They were hard-core entrepreneur types with more money-making schemes going than simply renting rooms. The son-in-law offered me black market gasoline obtained by a friend of his who worked in a state-owned gas station. I declined, both because it was illegal and because gas sold on the black market was frequently contaminated. Then the daughter wanted to know if, since I said I came to Cuba often, I could bring in DVD players. She assured me that she could sell them at a nice profit for both of us. She said she already had a supply of Spanish-language movies, as these were being brought back by doctors returning from humanitarian missions in Venezuela and elsewhere. The problem was that not enough Cubans had DVD players, and if I could help at that end...

I went to bed much later than I had intended, irritated by more than tiredness. I could not stop thinking about the old man, how he and his young compañeros had risked their lives to bring about a more just, less materialistic society, only to have his already-comfortable kids take over his house and focus on making money to buy consumer crap instead of trying to make Cuba a better place for everyone.

By now the reader must be as exhausted as I was that night, wondering how much longer this chapter is going to go on, and if all of this really could have happened in a single day. It could. It did.

So what is the point, literarily-speaking, of dragging you from one side of Cuba to another with such a jumbled mixture of people and places, kindness and corruption?

The point is this: If you ever intend to travel in Cuba, really travel, as opposed to holing up in Havana or at some all-inclusive beach resort for the duration of your stay, what I have described here is how it will be. Your itinerary should be considered tentative. If you travel by car you will need to pick up Cubans in order to compensate for the lack of signage. Assuming you understand enough Spanish to converse with them, you will find out things you never knew to ask about how things work in Cuba. Everywhere you go, you will find an intermingling of genuine kindness and "subsistence corruption."

As the Cubans would say, *"Es Cuba."*

I got up early the next morning and crept quietly downstairs to avoid waking anyone. The first blush of sunrise was just showing on clouds above the tree-lined street when I stepped onto the sidewalk. And there, standing next to my car, was the old man. In his hand he held a glass of fresh-squeezed orange juice.

"You had no dinner," he said. "I thought you might like this to tide you over until you find breakfast."

I drained the glass gratefully, and told him how much I had enjoyed talking to him the evening before. I told him I would love to stay longer and talk more but had to be on my way. That last was not true. If it hadn't been for his obnoxious grown-up kids, so obsessed with techie toys and making money, I would gladly have stayed longer.

He nodded gravely, and said. "There's one thing more. Something I want you to have." He reached into the pocket of his white shirt and from it took a bill that he handed to me.

It was smaller than a dollar bill, red and black in colour, emblazoned with a soldier beneath a blazing sun marching toward distant mountains. In each corner the value was marked: $5. It looked like monopoly money.

"What is this?" I asked.

"It is Revolutionary script," he explained. "What we in the movement were paid with during the war, before we won and formed the government."

"Good heavens!" I exclaimed, examining the paper closely. "You can't give me this! Why—it's an antique! I'm sure it has value!"

"Yes," he said. "It has value. But not monetary value. As a veteran, I got this house. That was payment enough for my service. And my daughter," he gestured toward an upstairs bedroom. "She went to university. She is a computer programmer. That was not a possibility for me. I myself had only four years of schooling."

"I understand the benefits of the Revolution," I told him. "But I don't understand why you want to give me this…this memory."

He looked at me for what seemed a long time. At last he reached out and with age-spotted hands, folded my fingers over the script. "I want you to have it. Because you love our Revolution."

PART 6

REVOLUTIONARY LOVE

Serious travelers know that if you don't do your homework before you go to a place you will miss a great deal and fail to understand a lot of what you do see. So prior to beginning our Cuba explorations Derek and I read several histories and travel guides. Even so, we were constantly surprised. Cuba was in a state of flux so guide books, including the cycling guide we were about to write, didn't remain current very long. Not even the question of who was in charge down there could be easily answered.

To further confuse things, the mainstream media did not have many of the basics right: for example, who historically *had* been running things in Cuba. From the outset, foreign media portrayed Fidel Castro as the man who started the Revolution, led the rebels to victory and subsequently controlled the island single-handedly—a benign hand if the lefties were to be believed, an iron fist if the right wingers were to be credited. Cuban government insiders said all along that while Fidel always had enormous moral authority, and still does, he had never governed Cuba as a lone dictator.

But what did they know? If the *New York Times* and the rest of the foreign media said…

Still, you have to wonder how any reporter could have been so gullible as to believe that Fidel Castro, whose military experience at the onset of the war consisted of leading his troops into two bloody disasters, how this Castro, in a region he did not know, with a mere fifteen men, four rifles, and no transport, managed to defeat Batista's 40,000-man army, navy and air force?

He did it, of course, but definitely not alone. He wasn't even the one who laid the groundwork for the war that resulted with Batista's ouster. The people who did were an impressive lot and not all of them are dead. To understand modern Cuba it helps to know who the main mover-shakers were, a bit of what they accomplished before, during, and since the war, and who among them still influences life in Cuba. Assuming the reader is interested (and if you're not, you might as well skip this section), what follows is a short list. It doesn't include nearly all of them—just a few whose influence is quite visible on the island today. For example…

Celia Sánchez was organizing opposition to the tyranny *before* Fidel's attack on the Moncada barracks in 1953 and once he got out of jail, she supplied him with maps, recruits, weapons, and contacts in the Sierra Maestra. She was the chief strategist during the war and Fidel's closest advisor for twenty-one years afterwards, decades when she facilitated the most people-oriented projects of the revolution. When Fidel's family asked people close to Celia and Fidel the nature of their relationship, Fidel's sister Juanita says they were told, "Celia is Fidel's right hand, his left hand, both feet, and his beard." Celia Sánchez, Cubans said then and often say today, was "the soul of the Revolution."

Vilma Espín, a founding member of the 26th of July movement and its coordinator in eastern Cuba. In 1957, Vilma left the urban underground to fight alongside Raúl in the Sierra Cristal. After the war she held powerful positions in government, and until 2008 was president of the largest political group in Cuba: the Federation of Cuban Women.

Haydée Santamaría was another woman warrior, involved in combat from 1953 to the end of the war. After victory she developed the internationalist and populist cultural tone that characterizes Cuba today.

Fidel, Raúl, and **Che,** all commanders in the rebel army and part of the ruling elite afterwards. Che was involved in government for only five years, but his ideological nonsense and moral sensibilities are still apparent in Cuba. Fidel of course became prime minister, then president, and remained so until 2008. Raúl assumed the presidency upon Fidel's retirement, having been vice-president for thirty years and Minister of Defence for almost fifty.

Are you flummoxed by the fact that of the six mentioned above (and there were many others) only the last three have a noticeable media footprint? Wondering why the others, if they were important, have had so little press? There are two reasons, both having to do with things in Cuba that are upside down to what they are here.

In our First World universe, people with a shred of power, money, or ingenuity use at least some of it to get publicity. This is *not* how it is in Cuba. Revolutionary ethos holds that personal publicity is to be avoided, or at least not sought. The aims and achievements of the group, not those of any individual, are what ought to be highlighted.

There was also a practical reason for avoiding publicity. Before the triumph of the Revolution, to be known as an anti-Batista activist was to be a target. Early on, Celia Sánchez's danger to the dictatorship caused Batista to put a price on her head. Had the involvement of others like Vilma Espín, Marta Rojas, and brave little teenaged rebels like Teté Puebla been known, their days would have been numbered.

Many of those the police did identify, like Frank País and his younger brother Josué, were shot dead. Being a media darling was *not* the road to longevity.

However, the success of the Revolution required publicity. It needed the support of the Cuban people who couldn't be expected to support an armed uprising unless they knew it existed. Fidel had had exposure as a student radical during his university days, so he had more media experience than the others. The failed attack he led on the Moncada military post intensified his visibility. After time in jail for that caper, he split for Mexico to prepare for a new offensive. Upon his return, it was decided that he would command the guerrilla forces. This automatically made him the face of the Revolution. (At least, it was decided by movement leaders in the east including Celia Sánchez, Guillermo Gárcia, Vilma Espin, the País brothers, and those working with them. Anti-Batista fighters in western Cuba and around Trinidad weren't part of the decision to give Fidel the lead role, and some of them definitely objected.)

Celia was superb at keeping a low profile. She would have realized that it made no sense to put a publicity bull's eye on one of the others in the movement when it was already on Fidel. Thus it was arranged for *New York Times* correspondent Herbert Matthews to interview not Frank País or Vilma Espín who were busy coordinating the urban underground in Santiago, not Haydée Santamaría or Melba Hernández who had participated in the Moncada attack, and certainly not Celia herself who for four years had been organizing clandestine cells and recruiting fighters whose goal was to overthrow the tyranny. When a *New York Times* reporter, and later a CBS TV film crew, was brought in to publicize the movement, it was to interview Fidel Castro. It did not occur to newsmen then or later to see the women who guided them on perilous trip to and through the mountains to Fidel's hideout as anything other than gofers. If "the girls" said Fidel was *El Comandante,* how were foreign journalists to know otherwise? Thus the movement acquired a Face, and the media acquired its "Guerrilla Prince."

This is not to say that Castro lacked real power. Although he had almost none when he arrived back in Cuba from Mexico that changed as soon as Celia Sánchez and other 26th of July leaders decided to put their recruits under his command. But even as commander of the rebel forces, Fidel was *never* a one-man show. From the outset there were others who had just as much power if not more. So why have you heard so little about them all these years?

Because being "The Face" was Fidel's job, not theirs. Just as a decision was taken to make him the face of the Revolution, so was it decided after the war that he'd be the face of the new government—none guessing that this would ensure that he remain a target for decades to come. Fortunately he was good at being the face of the Revolution and equally good at avoiding assassination attempts. This did, however, lead to another problem.

Despite the revolutionary ethos that "cults of person-ality" were bad, one immediately began to form around Fidel. He tried to prevent that, first by elevating to hero status Camilo Cienfuegos, a handsome revolutionary com-mander who died in a plane crash six months after victory. That didn't work very well because Fidel, being so alive, still made better copy—and a better target. He was most useful to Washington and the media during the Cold War as someone who personified everything the capitalists feared about socialism.

Then Che was murdered. Both to promote Che's values and to protect Cuba's living leaders from the dangers and distractions of media attention, Che worship was encouraged. This didn't stop the media from glomming onto Fidel, but he did the best he could. In Cuba you find no monuments to Fidel, no t-shirts or other kitch with his picture. Only since retirement has his face appeared on the occasional billboard. Over the years Fidel has been endlessly didactic but he has never been a self-promoter.

As for other Revolutionary leaders, they fiercely resisted publicity during their heyday and continued to do so. Whether they are now living or dead, they played major roles in shaping modern-day Cuba, *and have done so with very little publicity.*

Until you wrap your First World mind around that—not easy, I know, because most of us imagine that to become a Very Important Person takes millions of dollars of publicity—you cannot understand Cuba.

The Woman Behind (and Ahead of) Fidel

Havana's Necrópolis Cristóbal Colón covers several city blocks. It gets both mourners and sightseers, a few of whom I passed after I left my bike in the *parqueo* and headed along one of the cemetery's pedestrian paths. I had not come to see the grave of a baseball player topped with the naked torso of an athlete or wonder how air crash victims might have felt about having their tombs decorated with a plane flying toward infinity. I did not pause to smile at the tomb of a lady who so loved the game of dominoes that the marble slab on her grave was in the form of a giant domino, or to marvel at the one decorated with a hermaphrodite angel. I was there to find the vault that contained the ashes of Celia Sánchez.

I had heard that it was in the mausoleum of the Armed

Forces, and had no difficulty finding that imposing white marble edifice. There were many vaults. Each had a brass handle and a plate engraved with the name of the person whose remains were interred there. I hunted for an hour without finding one for Celia Sánchez.

Finally, worn down by the heat and frustration, I stepped out onto the pedestrian path. A woman sat on a park bench. I asked her, without much hope, "Do you know where Celia Sánchez's tomb is?"

Silently she rose and went into the mausoleum. I followed. She pointed to a drawer with a bouquet of wilted roses stuck through the handle.

I started at the white marble. "There's no name."

"It is not necessary," she said. "Everyone who cares knows where it is."

"But still—" I began.

"She wanted it this way," she said firmly. She removed the wilted roses, stuck a yellow sunflower from her own bouquet through the brass handle, and walked away.

It was only later, when I got similar vibes from other Cubans, that I grasped the unspoken message in the woman's attitude. It was that while Fidel belonged to the world, Celia belonged to *them*. She had never wanted celebrity when she was alive, and did not need it to be remembered by her people.

All of the Cuba-related histories I had ever read skimmed over the name of Celia Sánchez, so on my first trips to Cuba I did, too. Naturally I noticed it on schools, hospitals, kids' camps, and the like, but every institution in Cuba carries the name of some dead hero so hers made no particular impression.

And I entirely missed places that honoured her without mentioning her name. I passed countless billboards, not the sloganeering ones seen all over Cuba, but ones with somewhat primitive original paintings of a field of sunflowers or a range of mountains or maybe a single white dove on a field of blue. Sometimes the sign would carry a line that translated as "You are not forgotten" or "You are with us still" or "We feel your presence." But more often no words at all. And no name.

I once spoke to a man who was touching up the paint on one such sign. He said these handmade memorials were meant to honour Celia Sánchez. When I asked how one could be expected to know that, he shrugged and said, "We know."

Parque Lenin is a pleasant area on the south side of Havana. It includes a lake, museum, playgrounds, horseback riding academy, rodeo arena, and more. I always found it a good place to road test a bike before heading out on a cycling trip. One day I asked a gardener whose idea this park had been.

"Celia Sánchez," he said. "With her own hands she helped plant this grove of mango trees, even when the cancer was killing her. She loved trees."

Later, in Ciego de Ávila province, I asked what that little Dutch-looking village of gable-roofed houses was doing in the middle of a cow pasture.

"It's worker housing. About thirty families live there," replied a ranch hand. I asked why it wasn't in the same cement-block cracker-box style as most other worker housing in Cuba. He said, "Because it was designed by Celia Sánchez. She had a different way of thinking."

Then there was a campismo I came across in Parque La Güira, in the mountains west of Havana. It wasn't the usual row of cement block huts either, but dozens of little tree houses, each just big enough for bunk beds where a couple of kids could toss their backpacks. Campismo Los Pinos was already in ruins by the time I discovered it, smashed by a recent hurricane. There was one elderly man there, a caretaker of sorts. I asked him how this campismo, so different from all the others, had come to be.

"It was Celia Sánchez's idea," he said. "She knew this place from the time of the October crisis, when the Western Forces, under Che's command, were stationed in El Cueva de los Portales. One day she came with some soldiers. While they rested, she climbed up the mountainside to other caves." He pointed above the forested area where we stood. "Those caves were to be used, too, just in case."

"Did she really think there was going to be a nuclear attack on Cuba?" I asked.

"We all did. But here we are." He smiled. "Later she had this campismo built so kids from the city could see that such beautiful places exist in Cuba."

I was about to leave when another question occurred to me. "You said she was here under Che's command. I thought *she* was a commander."

"Not *under* Che," he corrected me. "Celia was under nobody."

I guess I looked puzzled because he explained, "When the rebel army was formed, she decided that Fidel should be El Comandante, even though some in the 26th of July leadership had their doubts. Raúl, Che, and Camilio became commanders, too. As did she. She took that rank not to command men but only so none of them could command her."

"I see," I said, thinking to myself, *That's not in any history of the Revolution I've ever read.* "How do you know this?"

"She told me." He pointed to the ruins of a small stone house on the brow of the hill. "That was her place. It is where she stayed when she came here."

These are some of the things Cubans told me about Celia Sánchez and at first that was all I knew. From a little-known biography by Pedro Álvarez Tabío, from other documents, and from old timers who knew her, I later learned the following:

Celia grew up in the sugar mill towns of south-eastern Cuba, in the shadow of the Sierra Maestra. Having lost her mother at the age of six, she was especially close to her dad, a doctor who cared for mill workers, cane cutters, and destitute peasants alike. From her teens onward she shared her father's political and social justice concerns.

By 1950, when Celia would have been thirty years old, she was thoroughly outraged by the misery in which rural people lived and the way the oligarchy was hogging all of the island's wealth. She began organizing opposition to a government that had gained power by fraudulent means. Fidel, six years younger, was still in law school at the University of Havana, 900 kilometres away. It would be three years before they connected, and four more before they actually met.

Celia had the ability to organize opposition to the regime but there was no one to lead an armed resistance, which she had become convinced was the only way to topple Batista. When Castro attacked Moncada she immediately identified him as a man who could lead that armed insurrection. The problem was that Fidel had been captured after the Moncada attack and sentenced to fifteen years in prison.

Celia raised money for food and other essentials for the prisoners, and communicated with Castro about her hopes for a more just Cuba. From prison he sent a note that read, in part, "To never have seen you, to never have helped you, pains me very much. I close my eyes and what I see is Celia's Cuba, not Batista's, not the Mafia's, not America's. One day I plan to help you make Celia's Cuba a reality."

Obviously Castro could be no help as long as he was in

jail, so the first thing Celia had to do was get him sprung. This she did by organizing protests all over the country demanding release of the Moncada attackers. It took two years but Batista finally gave in to public pressure and granted amnesty to Fidel and his followers.

When Fidel was released in 1955, he headed to Mexico to train an invasion force. Although he and Celia still had not met in person, they had come to an understanding that she would organize for an armed insurrection that was to be launched in the southeast corner of Cuba—a mountainous region she knew intimately and Castro knew not at all.

On the day he was to return, Celia was waiting on the beach with trucks to transport him and his 81 men to safety in the sierra. The boat did not arrive.

Two days later it ran aground far away from the intended rendezvous site. The men had to wallow through mangrove swamps in chest-deep water for nearly a mile before beginning their march into the mountains. Batista's troops caught up with them in a middle-of-nowhere place called Alegría de Pío, and Fidel's second military adventure (Moncada being the first) likewise ended in bloody disaster.

Batista announced to the world that all the rebels including Castro had been killed, but Celia believed some must have got away. She sent a close friend, the mountain-savvy peasant Guillermo García, to search for survivors. Eventually sixteen of the original eighty-two were rescued and reunited on a remote farm, there to recuperate in the care of sympathetic peasants.

A month later, movement leaders went to the farm to meet with Fidel. Given his abysmal track record, not all of them thought it was a good idea to turn over to him the recruits and weapons that they had so painstakingly assembled. But after a meeting said to have lasted more than twenty-four hours, Celia concluded that Fidel was still their best hope for a successful guerrilla war. After all, who else had the confidence to imagine that it was possible to defeat Batista's 40,000-man military with fewer than 100 poorly-armed irregulars? Never mind that Fidel had a record of failure in the areas of strategy and logistics; those were the very things at which *she* excelled. It was agreed that Castro would take charge of purely military operations, while Celia would be in charge of just about everything else.

She first returned to the city to find more money, weapons, and recruits. When need arose for a fixed base where the rebels could care for their wounded, she dealt with that, too. Choosing an easy-to-defend mountain high in the sierra, she personally oversaw the construction of La Comandancia, with its men's barracks, women's barracks, storeroom, cookhouse, radio station, a hospital Che would run, and the cottage she and Fidel would soon be sharing.

On Celia's instructions, this command centre, which covers several acres, was left in its natural heavily wooded state. Small thatched-roofed buildings were scattered across the mountainside and tucked under trees to prevent them being seen from the air. So well concealed was this base of operations that Batista's planes flew over repeatedly for more than a year and never spotted it.

Historians have minimized or ignored Celia's role as a leader of the Revolutionary war, even though it was no secret. Batista knew enough to raise the bounty he had placed on her head to $75,000. At the height of the war, a CIA document reported that, "Celia Sánchez is one of the most powerful figures in the 26th of July movement. All functions not strictly military are under her jurisdiction. All intelligence agents report to her."

And Teté Puebla, who fought alongside Celia, said in

her autobiography, *Marianas in Combat,* "Celia organized everything. Her ideas touched almost everything in the Sierra. She was the soul of the Sierra, very capable yet very sensitive to the needs of others. She was in charge of just about everything, not only schools and hospitals but the general command post. She was in charge of the sewing shops, the armoury, the transport of goods, and messengers. If a woman was giving birth in the mountains or a peasant was ill and needed medicine Celia was in charge of it. After the revolution's triumph she maintained these concerns."

La Comandancia is there yet and can be visited by those with the stamina to make the climb—a worthwhile excursion for anyone who enjoys hiking in the mountains even if they have little interest in Cuban revolutionary history. It was here that one of the great love affairs of the Revolution unfolded; two people whose feelings for each other could only be intensified by their shared objectives: to bring about the overthrow of the Batista dictatorship, free Cuba from US domination, and create a genuine social and economic revolution in Cuba.

Celia and Fidel spent almost two years in a rustic and romantic two-room hut at La Comandancia. Then they came down from the mountains, fought their way to victory in Santiago, and soon thereafter entered Havana riding side by side atop a tank.

They moved into a simple two-storey apartment building on a tree-lined street in the Vedado section of Havana. More accurately, Celia lived there. Fidel did not then and perhaps still does not sleep two consecutive nights in the same place. When his day ended he was driven to wherever he chose to spend that night. If it was not to Celia's apartment then his driver would come for her and take her to where Fidel had gone to bed. Midnight or in the wee hours it did not matter. She would go through his pockets and retrieve scraps of paper on which he had written the things he thought needed doing or had promised people he would do. These she would carry to her office and at whatever hour of the night that was, begin at once to follow up. In the 21 years they were together in Havana before her death in 1980, she was known as the single most effective person in the government at getting things done.

Celia Sánchez resisted the totalitarian model of communism. She pressed for justice at all levels of society, initiating schools, hospitals, housing, campismos, and childcare facilities for the general population, while helping countless individuals resolve personal problems. Celia Hart wrote in an essay on Sánchez, *A Butterfly against Stalin*, "She had the magical power to join heaven and earth without showing off. She was a perfect mediator between the work of the revolution, its people and leader."

The burdensome bureaucracy that grew up after the war was Sánchez's great enemy. Had she lived longer she might have prevailed over demands for conformity and political correctness that often took precedence over humanitarian considerations. But her death in 1980 left Castro and all the rest of the revolutionary leadership to be influenced by others.

I have met nine Cubans whose life, they claimed, was changed by one of Celia's "small" decisions. Here a child orphaned by the war whom Celia had brought to Havana to be educated (one of many, I was told). Here a homeless family for whom she found a house. Here a man who recounted how as a wild teenager he had got in trouble soon after the war and was about to be sent to a "re-education" camp when Celia intervened and arranged him to be trained as one of the "barefoot teachers" in the newly-formed literacy brigade.

Many others told me that during the first decades after the Revolutionary government came to power, the best and often only way to cut through the inefficient bureaucracy was to get to Celia Sánchez.

Marta Rojas, a trusted friend of Fidel from the Moncada assault to the present day, has said that from the time Fidel and Celia met in February 1957 until her death in January 1980 he made no major decisions without her approval.

Fidel fooled around with other women during his twenty-three years with Celia but she seemed indifferent to this except when it interfered with what she saw as his duties. Then she would put a stop to it. Maybe she felt a bit like Jesse Jackson's wife who, when a reporter asked about Jesse's infidelities, said, "It doesn't matter." When the reporter pressed to know why it didn't matter, Mrs. Jackson snapped, "Because I *said* it doesn't. When I decide it matters, then it will. What matters now is that we share a family and a vision." Celia might have said of her relationship with Fidel, "What matters is that we share a Revolution and a vision."

Fidel and four other close friends were at Celia's side when lung cancer claimed her. The modest apartment where she lived remains off-limits to the public because, it is rumoured, Fidel still goes there sometimes to be alone. Or is it to feel less alone?

Wasn't it Hemingway who wrote in *A Farewell to Arms* that for true love there can be no happy ending? Surely Celia's death, four months before her sixtieth birthday, seems like an unhappy ending. But they did have almost a quarter century together, years characterized by purpose, intimacy, meaning, and mutual understanding. Maybe it was all that, and not the ending, that mattered.

Haydée Santamaría:
Cuban Pain and Cuban Art

I stood looking up at the art-deco building known as Casa de las Américas, not thinking about the fact that it has hosted many giants of Latin American literature or that the adjacent Santamaría Gallery, with over 6000 pieces, contains the world's most extensive collection of Latin American art. Nor was I thinking about what a remarkable achievement it was that a struggling country like Cuba should have an institution so prominent in the publication, exhibition, promotion, and support of musicians, writers, painters, sculptors, dancers and other artists. I was thinking about Haydée Santamaría, who spent two decades bringing all that about, and how one day in July 1980, she walked into her bathroom, put a gun to her head, and ended all the pain.

No matter how much love has come one's way or how much of the Revolution for which one has fought has been accomplished, there is no guarantee of a happy ending. If Haydée Santamaría ever dreamed there might be, she learned at an early age that it was not in the cards for her.

She was only twenty-six when she, along with her brother Abel, her friend Melba Hernández, and her fiancé Boris Luis, joined Fidel Castro in the attack on the Moncada military facility. By a combination of bad luck and bad planning it all went terribly wrong. Within the hour some were dead, some had fled, and some, including Haydée, Melba, Boris, and Abel were captured. Haydée watched her twenty-two-year-old brother Abel beaten and dragged away. Later she was brought a gouged-out eyeball and told that it belonged to him. She and Melba overheard a soldier speaking of how, when the testicles of one man had been cut off, blood filled his black-and-white shoes. Thus Haydée knew the fate of her fiancé, because Boris was the only one in the group who had not been able to acquire boots and had been wearing black-and-white street shoes.

Boris and Abel died under torture. The soldiers burned Haydée and Melba's arms with cigarettes, but neither woman would tell them what they wanted to know. Later they were put on trial. Haydée and Melba were convicted and sent to prison along with other captured survivors.

They were released in 1954, a year earlier than their male compañeros. They promptly resumed clandestine activities aimed at bringing about the overthrow of the Batista regime. When the men were released in 1955, some followed Fidel to Mexico where they began training for another attempt. Other survivors of the Moncada fiasco, including Armando Hart, remained in Cuba to work with Haydée and Melba in what by then was called the 26th of July movement. Haydée and Armando were married in 1956.

Six months after the wedding, those who had been in Mexico with Fidel arrived back in Cuba, where Haydée, Armando, and Melba had been working with Celia Sánchez and others. Haydée spent the next two years as coordinator of the urban underground, fundraiser, gunrunner, tactician, and guerrilla combatant.

When victory came in 1959, followed by the confiscation of the holdings of American companies (which at the time owned much of Cuba's arable land, mineral deposits, communications systems, electric company, banks, gambling casinos, and big hotels) the full weight of Cold War fear and fury was thrown at the new government. This took the form of everything from an armed invasion to countless acts of sabotage and murder.

While men in the leadership focused on typically masculine issues like military defence of the island and forging political bonds with foreign powers, Haydée saw the ideological blockade being built around them and realized how that might choke Cuba culturally. Almost overnight, she transformed herself from a guerrilla fighter to cultural emissary. From 1960 onward she sought to encourage revolutionary values by bringing art and culture from all parts of the world and making it accessible to all levels of Cuban society. She made it her mission to ensure that whatever happened militarily, Cuba would not be blockaded culturally.

When a Central Committee was set up in 1965 as Cuba's supreme governing body, Haydée and her husband Armando Hart were on it and participated in drafting the constitution that governs Cuba today. Haydée did not falter under the weight of her political role, family responsibilities (which included not only her own two children but the adoption of five more), and the task she had set herself to forge artistic and cultural links between Cuba and the rest of world. It was Che Guevara's death in 1967 that almost did her in.

She wrote in a letter addressed to the slain Che, "Today I feel tired of living. I think I have lived too much already. I do not see the sun as so beautiful. I do not feel pleasure in seeing the palm trees. Some-times like now, despite enjoying life so much and realizing that it is worthwhile to open one's eyes every morning if only for those two things, I feel like keeping them closed forever, like you."

She rallied, though, and continued her cultural work. She saw it as a revolutionary imperative to rectify decades of cultural elitism and bring art to the Cuban people. She brought many of the world's leading dancers, musicians, sculptors, painters and theatre groups to Havana's Casa de las Americas. Awards were made, books published, and scholar-ships were given to Cubans and foreigners alike.

Casa de las Americas offered refuge for artists fleeing persecution in their own countries—and remarkably, this included persecuted Cuban artists as well. Doctrinaire bureaucrats had begun to dominate the Cuban government and the *Nueva Canción* (New Song) movement came under attack for its political lyrics and challenging stance. Haydée shielded many talented young singers and warned the government against dogmatism in all of its forms. She had some notable victories, but...

Her voice was weakening. It would be finally silenced by three powerful blows. Her marriage to Armando was falling apart. On January 11, 1980, Celia Sánchez, who had been one of her closest friends and strongest allies in the struggle to prevent a Stalinist-type bureaucracy from dominating Cuba, died of lung cancer. Then Haydée was in a car crash that left her in continuous pain. A few months later, on the anniversary of the awful deaths of her fiancé Boris and her brother Abel, Haydée again must have felt that she had "lived too much already."

It was then that the gun came out and she fulfilled the wish she had expressed in that letter to Che following his death: that of wanting her eyes, like his, closed forever.

A sad postscript to this story is that soon after Haydée's suicide, the ideologues cracked down on Cuban intellectuals like never before. This silenced many and drove many out, weakening that sphere of Cuban life she had done so much to invigorate. It would be two decades before Cuban intellectuals could breathe again, albeit not without some wicked punches being landed by both sides. A renaissance is coming about now in no small part because the international aspect of her focus did survive and Casa de las Americas is still there. To the degree it is permitted and Cuba can afford, La

Casa functions as Haydée intended. It still gives scholarships to Cuban artists, brings world culture to Cuba, and is an essential destination for anyone even slightly interested in Latin American art.

Che's Legacy

Whether or not one agrees with Che's political views or his belief that humanitarian aims can be achieved by violent means, it is undeniable that he remained courageous and self-sacrificing to the death. The world has not given us all that many like Che, men who are not corrupted by comfort or hardship, war or peace, victory or failure.

Considering that Che·was only in Cuba for seven years—two during the war and five after—it is amazing that he is so celebrated on the island today. One day my friend Dianne and I were doing touristy things in Habana Vieja. We visited rooms devoted to Che in the Museo de la Revolución, strolled along the Malecón under a several-stories-high face of Che painted on the side of a building, and walked through an outdoor crafts market selling every conceivable kind of Che kitsch. Then we climbed the stairs to the roof of one of the old forts, Castillo de Real Fuerza, to check out the view.

Gazing across the harbour, Dianne's attention was caught by a towering statue of a bearded man.

"Look!" she exclaimed. "It's a statue of Che!"

I laughed. "Dianne, that's not Che. It's Jesus."

"No," she insisted. "It has to be Che. They've got his image everywhere."

I turned to a Cuban and said, "My friend thinks that's a statue of Che. Is it?"

The Cuban looked at us in amazement. "Your friend

can't tell the difference between Jesus Christ and Che Guevara?"

It is certainly not something a Cuban would be unclear about. More than a few doubt that Jesus ever lived, and even if they believed he did, might well grant Che the more honoured status. The giant Christ statue commissioned by Batista dominates Havana Harbour, but throughout Cuba many more monuments have been built to honour Che.

The first was the Bosque de los Mártires de Bolivia in Santiago de Cuba, created by Rita Longa in 1973, just five years after Che's death. It is an arrangement of interlocking marble slabs, each bearing the face of one of those who died with him in Bolivia. On Che's block there is no image, just his words: *Hasta la victoria, siempre.* Until the victory, always.

In the city of Holguín there is a gigantic metal sculpture by Enrique Avila Gonzalez that captures the essence of Che's passage through Cuba. It is an enormous steel representation of Che striding into the future, leaving in his wake empty cut-outs of where his body was.

However, those with deep feelings about the man and the values he urged will want to make a pilgrimage to Santa Clara to visit the awesome memorial created by Cuban sculptor José Delarra and Architects Blanca Hernández and Alberto Cao. There atop a fifty-foot pedestal stands a twenty-foot statue of Che in battle fatigues, asthma inhaler peeking out of a shirt pocket, rifle in one hand, the other arm in a cast, a reminder of it having been broken during the last weeks of the Revolutionary war. This memorial, which includes a museum and mausoleum, took most of the 1980s to build and involved the volunteer labour of 50,000 Santa Clarans. It is here that Che's remains, recovered from Bolivia in 1997, are interred. An estimated 200,000 per year come to pay their respects. The surrounding plaza, which holds 80,000 people, was too small for all who came to attend a memorial ceremony on the fortieth anniversary of his death.

Why the museums and impressive memorials? Why millions of Che t-shirts? Why memorabilia sold in hotel boutiques and in street crafts markets? Why crudely-painted images of Che looming over city streets, rural farms, kids' camps, and industrial wastelands? Of course, there is the fact that Che is dead, and nobody celebrates their *dead* war heroes like Cuba. But what exactly did he *do* for Cuba?

There was his role as a commander in the war, of course. Afterwards he had various responsibilities, including running the national bank. There is a story, probably a *chiste* (joke) that goes like this:

Fidel is discussing with his inner circle who will take what job. Some volunteer, some are appointed. Finally Fidel asks, "Is anyone here an economist?"

Che says, "I am."

"Okay," Fidel says. "You'll have to be president of the National Bank."

Later, as they are leaving, Fidel says, "I knew you were a doctor, Che, but I didn't know you were an economist."

Che exclaims, "Economist? I'm no economist!"

Fidel says, "But I asked! You said you were."

"Sorry," Che replies. "I thought you asked, "Is anyone here a communist?""

Who assumed what responsibilities in the new government may have been a little more considered than that, but not a lot. Although most of the leaders were fairly well-educated, few had much experience at anything other than opposition to the regime they had just defeated. The job assigned to Che was not an easy one. Batista and his cronies had cleaned out all the liquid assets they could grab, leaving a public debt of $1.3 billion, a deficit of $90 million, and only $500,000 in the national treasury.

Che called on the people to help by paying their back taxes. The response was tremendous. Within six months $232 million in taxes came pouring into the treasury, enough to wipe out the deficit. Instead of being in the red, the new government wound up with assets of $57 million and currency reserves of $147 million.

Che had definite ideas about agrarian reform and got on it right away. He crafted the first Agrarian Reform Law, limiting the size of farms to 1000 acres. The government expropriated all holdings over that and either kept them to run as government enterprises or redistributed the land to peasants in 67-acre parcels. The up side of this policy was that many peasant families received land through the redistribution. The downside was that the best farms were taken over by the state. Experienced farm managers were replaced by inexperienced ones and production plummeted.

Che headed the Ministry of Industry, too, and in that position his attachment to Marxist ideology led to even more disastrous results. He believed that moral incentives would induce greater production than material incentives, ignoring the fact that moral incentives have only worked in small religious communities. He also believed what every Third World leader then believed: that industrialization could thrust a nation economically skyward like a rocket. In fact, profitable industrialization almost always requires an abundance of resources and expertise—neither of which Cuba had.

Che also lacked—as most of us did in 1960—an awareness of how horribly polluting industry could be. That is why if you go to the town of Moa today and stand in the shadow of a gigantic Che statue at the entrance to a nickel-smelting plant named after him, you will be at Ground Zero for the most contaminated place in Cuba. There has been a reduction of toxic emissions in the past decade as Sherritt International, a Canadian mining company, has brought its own new-technology smelter on-stream just down the road, but Empresa Che Guevara still spews out a vast quantity of filth, making its environs Cuba's Number One eyesore.

Che's political influence in the realm of international affairs was as problematic as his influence in the economy. He believed that as he had helped Cuba overthrow its dictator, so Cuba should help other downtrodden people overthrow theirs. A noble ideal but Cuba did not have the resources to do that. Over the next twenty-five years its military interventions created many headaches for a nation that had enough problems already.

In short, the political and economic legacy of Che's five years in the Cuban government is mixed and messy. However, there is another legacy, more solidly positive, that derived from his humanitarian sensibilities. His thoughts are amply documented in books that can be found all over the world, as well as on the internet, so if you're interested, you can judge them for yourself. But there is no doubt whatever that they are taken seriously in Cuba.

Once you start examining evidence related to how Che thought, you can't help but wonder what made him the man he was. Was it seeing the level of poverty in Bolivia? Yes. Work among the lepers of Peru? Yes. Being in Guatemala when the US destroyed its democracy? Yes. But what about his experiences in Cuba? How formative were they? With this question in mind, I decided to visit places in Cuba where Che was known to have spent time.

I started in a mangrove swamp where the boat carrying him

and eighty-one others ran aground. Because of that near-fatal mishap, Che's first foot on Cuban soil wasn't on soil so much as on water. Today it's possible to visit the place without wading through swamp. You can follow a raised wooden walkway through a stifling tangle of insect-humming mangroves for a kilometre, imagining, as you do so, how much farther it must have seemed to Che and his compañeros with mud sucking at their boots and water up to their chests, besieged by mosquitoes and no idea how far it was to shore.

Once on solid ground, they hiked inland along a route I myself took—but not very far. I did not turn back because the trail was too rough but because I knew already where it led and did not want to go there; did not want to be reminded of how Che and 81 others, having shed most of their supplies to get through the swamp, chewed sugar cane to keep up their strength. Batista's soldiers only had to follow the trail of chewed cane stalks the hungry men had cast aside. They caught them in Alegría de Pío and most were killed. Che was one of sixteen survivors.

Peasants recruited by Celia Sánchez eventually found the scattered survivors and reunited them on a farm where they spent a few weeks in recovery. Then several leaders from the 26th of July movement showed up to meet with them and evaluate the situation. Che's assessment, recorded in his diary, was bleak. But Fidel was confident that a guerrilla war could succeed, and Celia concurred. Thus the war commenced.

Che, named one of the commanders, would participate in more marches and survive more battles. But once the Comandancia base camp was constructed, his primary responsibility was at the hospital he presided over, staffed by volunteers recruited by Celia Sánchez.

That hospital can be visited today, as well as a tiny shack

just down the mountainside where Che treated peasants, most of whom had never been seen by a doctor before. A man from the nearby village of Santo Domingo told me that they didn't call that shack a doctor's office; they called it the dentist's office because what Che did most often there was pull teeth. As a boy of eleven, this man said, Che had pulled one of his. He put his finger in his mouth and held it open wide so I could see the gap.

La Comandancia may be one of the best places to imagine Che, working there in the dirt-floored "dentist's office," or in the hospital that had no electricity or running water. He was almost two years in this place. Here he wrote, he fought, he healed, he thought. It is my personal belief that it was here that he became the man we think of as Che, and perhaps the one he thought of as Che.

At the very end of 1958, Dr. Che came down out of the mountains in command of a column of rebels and fought Batista's army all the way to Havana.

First, of course, there was Santa Clara, and if you go there you can see the troop train his men derailed and other reminders of that battle. Contrary to myth and memorial, the Santa Clara train episode was not a battle. It was a deal. The ranking officer on the train, Colonel Florentino Rosell, allegedly accepted $350,000 in cash from Che in order to surrender the train and all its weapons. What is known for certain is that after speaking with Che, Colonel Rosell took several briefcases to a waiting car, hightailed it back to Havana, and sailed his yacht to Miami, where he started a construction company and soon became extremely wealthy. Back in Santa Clara, Che took possession of the train, released the men on it (some then, some a short time later), and continued his victorious march to Havana.

And where was Fidel just then? Back in eastern Cuba,

waiting to take Santiago until Che reached Havana and captured Batista's main military base at Camp Columbia. This Che did on January 1, 1959.

Then the rebels had a government to form, and who among them knew how to do that? Gone was the camaraderie of living in the mountains, fighting battles, and tending the sick. In the city, chaos was the order of the day. Che wore many hats and his asthma plagued him. He was with a new woman by then, having divorced his first wife, a Peruvian, (or maybe she divorced him) to marry Aleida March, a fellow revolutionary. He traveled abroad incessantly trying to drum up international support for Cuba's new government and its economy, both of which were already being hammered by the USA.

Che did not participate in the battle at the Bay of Pigs in April 1961, because Fidel, knowing an invasion was imminent but not knowing where it would take place, charged Che with defending the western end of the island. A swift victory at the Bay of Pigs allowed Che to return to his civilian duties. But not for long.

In October 1962, it seemed to Washington that the Cubans, by allowing the USSR to put missiles on the island, were inviting annihilation. Cubans feared that despite the island's proximity to Florida, a nuclear attack might be on the agenda. Havana was evacuated and Che was again sent to Pinar del Río to defend western Cuba. As if there could be any defence against a nuclear attack.

If there is any place in Cuba to understand what kind of example Che left in terms of courage, it would be at La Cueva de Los Portales. Although he easily could have left prior to the expected nuclear destruction of Cuba, he did not. He accepted the Western Command and waited it out. It is possible to visit Los Portales today, although few people do. You can sit by the river that runs through the cave or at the long table in the underground chamber where Che and his men discussed strategy. You can go into a cell-like room in the cave which still has the narrow cot where he slept—if he slept—waiting for that part of the world known as Cuba to end.

It did not, of course. The end, for Che, was waiting for him in Bolivia.

Is that the sum of Che's legacy in Cuba? A brave military career that became bogged down in adventurism—but not before he had convinced Cuban leaders to invest in similar lost causes? An ideologically-driven industrialization policy that took decades to set right? Humanitarian values that are still being taught and widely practiced by Cuban children?

Actually, no. That is not all. One thing I haven't mentioned, the most important yet seemingly least remembered, is that Che fathered the Cuban health care system. He argued from the outset that (a) health care is a human right rather than a product to be sold for economic gain; and (b) its delivery is the responsibility of the government. Just as that view of medicine is being contested in the US today, so was it contested by doctors in Cuba in 1959. Che's views prevailed. Within two decades, Cuba had a population as healthy as that of any First World country, and was internationally admired for its health care contributions to poorer nations. One can't help but see that some of the benefits Che hoped to bring to suffering Third World people through force of arms have been brought to millions by the Cuban health care system combined with the internationalism that he espoused fifty years ago.

It was Fidel who, in 1998, won the World Health Organization's "Health for All" award; Cuba had reached all the WHO health goals set for developing nations. And it was Fidel who, in 1999, formalized Cuba's international medical assistance program by founding the Latin America School of Medicine (ELAM). There thousands of students from all over the world are trained as doctors, on full scholarships from the Cuban government, to go back and practice in their own needy countries. As of 2012, twenty-seven countries and sixty ethnic groups were represented among ELAM's 8000 students. This even included about 80 from the US who promised that after graduation they would return to work as doctors in their own poor, medically-underserved neighbourhoods.

And there is Operación Milagro. Fidel gets the credit for that, too, as well he should because he is the one who launched it. But what raised his consciousness on the subject of health care if not Che's eloquent argument—and example—that doctors should not profit from human misery, but should voluntarily work to mitigate it?

As of January 2010, Operación Milagro had resulted in at least 1,600,000 patients from thirty-five countries having their sight restored.

In 2008, a Cuban eye surgeon removed cataracts to restore the sight of a retired Bolivian soldier who forty years earlier had aimed a rifle at a wounded, unarmed prisoner named Che Guevara and riddled his body with bullets.

As for the question of legacy, one might ask which is more lasting: to be remembered for having launched those bullets into Che Guevara's brain, or for being the visionary who, in addition to launching more than a few deadly bullets himself, also launched a humanitarian medical program that brought the whole thing full circle?

Golden Oldies

Not all the great leaders of the Cuban Revolution are dead. Just to give you an idea, here are three who as of 2012 were still with us but may not be much longer. However physically fragile they are, their mental acuity remains intact. During first decade of the 21st century and beyond, they have continued to influence Cuba's top leadership in both subtle and overt ways.

Melba Hernández, born in 1921, describes herself not as a lawyer but as a revolutionary. She was both by the time she participated in the 1954 attack on Moncada. When she and other survivors of the uprising were to go on trial for treason, Fidel appointed Melba to be his lawyer. She argued in court that citizens have a duty to overthrow a leader who abandons democratic principles and engages in the kind of violence against citizens that Batista had. She offered irrefutable evidence that, following the Moncada attack, prisoners had been tortured and murdered. She lost the case, so Fidel and the other rebels who survived the attack were sentenced to prison. Melba, along with Haydée Santamaría, served seven months before being released by Batista in an effort to appease opposition to his brutal regime.

Upon her release, Melba stated, "We went to Moncada moved by a sacred love for freedom, and we are ready to give our lives for its principles." With that, she returned to clandestine activities aimed at ending the Batista regime. She helped lead the 26th of July movement and started distributing revolutionary literature. Castro, still in prison, used her as his primary representative. Melba eventually received and published the full text of the speech Fidel had delivered at his trial for the attack on Moncada, called "History Will Absolve Me."

When Fidel was released from prison in 1955, he went to Mexico to train men who expected to join other guerrilla fighters being organized by Celia Sánchez and Frank País in southeast Cuba. Fidel, finding it necessary to go to the US to raise funds to equip his recruits and transport them back to Cuba, left Melba in charge of training activities in Mexico. While in Mexico she became engaged to another rebel leader, Jesús Montané. When Castro returned from his fund-raising trip, he moved in with them.

In the 1960s, after the revolutionary government took power, Melba formed the Cuban Committee for Solidarity with Vietnam, Cambodia, and Laos. She travelled to Vietnam to observe the situation first-hand, and said she was certain of an eventual Vietnamese victory. For several years she served as Cuba's ambassador to Vietnam and Cambodia. From 1976 to 1986 she was a member of Cuba's highest legislative body, the National Assembly. She was re-elected to the National Assembly in 1993 but has since retired.

Ninety-one years old in 2012, Melba Hernández is now more icon than activist, but she is listened to with respect by Cubans of all ages when she speaks, as she often does, of the need for Cuba to remain independent and to pursue socialist humanitarian values.

Marta Rojas was, in July 1953, a twenty-five-year-old journalist wandering around Santiago looking for something to write about. She heard gunshots and hurried toward them. On a street near the Moncada military facility she came upon what would not only be the story of her life but the turning point of her life. She was the first to report on the rebel attack, and attended every day of the trials held for Fidel Castro and his fellow fighters.

Marta's notes, smuggled out at great personal risk, were

later published as *El Juicio del Moncada* (The Moncada Judgement). Given heavy censorship that prevented the Cuban people from knowing the facts surrounding that event, the political and historical importance of the information Marta recorded and made public can hardly be overstated.

Marta's coverage of revolutions-in-progress began in Cuba but did not end there. Later she traveled to Vietnam to cover that war from North Vietnam's perspective. She interviewed Viet Cong fighters, military officers, and Ho Chi Minh. She also talked to ordinary Vietnamese, many of them victims of napalm and Agent Orange rained on the population by the US Air Force.

After the Vietnam War ended, Marta continued working as reporter for Cuba's principal periodical, *Granma,* covering conflicts in Haiti and Guatemala.

She then became manager of *Granma's* mostly-male editorial board, a post she held for seventeen years. Was that difficult? Marta merely called it "a challenge." She insisted she never felt hostility from male colleagues but admitted, "I had to fight to get what I wanted. I made myself respected by my behaviour and discipline; by my example."

In addition to articles on important political issues, Marta wrote about the role of women in society, exploring issues of machismo, sexuality, and sexism. In her seventies she turned to novels: *Santa Lujuria* (Holy Lust), *El Columpio de Rey Spencer* (Rey Spencer's Swing), *Inglesa por un Año* (English for One Year), *El Harén de Oviedo* (Oviedo's Harem), and *El Viaje* (The Journey).

Marta Rojas, who will turn eighty-five in 2013, has not abandoned either the journalism where she first made a name as a gutsy writer or the complex fiction that now absorbs her. She remains one of the most respected voices in Cuban literature.

Esther "Teté" Puebla was only fifteen when she joined the guerrillas in the Sierra Maestra. Her battle skills and bravery under fire were so inspiring that she rapidly rose to the rank of captain in the rebel army's Mariana Grajales Women's Brigade. When male soldiers complained that women were being given weapons when many of the men didn't have a gun, Fidel snapped that it was because the women were better fighters.

Like most of the women who held commissions during the guerrilla war, Teté Puebla remained in the army after the revolutionary government came to power. And like other commanders, she took on other responsibilities. In 1969 she was designated director of the Guanicanamar Cattle Plan in a rural region of Havana province.

In her autobiography, *Marianas in Combat,* Teté wrote: "Castro said he was putting me in charge to demonstrate that women could lead as well as men, to show that women could lead an agricultural project, and, in short, that women could head up any front and carry out any task of the Revolution."

Teté and Fidel may have thought she could do it but the peasants said flatly that they would not work with her. One of the men said, "She might be a captain, the Commander might have brought her, but I'm *not* working with a woman."

Yet according to Teté, "After a month the peasants were working with me. The fact that I worked the same as they did, during the day, the night, Saturdays, Sundays, and so on, gave them confidence, so they understood that I could be a farmer. I had to show that I was their equal in order to demonstrate that women could do anything."

Now in her seventies, Brigadier General Teté Puebla is the highest-ranking woman in the Cuban army. In 2009, she was one of the keynote speakers at a Caracas conference.

She didn't dwell on history, but pointedly reminded the crowd that 40,000 Cuban men *and* women volunteers are currently working in Venezuela in the spheres of health, education, agriculture, and sports.

These are a few of the courageous women who fought on the battlefield and off to revolutionize Cuban society. Yet even the accomplishments of this remarkable few are little known outside their native land. Not knowing who they were, what they sacrificed, and what they accomplished is not their loss. It is ours.

Raúl's Vilma & Vilma's Raúl

In the 1940s, old Señor José Espín, vice-chairman of the Bacardi Rum Company in Santiago de Cuba, could not have imagined the trajectory upon which his teenaged daughter Vilma was about to embark. Vilma had the refined manners of her French mother and all the privileges accorded the wealthy elite of pre-Revolutionary Cuba. She was on the girl's volleyball team and a member of the school choir. Her prettiness belied her toughness. And she was smart. When she entered university, it was to study chemical engineering.

That would have been around 1950, just before her passion for politics surfaced. In 1952, Vilma participated in a student protest against Batista's military coup. When Batista ignored nationwide protests and made himself president anyway, she joined a clandestine movement aimed at booting the bugger out.

It is possible that Vilma's parents got wind of her dangerous activism because in 1955 they sent her to the US to do postgraduate work in chemical engineering at MIT. She spent a year there—or mostly there. At one point in

1955 she did travel to Mexico, and there for the first time met Fidel and Raúl Castro, who were training troops for a future guerrilla war against Batista. They said they would return to Cuba the following year, so in 1956 Vilma abandoned her studies and went home to help Celia Sánchez, Frank País, and others to prepare for the arrival of the Castro brothers and their men.

Vilma initially worked as deputy to Frank País who headed the eastern Cuba wing of the urban underground. But when Frank began to attract too much attention from the authorities it was decided that Vilma would replace him as director. Her home became the Santiago headquarters for the urban underground.

The Castro group arrived from Mexico on December 2, 1956. The men were of no immediate help since most of them were killed within the week and the sixteen survivors did not have enough rifles to go around. However, the movement turned over to Fidel all the weapons and volunteers it had, and charged him with initiating military actions against Batista's forces. This freed Vilma, Celia, and others in the urban underground to focus on raising more money, buying more weapons, and recruiting more men and women to the cause.

In the spring of 1957, Celia, with a price on her head, was forced to flee to the mountains. Vilma continued their clandestine work in the city until the summer of 1958. Then, with Batista's men closing in on her, she joined the guerrillas, too—not those Fidel commanded in Sierra Maestra but the ones commanded by Raúl in the Sierra Cristal.

It was a dangerous time, as Raúl's troops were being bombed repeatedly by Batista's air force. It must have been a romantic time as well, because during those six months

Vilma Espín and Raúl Castro became a couple. Vilma said later, "I was twenty-eight and had never had a lover. He said I had bewitched him with my singing."

In January 1959, three weeks after the victory of the Revolution, Vilma and Raúl were married. From the outset she held a position of power in the new government. Initially she headed the Center for Industrial Development of the Food Industry. A year later she founded a non-governmental agency called the Federation of Cuban Women (FMC).

With Vilma at its head, the FMC soon became one of the most powerful organizations in Cuba. It encouraged women's political participation, set up programs to fight illiteracy and improve women's skills, developed a network of daycare centers, created the Childhood Institute to assist pre-school children, and in 1974 got legislation passed that guarantees three months of paid maternity leave. The FMC also insisted on changes to Cuba's Penal Code, thereby establishing severe punishment for violent crimes, especially rape and sexual assault.

Along with gender equality in the workforce and in education, and free access to contraception and abortion, Vilma and her politically savvy minions were responsible for the most radical piece of family legislation ever promulgated in a Hispanic country—the Cuban Family Code of 1975— which *requires* men to share housework and child care.

Fifteen years later, Vilma told *LA Times* reporter Don Schanche, "Of course there are still vestiges of machismo within the heart of the family, and even some women in positions of leadership still have old-fashioned ideas, but we have to fight to see that men and women share the house-hold tasks."

The rights of women and children were Vilma's main things, but not her only focus. She was one of the first to fight against the persecution of gays in the 1960s, when machismo-Leninismo was in full swing and such work was groundbreaking and dangerous. In 1979, she pushed through legislation that decriminalized homosexuality.

In her "spare time" Vilma led many international delegations. I saw her only once, in 1975, at the International Year of Women conference in Mexico City. There was a sharp division among delegates that broke not along ideological lines but along First World/Third World concerns. First World women focused on issues like equal representation in the professions, equal pay, daycare facilities, Lesbian rights, etc. Delegates from poor countries were more concerned with food security, access to birth control, and laws that protected women against being treated as chattel. One of the things Vilma said, when she rose to address the delegates at that conference, was, "We [in Cuba] have already obtained for our women everything that the conference is asking for. Women are part of the people, and unless you talk about politics, you are never going to change anything."

I heard her say that. Cuba-sympathetic though I was, I did not believe it. I doubt anyone else at the conference did either. Vilma got no mention in the international media about it, nor was there any flood of journalists—or feminists, for that matter—to Cuba to see if it was true. As I would learn when I got there myself some long time later, just about all of what she claimed in terms of women's rights in Cuba *was* true.

In a 2007 article in *The Nation* magazine, Rosa Elizalde quoted Vilma's response to a question about the re-emergence of prostitution in Cuba in the 1990s. "Don't forget that jineteras are not mere prostitutes. They are *our* prostitutes," she said. "We must not demonize them because we run the risk of attacking the victim instead of attacking the wrong."

Vilma, a political animal to the end, died in 2007 at the age of seventy-seven. For fifty years she had worked to improve the lot of groups that her male colleagues supported only with persistent nudging. Her constituency outnumbered even that of her husband, as the Federation of Women includes eighty percent of all adult Cuban females, or about two million members—ten times more than the 200,000-member military commanded by Raúl.

So where was husband Raúl during all this? Not merely fathering their children, three daughters and a son. Raúl has long been a power in his own right. As of January 2009, he had commanded the Cuban armed forces for a full fifty years.

As a child, Raúl was as much a rebel as Fidel, resulting in his expulsion from school at the age of six. His exasperated father sent him off to Santiago to attend the Jesuit school where Fidel was enrolled, there to room with his four-years-older brother. Fidel, recollecting this sixty-five years later, seems not to have minded or paid a lot of mind to Raúl.

"He was just a little guy," Fidel said, adding that he often found himself in the role of playground protector to Raúl.

This earned him the undying loyalty of "little Raúl." Loyalty, I would venture to say, is Raúl Castro's most obvious quality.

Just about everything Fidel undertook after that he did with Raúl at his side. Raúl participated in the Moncada attack. He drove the car that *didn't* get lost, with the men who *did* achieve their objective, although they were all captured later and ended up in prison along with other survivors. It was Raúl who first met Che Guevara in Mexico and brought him into their circle. Raúl made the dangerous boat trip from Mexico back to Cuba, and was one of the sixteen to survive the Alegría de Pío massacre. He led the Second Front during the war, and after-wards became Minister of Cuba's Armed Forces.

So why was so little made of him in the foreign media? Well, look at any picture you can find of him and Fidel. There he is, nearly a foot shorter and not as good-looking. How many guerrilla princes does a revolution need anyway? Not one of the leaders of the Cuban revolution was interested in personal aggrandizement. If they had been they would have been scorned by the others because it's antithetical to revolutionary values. But the foreign press would have their guerrilla prince who, like it or not, was Fidel. Raúl wasn't even in the running. Like Vilma, Celia, Haydée, Melba, Marta, Teté, Juan Almeida, and all the others who survived the war and were part of the top echelon of power in Cuba for decades afterwards, Raúl eschewed publicity and just did his job.

The personality Raúl brought to his work was that of a man who obeys commands and expects his commands to be obeyed. When it comes to rules, I doubt that the word "flexible" applies to Raúl. I have heard soldiers who served under him call him "a hard man." Whereas Fidel has a history of being magnanimous with his enemies, Raúl does not. Perhaps it was for this reason that Fidel himself did not over-see the roundup of war criminals. (The winners always get to decide who the criminals are after a war, right?) He turned that chore over to Raúl and Che. Around 500 were brought to trial, sentences delivered, and where those sentences were death, Raúl and Che had them carried out.

Besides running the military, Raúl has always had polit-ical responsibilities. In 1972, he was made first deputy pre-mier, and when the government was reorganized in 1976, he became Cuba's vice president. That too kept him in the background, but by temperament and choice as much as by the position. He is usually described as "reticent," although not shy and certainly not weak.

Up until the end of the 1980s, Cuban troops were sent to support one side or another in conflicts in various foreign countries. US leaders supposed that this was at the urging of the USSR, but declassified documents have now revealed that such Cuban "adventurism" drove Soviet leaders at least as crazy as it drove those in Washington. However, for more than twenty years now the Cuban military has been for, and only for, defence of the island.

Raúl's strict discipline may get him labelled as "hard" but even the CIA admits that he runs a professional army. And it is respected, not feared, by the Cuban people. Unlike the military in other Latin American countries, the military under Raúl has *never* been used against the Cuban people. All Cuban males between the ages of 18 and 28, minus homosexuals and those deemed physically unfit, serve a requisite two years. Those who make the military their career get numerous perks, such as priorities in housing, free holiday camps that are nicer than ones open to the general population, and PX-type stores where more consumer goods are available at much lower prices than to the public. There is some small irony in this. Raúl was one of the few card-carrying Communists in the top leadership, yet he never believed that moral incentives were enough. From the outset, he saw to it that his soldiers had material incentives as well.

Veterans come in for benefits, too. I have rented rooms in the homes of three veterans, one an old man from the Revolutionary war, one a veteran of the Angola civil war, and one a veteran of the Ethiopia conflict. None were officers. All told me they received their houses from the government specifically because they were war veterans.

In the early 1990s, when a lot of career military men were retiring, and Cuba faced a food shortage, Raúl came up with an admirable idea. Laws had just been changed to allow farmers to sell their produce on the open market, so Raúl arranged for free land and start-up funds to be given to any veterans' group of five or more who wanted to form a cooperative and raise vegetables. When I am in Cojímar, a town just across the harbour from downtown Havana, I often buy vegetables from one such veterans' co-op, located about a block from Hotel Panamericano.

Foreign media rarely mentioned Raúl until, during Fidel's life-threatening illness in 2006, he became Cuba's acting president. Even then the focus remained on Fidel. (Once a prince, always a prince, eh?)

Somehow First World media gurus couldn't seem to grasp the fact that Raúl, a commander during the Revolution, in charge of Cuba's military for fifty years, and vice-president for thirty years, just might be capable of making independent decisions. Even after Fidel retired in 2008 and the National Assembly elected Raúl to succeed him as president, Fidel continued to get more coverage in the foreign press—and does to this day.

When Raúl was asked recently why he has remained so much in the background, he gave a reasonable explanation: "Many tasks related to defence should not be made public and have to be handled with maximum care, and that has been one of my fundamental responsibilities."

Upon becoming president of Cuba, Raúl didn't move into a presidential palace. (Cuba has no presidential palace.) He still lives in the Havana suburb of Jaimanitas in a nice but not extravagant house called La Rinconada (The Little Corner).

Although Vilma has been dead since 2007, they were married for forty-eight years, so Raúl probably is still trying to get used to her absence. For decades Raúl had a habit of inviting as many of his and Fidel's children and grandchildren as could make it for Sunday dinner at La Rinconada. I guess he still does that. When the youth is gone, and the partner, and someday the power, at least there will still be the kids, right?

The Juniors

Nepotism is rampant in most South American countries but it is not the norm in North America or in Cuba. It's true that by hook and crook, one of George Bush's sons became president of the US, and Robert Kennedy almost certainly would have followed his brother John into the presidency if he had not been assassinated. In Cuba, the younger brother survived assassination attempts and did succeed his older brother as president in Cuba, but nepotism remains as uncommon Cuba as in the US.

The children of those powerful first-generation revolutionaries, known in Cuba as *"hijos del papa"* (children of the daddy) are today middle-aged. Like most Cubans they are educated professionals, and like most Cubans they work for the state. But their involvement in politics is minimal or non-existent. They have practically no influence in the area of policy. Still, you might be interested to know how the lives of some of them have unfolded.

Haydée Santamaría's two grown children, Abel and Celia Hart, became part of that family's legacy of tragedy when, in 2008, their old VW bug spun out of control on a Havana street flooded from a recent hurricane. It hit a tree, killing both. Although Celia was a physicist, some believe that political writings aimed at persuading the different Latin American leftist tribes to listen to one another will turn out to be her main contribution. No one pushed harder for unity on the left than she.

Che Guevara's eldest daughter Hilda, a librarian in Cuba, died at the same young age (thirty-nine) as her father. In her case the killer was cancer.

Che's eldest son Camilo is now in his fifties. Until recently he headed Cuba's Ministry of Fisheries. He hardly ever comments on political issues outside his official sphere of influence—an exception being when he criticized Israel's bombing of Lebanon. In 2008, in Vienna for an exhibition of photos of his famous father, Camilo walked away from an interviewer who showed no interest in the exhibit but persisted with questions about current Cuban policies. Camilo has expressed revulsion at the merchandising of his father's image.

Camilo's brother Ernesto likewise took a public stand against the Israeli bombing and occupation of Lebanon. Ernesto was for a time a member of the National Guard. I am not sure what he is up to now besides riding his Harley, said to be one of only 120 Harley hogs in Cuba (although there are known to be many more in need of parts to get them back on the road). Ernesto has put his name to several books about Che's life, but it may be that he did not write more than captions to the photos.

Che's daughter Aleida is a paediatrician based at the William Soler Children's Hospital in Havana. By becoming a doctor and volunteering on medical brigades in Angola, Ecuador, and Nicaragua, Aleida comes closest of any of Che's children to following in his footsteps. But not, some

Cubans say, close enough. Che, when utilizing his medical skills in poverty-stricken countries, lived as the locals did. Aleida not only does not live like the locals; she often stays in different and better facilities than her medical colleagues. However, one cannot discount the fact that this may be necessary. Che never had to cope with the harassments of fame. His offspring do, especially when they are out of Cuba.

Aleida is a frequent speaker at international conferences on behalf of Che's values and those of the Cuban Revolution. On one occasion, when she was to speak at Tehran University, a member of the host organization introduced her by quoting from a Farsi book on Che's life. It concluded that Che was a godly man and finally met God. Aleida took the microphone and said angrily, "I don't know what book you are quoting from but my father was a Communist who did not believe in God and as far as I know, never met God in the end either!" The students broke out in a frenzy of applause and shouts of approval. Aleida was surrounded by Iranian intelligence agents, taken directly to the airport, and expelled from the country.

While children of the revolutionary elite don't earn more than other Cubans, they do receive more than a few non-monetary perks, and are widely perceived as being excessively favoured in their chosen profession. For instance, Che's daughter Celia is a marine biologist. A veterinarian with a speciality only in sea horses, she is responsible for animal health at Havana's Acuario Nacional. Given the number of deaths among dolphins in her care at the aquarium, one is inclined to conclude that she is not qualified for such a post. The fact that she has not spoken out against Cuba's ongoing practice of capturing wild dolphins has done neither her nor Cuba's reputation any good internationally.

I like to imagine that it was partly in reaction to such insensitivity that Che's granddaughter Lydia went off on her own revolution. This took the form of posing for a poster for the radical animal rights organization PETA wearing only a red beret and bandoliers made of carrots—this part of a campaign to start a "vegetarian revolution" in South America.

Fidel's eldest child, Fidelito, was born in 1949. Fidelito earned a PhD in nuclear physics from the University of Moscow, and was then appointed executive secretary of the Cuban Atomic Energy Commission in 1980. It was a reasonable enough choice in view of the fact that Cuba had few nuclear physicists and even fewer who were fluent enough in Russian to communicate with the Soviet experts who were about to provide the island with a nuclear power plant. However, Fidelito was fired in 1992.

"There was no resignation," Fidel said flatly. "He was fired for incompetence. We do not have a monarchy here." The public was never told the nature of that incompetence but it might have been Fidelito's failure to get the power generating plant up and running in a timely fashion—as in, before Soviet aid was suspended. The collapse of the Soviet Union and withdrawal of its support for Cuba's nuclear energy program caused the reactor to be mothballed in a state of incompletion.

Later Fidelito worked as a consultant to Cuba's Ministry of Basic Industries. His chubby self is often seen in public with his father but he has no political power. Occasionally he lectures on such arcane subjects as nanotechnology, and recently wrote (or had his name put to) a book on climate change, which has caused some media to dub him "Cuba's Al Gore."

Fidel has five sons by his wife Dalia Soto de Valle. Angel and Antonio are both medical doctors. Alexis and Alejandro are computer programmers. Alexander was trained as a computer programmer but left that line of work in favour of photography. They all live better than the average Cuban—or worse. That is to say, they are not rich but do have all their material needs met to the level of an upper middle-class family in North America. On the downside, security concerns necessarily limit their freedom of movement. They are never seen on television and rarely photographed. Their main perk as "hijos del papa" is in the area of career. For example, Antonio "Tony" Castro is the Cuban National baseball team's doctor, even though he is an orthopaedic surgeon specializing in the hand, not a sports medicine doc. As for Alex, after he switched from computer programming to photography, he was able to exhibit his pictures at Havana's historic Hotel Nacional, where they would catch the eye of big-spending foreigners. Of course, many Cuban artists have been selected to exhibit at Hotel Nacional, and anyone who has seen Alex's photography would have to agree that they are good enough to have been selected on merit alone. But mention the Hotel Nacional exhibit to a Cuban and you will likely get a sidewise smile and a murmur, "Naturalmente. Es hijo del papa."

As for *hija* del papa, poor Alina comes to mind. According to her mother Naty Revuelta, Alina was fathered by Fidel. This may or may not be true. What is demonstrably true is that Alina has kept herself in the media limelight for decades by trading on her presumed Castro parentage. Pretty tacky but given her upbringing what could you expect? Her Fidel-besotted mother proclaimed Alina to be El Comandante's out-of-wedlock daughter, while the grandmother with whom little Alina lived routinely made bitterly anti-Castro remarks. As a child, Alina found Fidel's fatherly attentions quite deficient. She didn't like the baseball game he took her to, didn't think the cake he brought her for her *quinceñero* was any better than what other girls got when surely he could have afforded better, and said he didn't take much notice of her—which he probably didn't. She did get the model's training she wanted and was sent abroad to model Cuban clothing designs. But Cuban *fashion?* There's a career non-starter if ever there was one. The best Alina could do, which she did do, was to leave Cuba for the US where she embarked on a career as a professional Fidel-hater. Her book on the subject is surpassingly awful, but she has managed to keep a toehold in the media. She hosted an anti-Daddy radio show in Miami for a while, and in 2006 was hired as a "Cuba expert" on CNN's cable news network.

Fidel is alleged to have several other children by various short-term lovers, but he *never* speaks of his personal relationships and as it appears to be in no one's interest to do DNA testing, the public is never likely to know (nor does it need to know) how much truth there is to any of those claims and rumours.

Raúl Castro and Vilma Espín have four children: Alejandro, an engineer and national security advisor for the Ministry of Interior Security; Deborah, an engineer and advisor in the Ministry of Education; Nilsa, also an advisor in the Ministry of Education; and Mariela, director of the Cuban National Center for Sex Education (CENSEX).

Mariela is most often in the news, usually having to do with the activities of CENESEX, a Cuban organization which campaigns for AIDS education and recognition and acceptance of homosexuals, bisexuals, transvestites, and transsexuals. Mariela sponsored the 2008 resolution that approved free sex change operations within the state health system and says she has spoken to Cuba's president (her father) about the need for a change in the law that bars gays from the military. Raúl is said to have warned her of the need to "go slow" to avoid a backlash against the very groups for which she is trying to gain greater acceptance.

While being the daughter of such politically powerful parents as Raúl Castro and Vilma Espín certainly helped Mariela to achieve her current position, she told an interviewer that being the president's daughter was *not* helpful in terms of achieving her agenda. Although she has access and keeps Raúl informed, she complained that when it comes to implementation "most government officials are afraid to consider my proposals for fear of being accused of favouritism."

Mariela sees legislation as a means of bringing about necessary social change and does not hesitate to offer her opinions on political issues. She has publicly accused the Cuban Communist Party of discrimination against homosexuals. Although not an advocate of a multiparty system, she has made speeches both in Cuba and abroad about the need for more participatory democracy, and has urged giving young people a greater voice. She has also authored nine books. If she isn't listened to yet, that is not to say she won't be heard in the future. It seems to me that Mariela Castro is one "hija del papa" who bears watching—if only because, like her politically-savvy mother, she is hell-bent on getting laws implemented that will impact and perhaps improve Cuban society.

A Most Romantic Man

Fidel Castro is the most romantic man of our time. I use that adjective not merely because he has loved a few women and a great many more have loved him. The proof of his being a deeply romantic man lies in what he tried to accomplish.

His personal history proves that he truly believes in revolution, and when you get right down to it, few ideas are as romantic as the one that holds that it is possible to revolutionize (completely change) an entire society and remake it into something way better than what it was.

This romantic notion resulted in two decisions that were disastrous for the Cuban economy. One was that the state should run even small businesses, thereby "saving" its citizens from the corrupting influence of self-serving commerce. This it did, without noticing that people have been bartering the whole of human existence and are as hard-wired for trade as for sex; thus trying to prevent folks from engaging in trade is about is likely to succeed as trying to prevent them from engaging in sex.

The other disastrous decision was to help several countries in their attempts to get out from under the thumb of their oppressor. Cuba's involvement in conflicts in Ethiopia and Angola cost the nation dearly. Resources were expended that might have been utilized to create economic self-sufficiency. This failure to become food and energy self-sufficient was the principal cause of the extreme poverty that afflicted Cuba during the decade that followed the withdrawal of USSR subsidies in 1989. For at least two decades prior, Cuba had had the resources to develop greater economic self-sufficiency but had not made that its top priority.

Castro and his closest advisors had better reasons than most to feel romantic about revolution. But the belief that little Cuba could rescue other nations from themselves, and the notion everybody in Cuba would be willing to work *entirely* for the general good rather than private gain—these were foolishly romantic notions that flew in the face of common sense and human nature.

Romantic that he is, Fidel went further. At Che's urging, he set his government the task of creating a "new man" (this retro phrase meant to include women as well). Basically the objective was to get people to change their attitudes to the extent that they were willing to work for moral incentives rather than material ones. Che convinced Fidel that moral incentives would bring out the best in people, causing them to approach life in a hard-working, self-sacrificing, egalitarian way.

If there is anything more romantic than the belief itself, it is the notion that such a radical "attitude revolution" can be achieved quickly. If the idea seems preposterous, just remember that both Fidel and Che were men who thrived on self-sacrifice and hard work. Since they were that way by nature, they probably didn't perceive it as something all that difficult to get others to accept. They honestly believed that greed and inequality in the Cuban society were products of colonial domination and savage capitalism. Surely that could be turned around in a couple of years, because, well, wouldn't people *rather* live in a society where the nation's resources were divvied up more or less equally and everybody could count on everybody else?

Apparently not. If Jesus Christ's straight-forward instructions along those lines didn't inspire his followers to go that route, one wonders why Fidel though he could persuade Cubans to do it.

My conclusion is that Castro believed that just because he is a romantic. Here I am applying both of the two most common definitions of a romantic: (a) one given to things that are far-fetched and not very practical, and (b) tender or intimate in mood.

Fidel is surprisingly good at creating intimacy. I suspect this has been as least as much a factor as his intellect in what some would call his charisma and others (especially female others) call love. That is really what you want to hear about, right? Not psycho-political speculations, but about the women in his life. So okay, let's get that out of the way.

There was his first wife, Mirta Díaz-Balart, who was a twenty-year-old philosophy student at Havana University when he met and married her. Neither of them knew that Fidel had already found the love of his life, and as it was not a woman there was no way Mirta could compete. Like good bourgeois newlyweds, they took the $1000 wedding gift from Mirta's Uncle Batista and went off to the US for their honeymoon. After that Fidel became involved with his true love—*La Revolución*.

Five years into their marriage came the ill-fated attack on Moncada and Fidel's quick imprisonment. Mirta did not leave him at once, but she must have felt that a husband jailed for trying to overthrow the resident dictator, who just happened to be her uncle, didn't have much of a future.

Had she stuck around five years longer she would have seen how wrong she was, but Fidel being locked up wasn't the only stress on their marriage. He was, just then, being romantically pursued by one Naty Revuelta, a doctor's wife who had assisted the revolutionary underground in important ways. Fidel was writing to Naty from prison just as he was writing to Mirta, and while his letters were predominately pleas for more books (he was in solitary confinement most of the time), his essentially romantic nature caused him to include in letters to both women phrases that clearly qualified as "tender and intimate." Someone, likely a prison administrator with a vicious sense of humour, sent a letter meant for Mirta to Naty and vice versa.

Mirta's flip-out over that was matched by Fidel's flip-out when he learned that *she* had betrayed *him*, not by taking a lover but by getting herself on Batista's payroll. At first Fidel refused to believe it but when presented with proof that his wife was accepting money from the very man who had put him in prison, he demanded a divorce.

Given his poor prospects, his anger with her, and those written declarations of affection for Naty, Mirta must have been as ready as he for a divorce. However, she was not ready to hand over their son. For the next five or six years they behaved like any bourgeois couple in the throes of divorce, fighting tooth and nail for custody of Fidelito.

Divorce proceedings were underway by the time Fidel was released from prison in 1955. Naty was waiting in the wings—or actually, in a bedroom. A night spent with Naty was to become a defining moment in her life, one that she claimed resulted in the daughter she gave birth to nine months later. Fidel, however, was not distracted by their brief intimacy or its aftermath. True to his real love, La Revolución, he promptly headed to Mexico to train a handful of men he romantically imagined would defeat Batista's large, well-equipped army.

Of course, there were women in Mexico, too. One was a beautiful eighteen-year-old to whom Fidel, then twenty-nine, became engaged. However, after he bought her a swimsuit to replace a bikini he considered inappropriate, she broke up with him and married her former fiancé. (One can imagine that the teenager might have been disillusioned to discover that this dashing revolutionary was more fashion-conservative than her mother.) A year later Fidel returned to Cuba, met Celia Sánchez who was six years his senior, and fell for her like no other.

Fidel never stopped loving Celia, nor did he ever cease

to heed her advice. Some say that near the end of her life she told Fidel, who was then fifty-four, that he should marry forty-year-old Dalia Soto del Valle, a long-time friend of both of them, who had been a teacher in the literacy campaign. Fidel has never confirmed this or anything else about his personal life but he did marry Dalia six months after Celia's death. They have by now been together for more than thirty years and, in an unpretentious four-bedroom home in the west Havana suburb of Jaimanitas, raised five sons.

End of synopsis of Fidel's romantic involvement with women. But more to come about his romantic dream that an attitude revolution could be achieved in his country, and his deep attachment to the Cuban people upon whom he superimposed that dream.

From remarks about Fidel that one hears in North America, it's easy to conclude that he is the most hated man in Cuba by Cubans. But that view comes mainly from US government officials who want him to disappear and Cubans who have left Cuba in part because they didn't like living under a government headed by him. On the island, where more than eleven million people do live under the Castro government, you don't encounter the same unremitting hostility.

This is not to say that there are no criticisms of Fidel. I often heard complaints that he induced laws that prevented private businesses from flourishing; showed too much tolerance for an inefficient and often oppressive bureaucracy; and gave too much attention to social justice goals abroad when there was so much that needed to be done right there on the island.

However, the comments I heard most frequently were ones that indicated tremendous admiration for Fidel for having faced down the US and kept Cuba independent all these years, along with a belief that it was past time for him to step aside. He did step aside 2008. Now that the Cuban people no longer see him as responsible for many of their problems, they are able to love him more—or at least resent him less.

Or put another way, the remarks about Fidel that I have heard over the past fifteen years have almost always reflected a mixture of love and frustration. I have also heard and read many speeches by Fidel. They are likewise a mixture of love and frustration toward a people who simply will *not* live up to his romantic ideal of a culture where materialism and me-firstism has been completely replaced by values of sharing and caring.

Yet however disappointed the people may be in Fidel, and he is in them, I am fairly certain that for both, a strong romantic attachment remains.

The year was 2003. I was at Havana's Palacio de las Convenciones attending an organic agriculture conference. I was at the back of the auditorium, as a tendency to claustrophobia causes me to always select a seat near the exit. When the lecture ended, I was first out the door. Just then a conference room door across the hall opened and out walked Fidel.

With him were two men, a grey-haired military officer about a foot shorter than Fidel and a slender dark-haired young man in casual clothes with an ear plug and a walkie-talkie. I stopped and stared, not surprised by seeing Fidel so much as surprised to see him not surrounded by a great crowd of people, which is how I had seen him before.

Others from the conference room I had come from began pouring out. Fidel was by then further along the corridor. He was walking away from us but the recognition was instantaneous. A murmur went up. "Fidel! Is that Fidel? Yes, look! It's Fidel!"

Although no one was speaking loudly, the many voices carried his name. He turned and gave a small wave. The military minder touched his arm, urging him to continue. He did, until a woman right beside me shouted, "FIDEL! FOR LOVE!"

He paused, and although the military attaché again touched his arm to keep him moving, Fidel turned and walked back to where we were standing.

The woman who had called out to him began speaking in rapid Spanish. Her name was Monica, she was from Venezuela, and oh my god, did they have problems! Half the people were illiterate, the police were corrupt, doctors charged more than people could afford to pay, and on and on she went. "You must help us, Fidel! Please! You can; I know you can. Venezuela has the money! What's needed is the political will. You dealt with these problems here; now please help us deal with ours! Please!"

As she spoke, her words like bullets fired from an automatic rifle, Fidel stood directly in front of me, listening intently to her. For some inexplicable reason I touched his sleeve. The military attaché quickly brushed away my hand. I blushed, partly because the touch seemed to reflect an embarrassing groupie impulse that I hadn't been aware of having, and partly because I imagined I had violated some protocol, like, you know, no commoner is supposed to touch the person of a British Royal.

Fidel, who had not taken his eyes from the Venezuelan woman, looked at me for an instant, his gaze bright, curious, and warm, creating a sense of intimacy that I would not have believed possible. He took my offending hand in both of his and held it while simultaneously giving Monica's words his full attention in a way that must have made her feel a similar sense of intimacy.

She spoke rapidly for several minutes. When she paused for breath he said, "Write to me, Monica. Put all you have just told me in a letter to me."

Then he looked over both of our heads, his eyes roaming the crowd in a way that I am certain made many of them feel a sense of intimacy with him, too. "What are you doing here?" he asked, as if nothing could have interested him more.

Someone said, "We're here for the organic agriculture conference."

He smiled. "Good. You grow it and I will eat it." With that he turned and walked away from us.

Now, I am not a great celebrity watcher but I am a crowd watcher. I hadn't been well-placed to watch this crowd, so as soon as Fidel began walking away I turned around to look at the two hundred or so people behind me. No one jostled or shoved past me to follow him. The Americans in the crowd (most of the foreigners were Americans) seemed stunned, as if they couldn't believe that the man walking down the long empty corridor of a public building with only two security escorts could really be the demon Fidel Castro. The faces of Cubans reflected no surprise, just a kind of quiet affection mixed with pride. For a couple of minutes there was a low buzz of excitement, then people turned their attention to the program to see where in the convention center the next event on the organic agriculture schedule was to be held.

I ducked into the room that Fidel had come out of to see what kind of meeting had been going on there. I found a group of doctors and other health workers who were about to leave for Argentina to assist flood victims. Fidel had been giving them a send-off speech, something they said he often did when volunteers left on humanitarian missions.

When I came back into the hallway, I heard the commotion of an excited crowd in another part of the building. I thought to myself, *Fidel is still here!*

I followed the sound, hoping to get there before he left. The sense of intimacy he had established with delegates to the organic agriculture conference seemed implausible even though I had felt it myself. This time, as an observer rather than participant, maybe I could be more objective.

The scene was very different. In the middle of a huge room was a vehicle ramp leading down to the parking garage. Fidel and his elderly companion in the military uniform had just started down the ramp. Above, crowded at the railings that ran along three sides of the ramp, were several hundred people. A few were from the organic agriculture conference. The others, I presumed, were there for other events or were convention center employees. It was a more exuberant crowd and more of them were Cuban. There were shouts of "Fidel! Vive Fidel!" Castro waved and continued walking. He was about half way down the ramp when a Cuban woman leaned over the rail and shouted in Spanish, "Fidel! Here is a poem I have written for you!"

He stopped and looked up. She began to recite. It was about how the people believed in him because he had made them believe in themselves, had demonstrated what it meant to love ones country, and how they would never give up, ever, and Cuba, great as it was, would be greater yet. I won't try to record it here because I didn't take notes and would probably get it wrong. I can say that it was heroic in tone and probably not good poetry, but beautifully recited with intense emotion.

When she finished there was silence. Fidel bowed his head and I think he said, "Gracias."

Then he looked up. As before, his eyes swept the crowd in a way that convinced me he was seeing individuals and, incredibly, in this most public setting, creating a sense of intimacy.

His gaze stopped at a woman standing in the throng on the opposite side from me. "Monica," he called up to her, "don't forget to write."

Less than a year later Cuba began a literacy program in Venezuela, and Operación Milagro embarked on a project of restoring sight to hundreds of thousands of blind Venezuelans. This would seem to indicate that the help Monica begged of Fidel for her country was already in the pipeline. Still, there was that gesture of acknowledging her concern and an indication that he would give it personal attention. I suspect this has long been an aspect of his relationship with people, and is part of what makes so many feel a connection to him.

But at other times I am pretty sure that Fidel has been as angry with the Cuban people as they have been with him for having failed to deliver a better Revolution. Lovers, as it were, deeply disappointed in each other.

What I saw that day reminded me of an elderly couple, one where each partner has failed in many ways but who have meant so much to each other for so many years that a deep reservoir of love remains.

Or maybe love is not the right word. Maybe the tenderness I sensed between the crowd and the man was just a lingering whiff of those romantic dreams that once, long ago, both believed were possible.

PART 7

CUBA MANANA

There is not much to suggest that the offspring of Cuba's most powerful revolutionary leaders will be among the nation's future mover-shakers. In fact, the nation's new leaders are already positioned. They come from the ranks of 50- to 65-year-olds who earned their spurs not in the Sierra Maestra but on bureaucratic battlefields. All I can tell you about these verbal battles is that there are a great many of them going on regarding which road Cuba should follow, how far, and how fast. I doubt that anyone outside the conference rooms, or even inside them, can predict what the outcome will be.

My personal hope is that the "young old" who are already beginning to replace the "old old" will go on encouraging the humanitarian, egalitarian, and sharing values of the Revolution—albeit with more tolerance for diversity and less pressure for conformity. I hope for that because I am certain that the values the new Cuban leadership endorses will have a greater impact on their nation than anything the US government or any other foreign power tries to do to force change in Cuba.

I have encountered in Cuba not only a belief in sharing but widespread practice of that value. I have seen it among those with few possessions, where a family with only a pot for boiling crabs and a sack of yucca roots shares with two hungry cyclists. I've seen it among homeowners who insist that guests take the best bed and the only pillow in the house. I have also seen such sharing manifested at official levels by a decision to care for more children from the Chernobyl disaster than all G-8 countries combined; to send abroad over 100,000 Cuban medical professionals to serve in 101 countries; to restore the sight of more than 1.5 million people from countries poorer than Cuba; and by having, right now, at least 160,000 students from Africa, Asia, and Latin America enrolled in Cuban medical schools. That is a serious amount of sharing for a nation as poor as Cuba.

I am not claiming—even Fidel does not claim—that in Cuba a "new man" has been created, one willing to share everything he has and never lust after material possessions. Cubans have the same "blue jay" compulsion we do, which causes them to covet shiny objects. Given half a chance they will fill their nests, just as we have, with more objects than are really needed or are good for the planet.

Still, revolutionary efforts to turn people's heads around, convince them that it's better to share what they have than to hoard, and that working for the good of the community is more respectable than to amass personal wealth, has impacted Cuban culture. As Derek remarked on one of our cycling trips, "Cuba seems to have the lowest ratio of assholes to humans of any place I've ever been."

There is something about the generosity of the Cuban people that makes some of us want to embrace the ethic of generosity ourselves and get the good feeling that comes with it. Some of us even give it a try—not as a way of life, of course, but for a short time. It can be a kind of "vacation" from our own materialistic culture where anyone who wants too little or shares too much is considered a little crazy.

When all is said and done, maybe that's the only way to understand Cuba: as a place that is kind of crazy because for half a century its culture has been influenced by men and women who had the crazy notion that if they managed to remove certain kinds of economic pressures and ensured basic necessities and provided a good education for all citizens, the majority of Cubans, the poor and the powerful, really would be nicer to each other.

Of course it's nonsense. I don't believe it for a minute. But even as I write this, I'm planning my next trip to Cuba, because...

...to be perfectly honest, when I am there, standing on the street with my bike in the pouring rain and total strangers take me in, or a woman who has waited hours for a ride relinquishes her seat to an elderly man, or a teenager gives away a piece from his bike that won't be easy to replace, and even women and children can safely hitchhike, Cuba *feels* like a kinder place.

-end-

ACKNOWLEDGEMENTS

One rarely travels alone in Cuba. It is to those who have travelled with me there that I am most deeply indebted. I am particularly grateful to the hundreds of Cubans I picked up hitchhiking and had the pleasure of talking with for as long as we travelled together. In most cases we never learned each other's names. They will never know how much they contributed to my understanding of Cuba's diversity and complexities.

A few old friends have also "vacationed" with me in Cuba, hardy souls who had no clue what they faced in terms of miles covered, modes of transport, roads and not-quite-roads that I would choose to follow. These I *can* name: Chantal Cutter, Brenda Birrell, Dianne Dennis, Larry Doell, Terri Nash, Rhonda Walsh, and Alan Sudbrock. To them I owe not only thanks but sincere apologies for what they endured by sharing my version of interesting travel. And then there is Derek Choukalos, who roamed around Cuba with me more than anyone else. He has facilitated my travels, my ideas, and my writing in every possible way. Sometimes travel buddy and full-time partner, Derek is my muse and my wings.

Finally I thank Kristen MacQueen for introducing me, by e-mail, to her mother-in-law and noted Cuban historian Alicia Céspedes Carrillo, who in turn sent me a biography of Celia Sánchez, *Celia,* by Pedro Alvarez Tabío, and one of her own books, *Un Antiguo Conflicto.* Many serious works contributed to my understanding of Cuba, but these two were especially important because I had not heard of them before and didn't know where to find them. The efforts Alicia took to acquire them for me in Havana is a perfect example of the Cuban tendency to helpfulness and sharing, even with total strangers.

ABOUT THE AUTHOR

Rosa Jordan grew up in the Florida Everglades, attended university in California and Mexico, and immigrated to Canada in 1980. After a decade of freelance journalism and other subsistence jobs, she authored the autobiographical *Dangerous Places: Travels on the Edge*. Next came four young adult books and her first novel, *Far from Botany Bay.*

Meanwhile she set out to cycle the Cuba's 5000-km coastline. That resulted in two travel guides co-authored with her partner Derek Choukalos: Lonely Planet's *Cycling Cuba* and *Cuba's Best Beaches.*

In 2012 came the publication of *The Woman She Was,* a novel set in Cuba, and now *Cuba Unspun,* this non-fiction narrative.

Cuba Unspun recounts travels through known and unknown parts of the island and conversations with Cubans from every walk of life. As with her other books, Jordan explores the culture physically and intellectually, with particular attention to ways in which political and social realities intersect with personal courage and compassion.